365 DAYS OF HEALING

Powerful Devotions and Prayers
To Help You Recover and Keep You Well

BY
MARK BRAZEE

Harrison House
Tulsa, Oklahoma

13 12 11 10   10 9 8 7 6

365 Days of Healing:
Powerful Devotions and Prayers To Help You Recover and Keep You Well
ISBN 13: 978-1-57794-817-9
ISBN 10: 1-57794-817-3
(formerly ISBN 1-57794-599-9)
Copyright © 1999, 2003, 2006 by Mark Brazee
Mark Brazee Ministries
P.O. Box 470308
Tulsa, Oklahoma 74147-0308

Published by Harrison House, Inc.
P.O. Box 35035
Tulsa, Oklahoma 74153

Foreword

I was saved in 1972 while attending Michigan State University. I grew up in a good, Christian home, and as far back as I can remember, I had a love for God.

As a child I knew I had a call of God on my life; however, I ran from God as long and as hard as I could for years. Being a Christian seemed to me to be a boring life with no apparent benefits—except that at the end one would go to heaven instead of hell. I wanted in on the heaven part! But I could not understand a God who would pay the price to purchase me and to cleanse me from my sins and make me new inside yet leave me to fend for myself down here on earth.

When I finally surrendered my life to God and asked Jesus into my heart, I found a life of excitement and adventure beyond my wildest dreams. I also found that God doesn't leave us helpless down here; in fact, I found just the opposite.

After being saved, I returned to my hometown and started working in the real estate business. Suddenly I began encountering great financial difficulty. After trying everything else, I opened my Bible to see what God had to say about my finances—if anything.

To my amazement, I found that God had already taken care of my financial needs, and through the truths I found in His Word, He would give me faith to walk in His blessings of an abundant life.

I also discovered Philippians 4:19, which says, "But my God shall supply all your need according to his riches in glory by Christ Jesus."

Over a period of time the truth of that Scripture settled down into my heart, and my financial situation began to change. God had become my source of supply, and He has been faithful to me in the area of finances for more than twenty-five years.

Through that experience, I discovered that God would not only save me but He would also bless and take care of me. But at times I had needs in my physical body as well. Would God make provision for them?

I decided to search the Scriptures and see if healing was a part of what Jesus had provided for me through His death, burial and resurrection. And as I studied God's Word in the area of divine healing, I found truths that have changed my life.

Consistently "feeding" on God's Word on the subject of healing produces faith in anyone's heart. Jesus said that all things are possible to those who believe (Mark 9:23), and that includes healing for the body.

I believe that the daily nuggets of truth in this book on God's healing plan will both produce healing to all of your flesh and keep you in divine health all the days of your life.

Preface

Suppose you went to the doctor to receive relief from pain or sickness and he told you, "I have a new wonder drug I'm going to prescribe for you. There are no side effects, and it's guaranteed to heal you of your condition. Not only that, but it will actually bring health to every part of your body, no matter what the problem or ailment! However, you have to faithfully take it exactly according to instructions."

After hearing that, I bet you'd listen very carefully as the doctor explained how to use this wonderful medicine. You'd want to take your prescription just as instructed so you could receive its full benefits!

You may say, "Well, that's a nice thought, but it's all hypothetical. There is no such wonder drug that can do all that."

I have some good news for you—that imaginary prescription isn't imaginary! The medicine that the Great Physician has provided for you does all that and more!

You see, God says that when you attend to His Word, it's actually life to you and health, or medicine, to your flesh. (Prov. 4:20-22.) When you take God's medicine according to His instructions, it goes to work in your body to drive out pain, sickness and disease. And it doesn't stop until it's made you whole from the top of your head to the soles of your feet!

But in order to walk in divine health, you have to take your medicine every day according to the Great Physician's prescription. That's where this daily devotional comes in.

365 Days of Healing provides a daily dose of God's medicine for you to take as you're on your way to health and wholeness. Make sure you take your divine prescription as instructed. In other words, don't just read your daily dose and then forget about it as you go on your way. Read it over and over. Meditate on its truth until it's planted down in your spirit. Throughout the day, release your faith by saying the confession at the end of each devotion out loud.

As you do so, faithfully acting on the Word you are learning, your health will improve. In fact, I believe it won't be the same at this time next year, but you'll see the effects of God's medicine at work in your body for 365 days—making you healed, strong and whole!

Plant God's Word in Your Spirit

If ye abide in me, and my words abide in you, ye shall ask what ye will, and it shall be done unto you.

—John 15:7

Many people in the body of Christ today aren't walking in health. They may believe in their heads that healing belongs to them, but they haven't received the revelation of it in their spirits.

To walk in health, we need the basic truths in God's Word on healing lodged deep down inside us so they can become an effective, working part of our lives. Only then will healing manifest in our bodies.

When I was just beginning to learn how to live by faith, I walked around confessing, "I know I'm healed. I believe I'm healed." The problem was, my body still felt sick! But I kept reading, studying and meditating on the Bible, and God's truth about healing finally dropped down into my spirit. The stronger the Word of God grew on the inside of me, the more I was able to walk in health. Of course, I still have "opportunities" to be sick, but now I choose not to accept them.

What more could we possibly need to know than, "Surely he hath borne our griefs [sicknesses], and carried our sorrows [pains]...and with his stripes we are healed" (Isa. 53:4,5)?

So when the devil tries to offer you some symptom, just say, "No, I'm not taking that. That isn't mine. Jesus took my sickness 2000 years ago!"

Confession

Father, I abide in You, and Your words abide in me.
I choose to believe Your Word, which says healing and
health belong to me. I walk in divine health because
Jesus took my sicknesses and carried my pains.

Don't Wait on God for Your Miracle

What if you need a miracle, but God doesn't move sovereignly through the gifts of the Spirit to give you one? Don't be surprised if He doesn't; He never promised He would. In fact, God didn't design the gifts of the Spirit for the Church. He intended them to be divine "advertisements" or signs to an unsaved world.

For therein is the righteousness of God revealed from faith to faith: as it is written, The just shall live by faith.

—Romans 1:17

Of course, God loves us so much that He does manifest spiritual gifts among Christians for our blessing, but He doesn't expect us to sit and wait to be blessed by a sovereign move of His Spirit.

How do I know that? Look at 2 Corinthians 5:7: "For we walk by faith, not by sight." Notice this verse does not say, "For we walk by the sovereignty of God, and we hope He operates quickly." Nor does it say, "For we sit back and wait for God to move on our behalf, even if it takes forty years." No, it says we walk by faith—not sight.

What happens if a person walks by faith? The same thing that happened to the woman of Canaan in Matthew 15:28: "O woman, great is thy faith: be it unto thee even as thou wilt."

God expects believers to *believe*—and use faith to initiate miracles. So don't sit back and wait! Go to God's Word and find out His will; then reach out by faith and take hold of what already belongs to you.

Confession

I walk by faith and not by sight. Jesus' body was broken for me so I could live free from sickness and pain.
I receive my healing now by faith.

Take God's Medicine

My son, attend to my words; incline thine ear unto my sayings. Let them not depart from thine eyes; keep them in the midst of thine heart. For they are life unto those that find them, and health to all their flesh.

—Proverbs 4:20-22

In the original Hebrew, this Scripture literally says God's Word is medicine to our flesh. (A marginal note in my *King James Version* Bible substitutes the word *medicine* for the word *health*.) So think about this: What if someone invented a medication that could cure anything wrong with the human body? He'd be rich overnight! People would take that medicine diligently. And yet, if we'd just give God's promises on healing the same credibility we give the medicines developed by medical science, we would have 100 times the results!

(Now, I'm not against medical doctors. In fact, I have several doctors in my close family. Thank God for doctors! They keep people alive until people discover there's a better way.)

God's words may be medicine to all our flesh, but like any other medicine, we have to take it. If we just put it on the shelf and look at it, it won't do any good.

How do we take God's medicine? We hear it and hear it and hear it. Romans 10:17 says, "So then faith cometh by hearing, and hearing by the word of God." When we continually hear God's Word, our faith hooks up and releases God's power—and we rise up healed!

Confession

God's Word has the power to effect healing in my body. I hear the Word and faith rises in me, releasing God's power and producing what I need.

Keep Your Faith Hooked Up

Years ago my wife, Janet, and I held four nights of meetings in Capetown, South Africa. We noticed the first night that a lady in her fifties was led to the front for prayer and then led back to her seat afterward.

After the last meeting she shared her testimony with us: "I've been blind for thirteen years and suffered with migraine headaches for a long time. I was instantly healed of the headaches the first night, but as I walked back to my seat I still couldn't see a thing.

And Jesus went forth, and saw a great multitude, and was moved with compassion toward them, and he healed their sick.

—Matthew 14:14

"But I kept coming back each night to feed my faith," the woman continued. "The first night all I could see was a mass of gray. But tonight, I can tell what color your suit is. And by the time you come back, I'll see you!"

This woman kept her faith hooked up once she realized God wanted her healed. Knowing it is God's will to heal us is the same foundation we all must stand on. In fact, you can take a stand right now on God's Word by saying from your heart, "Father, I believe I receive my healing! It's mine now, and I thank You for it in Jesus' name."

You may not look or feel any different, but believe you *are* different. Keep your faith hooked up and hold fast to your confession of faith. Healing may come instantly or over a period of minutes, hours, days, weeks or even months—but it will come!

Confession

God is able and willing to heal me.
Therefore, I believe I receive my healing.

Put Your Faith in God

My son, attend to my words; incline thine ear unto my sayings. Let them not depart from thine eyes; keep them in the midst of thine heart. For they are life unto those that find them, and health [medicine] to all their flesh.

—Proverbs 4:20-22

Someone may ask, "If I believe I'm healed, do I need to throw my medicine away?" If you have to ask, you better not. After all, you aren't healed because you throw your medicine away; you're healed because you believe God.

Some people hear a message on faith and then go out and smash their glasses to pieces. They say, "I believe I'm healed," and then they walk into walls for six months until they get a new pair of glasses.

Yet, the glasses don't heal your eyes; they simply enable you to see while God heals your eyes. So every time you put your glasses on, make a practice of saying, "Thank God, I believe I'm healed."

Or if you're taking medicine, every time you swallow a dose say, "Thank God, I believe I'm healed by the stripes of Jesus." The medicine doesn't heal you, but it helps keep your body working right while God does the healing.

Now, if God tells you to throw your medicine away, obey Him. In that case, however, you'll know it's God and you won't have to ask anyone else. So until then, keep taking your medicine. And meanwhile remember—your faith is in God, not the medicine.

Confession

Medicine may be helpful, but God's medicine—His Word—
is much more effective. I believe God's medicine is
working in me now, making my body completely whole.

Having Done All–Stand

I know a lady who learned after she became pregnant that a childhood case of rheumatic fever had permanently damaged her heart. Her doctor put her on heart medication indefinitely.

Later the woman discovered Mark 11:24 that says, "What things soever ye desire, when ye pray, believe that ye receive them, and ye shall have them." She fed on that Scripture until faith rose in her heart, and she believed she received healing for her damaged heart. For two whole years every time she took her medicine she'd say, "Thank God, I'm healed by Jesus' stripes. Medicine doesn't heal me; it just keeps my heart beating right while God does the healing." She kept standing on the Word.

Wherefore take unto you the whole armour of God, that ye may be able to withstand in the evil day, and having done all, to stand.

—Ephesians 6:13

One day the lady went to her medicine cabinet when suddenly the Holy Ghost spoke to her: "You don't need the medicine now. Throw it away." (Notice that she didn't stop taking her medicine until she knew God told her to.)

Later she went to another heart specialist who conducted more tests and concluded, "There must have been a mix-up in the original diagnosis because your heart is fine!" Now, heart damage doesn't just disappear. No, this woman supernaturally received her healing.

We all want quick results to our prayer of faith—and at times we receive them. But if our answers don't come quickly, we must do as Ephesians 6:13 says, "having done all, to stand."

Take hold of God's Word, stand in faith—and then keep standing.

Confession

Medicines help me, but Jesus is my healer. I say with confidence, "God's Word works, and it's working in me now!"

Be Free From Condemnation

Beloved, if our heart condemn us not, then have we confidence toward God. And whatsoever we ask, we receive of him, because we keep his commandments, and do those things that are pleasing in his sight.

—1 John 3:21,22

Condemnation and disease go hand in hand. The devil puts condemnation on you to make you feel bad and to destroy your confidence in God so you can't receive from Him.

God is never the One who shuts you off from receiving. But if you allow condemnation to operate in your life, it will stop your faith from working every time. Condemnation dogs your trail, making you say things like, "Well, God wouldn't heal me. God wouldn't do anything for me. I'm unworthy. I've made mistakes. Something is wrong with me."

The enemy likes to put you under condemnation for past sins, failures and mistakes until you lose all your confidence in receiving from God. The devil knows that if he can just put you under condemnation, he can keep you wrapped around his finger with sickness and disease.

But always remember that the devil is the one who condemns—not God. The Holy Ghost and your own spirit will only convict you of sin in order to draw you to repentance. Condemnation *always* comes from the kingdom of darkness.

So get yourself in position to receive from God—absolutely refuse to allow condemnation in your life.

Confession

I'm a child of God. My Father never condemns me,
so I do not allow condemnation in my life.
I hold fast to the truth that my Father loves me.

Freedom From Condemnation Changes Your Life

One time during a service, the Spirit of God suddenly spoke to my spirit: There's someone here who fell several years ago and injured the bottom of her spine. Call her up here; I want to heal her. I spoke out what I'd heard and immediately a lady came forward. "God just wants you to know He loves you," I told the woman. Then I laid hands on her and prayed.

There is therefore now no condemnation to them which are in Christ Jesus, who walk not after the flesh, but after the Spirit.

—Romans 8:1

The next day this woman shared her testimony: "Some bad things happened to me as a young child that didn't happen to my friends. Because I had no teaching, I assumed that God caused these bad things to happen to me. I formulated the opinion that there was something 'evil' about me, although I didn't know what it was."

I always thought, *God loves my friends, and good things happen to them, but He doesn't love me.*

But today at work, it suddenly registered to me: *The pain is gone! God called me out, and I was the only one in a whole crowd who had those symptoms. He healed me from the top of my head to the soles of my feet. From now on, my life will be different because I know God loves me."*

When God moved on this woman's behalf, He instantly healed her from pain and sickness and freed her from a lifetime of condemnation. And, as she testified, that new freedom changed her life forever.

Confession

My Father loves me; He doesn't condemn me. His best for me
is that I walk in healing and health, and I walk in His best.

Hold Fast to Your Healing With the Hand of Faith

Behold, I come quickly: hold that fast which thou hast, that no man take thy crown.

—Revelation 3:11

Many times people go to large meetings and get healed. But six weeks or six months later, the same symptoms return to their bodies and some end up worse off than before they were healed.

You may say, "Well, I thought God healed them." Sure, He did. But the Bible says, "Prove all things; hold fast that which is good" (1 Thess. 5:21). Healing is good, so we have to hold fast to it. And the only way to hold fast is with the hand of faith.

If you're in a big meeting and God moves with a gift of the Spirit to miraculously heal your body, don't turn it down. But once you're healed, run back home to your Bible and feed on God's Word. Get full of the Word on the subject of healing. Then if the enemy tries to steal your miracle, you'll be able to say with authority, "No, devil, you're not taking away my healing! God gave it to me. It's mine, and you're not stealing it!"

Rise up and take a stance of faith. Refuse to be moved. Hold fast to your healing with the hand of faith.

Confession

Healing belongs to me. I meditate on the Word, which is greater than any sickness or disease. The devil can't make symptoms stick, because God's Word in me drives them out.

Healing Is God's Will

Some people say, "I know lots of people who prayed for healing, and they didn't get healed." But faith begins where the will of God is known. Did those people know that healing is God's will? Did they know it's God's will they prosper and be in health, even as their souls prosper? (3 John 2.)

Your faith will never operate beyond your knowledge of God's will. Therefore, faith is simply taking God at His Word, which is His will.

So feed on the Word, and establish the truth in your heart that healing is God's will. Then you'll be able to say with confidence, "Father, You said it, I believe it, so that settles it."

For unto us was the gospel preached, as well as unto them: but the word preached did not profit them, not being mixed with faith in them that heard it.

—Hebrews 4:2

Act like God's Word is true—and receive your healing by faith.

Confession

I know my Father wants me healthy. His Son, Jesus, bore my sickness and pain so I wouldn't have to bear them. I receive the healing Jesus purchased for me.

Don't Waver

If any of you lack wisdom, let him ask of God, that giveth to all men liberally, and upbraideth not; and it shall be given him. But let him ask in faith, nothing wavering. For he that wavereth is like a wave of the sea driven with the wind and tossed. For let not that man think that he shall receive any thing of the Lord.

—James 1:5-7

When we ask God for something we must ask in faith, believing we receive our answer and not wavering in doubt. James said the person who doubts won't receive any thing of the Lord.

Well, wouldn't healing be included in "*any thing*"? So we could say the man who doubts won't receive *healing*. What man? The one who doesn't ask in faith. And where does faith begin? Where the will of God is known.

Sometimes I think we ministers pray for people in healing lines too quickly—before we know if they're ready to stand in faith. For instance, many folks say, "Well, I sure would like to be healed."

I ask them, "Do you believe it's God's will to heal you?"

"I hope so," they respond.

Their words show they're only hoping they'll be healed, but they're not in faith. And the more they're prayed for without results, the less they expect to receive the next time someone prays for them.

Don't let that happen to you. Spend time in God's Word. Find out what His will is regarding your need. Then pray the prayer of faith without wavering in doubt, and your answer will surely come to pass.

Confession

I confidently pray in faith for healing. I believe I receive my answer because God's Word says by Jesus' stripes I'm healed.

Real Faith vs. "That Faith Business"

Sometimes people say, "I tried that faith business, but it didn't work." Yet these people never could have been in faith to begin with. If they'd really been in faith, they'd still be in faith. If they really believed they received their answer when they prayed, they'd still be believing. But if they were just hoping and praying that "that faith business" works, then it won't.

Why is that? Because real faith involves:

For whatsoever is born of God overcometh the world: and this is the victory that overcometh the world, even our faith.

—1 John 5:4

- Stepping out and believing God for what you know to be His will for your life.

- Finding out God's will regarding your need and then trusting Him to bring it to pass.

- Believing that God said what He meant and meant what He said and then trusting Him to do what He said.

- Acting like God's Word is true and expecting Him to do the same.

So forget about "trying" faith. Either you believe the Bible, or you don't. Hope will give up, but faith has tenacity. Real faith digs its heels in and says, "I know what belongs to me, and I'm not going to live without it!"

Confession

I believe what God says will come to pass. I don't just hope to receive what I pray for; I know when I pray according to God's will, I receive what I've asked for.

Discern the Lord's Body

For he that eateth and drinketh [communion] unworthily, eateth and drinketh damnation to himself, not discerning the Lord's body. For this cause many are weak and sickly among you, and many sleep.

—1 Corinthians 11:29,30

The major reason many sick people stay sick is that they don't know whether or not God wants them healed. They don't understand why Jesus' body was broken. They are "...not discerning [not fully understanding or duly appreciating] the Lord's body."

Many people don't realize Jesus' body was broken for their physical health as much as His blood was shed for the forgiveness of their sins. Therefore, they don't know it's God's will to heal them.

I've heard people say, "Oh, yes, I believe that God can heal today. But sometimes He does, and sometimes He doesn't. We can never know who will receive their healing and who won't."

Yet that isn't faith. Faith begins where the will of God is known.

Discern the Lord's body rightly; understand that it was broken for you. Feed your spirit with the truth that by Jesus' stripes you were healed. (1 Peter 2:24.) Keep meditating on that truth until you know that you know God wants you healed. Then you can be sure when you ask God for your healing that you're truly praying the prayer of faith.

Confession

Jesus' body was broken for my physical health as surely as His blood was shed for my sins. I believe I receive healing in my body now.

Don't Leave the Door Open

If you were to leave the front door of your home wide open, any kind of animal—even a skunk—could walk right in. Spiritually speaking, Christians sometimes leave a "door" open to their lives for the enemy's "skunk" to enter.

Perhaps you're having trouble with obstacles the devil keeps throwing your way and you've done everything you know to do. Well, check to see if you've left a door open. For instance, by that I mean, are you walking in love? Are you harboring unforgiveness in your heart toward anyone?

As the bird by wandering, as the swallow by flying, so the curse causeless shall not come.

—Proverbs 26:2

You see, unforgiveness stops faith from working, because faith works by love, and love always forgives. (Gal. 5:6.) We may be trying to believe God for healing, but if we harbor unforgiveness in our hearts faith will not work.

Sometimes people think they just can't forgive. They claim that the devil won't let them. No, it isn't the devil who won't let people forgive; it's their own flesh—and the flesh can always be put under.

Forgiveness is not a *feeling;* it's a *decision.* We may have to reinforce that commitment to forgive again and again, but it's well worth the effort. When we keep all our doors shut, no skunks can get in to steal our blessings.

Confession

I refuse to walk in unforgiveness and open the door to the devil.
I won't allow the enemy's curse to come back on me.
I choose to forgive, no matter what anyone does. I walk in love.

Forgiveness and Healing—
Both Are Yours in Christ

*Bless the Lord,
O my soul, and
forget not all his
benefits: who
forgiveth all thine
iniquities; who
healeth all thy
diseases.*

—Psalm 103:2,3

Scriptures from Genesis to Revelation show that both forgiveness and healing were provided on the Cross. These Scriptures show that when you're forgiven, you can be healed as well. And when you're healed, you can also be forgiven.

Forgiveness and healing go hand in hand and cannot be separated. We are made righteous through the shed blood of Jesus Christ, and we are healed through the stripes He bore.

You may ask, "But what if I'm sick today as a result of living in sin in the past?" Even if sin opened the door to sickness, you can be forgiven and healed at the same time because of God's love and mercy.

So don't take one part of Jesus' redemptive work and leave the other behind. If one part of God's plan of redemption is for today, then all of it is for today. Jesus' body was broken for you as surely as His blood was shed for you. You have as much right to be healed as you do to be saved and forgiven from sin. It's a package deal, and it all belongs to you!

Confession

When I received Jesus as my Savior, I also received Him as my Healer. I meditate on all of His benefits. His blood was shed for my sins, and His body was broken for my healing.

Healing Belongs to You

At the moment you found out Jesus' blood was shed for your sins and you believed in your heart and confessed Him as Lord, *nothing* could stop your salvation.

Well, the same should be true when you make a declaration of healing by faith. You find out the truth in God's Word that Jesus' body was broken for your healing; you believe and confess Him as your healer. Then nothing can stop your healing.

And when he had given thanks, he brake it, and said, Take, eat: this is my body, which is broken for you: this do in remembrance of me.

—1 Corinthians 11:24

For too long, Church tradition has taught people only half of redemption. All over the world, ministers have preached "whosoever will" shall receive salvation. But many of those same people have also told Christians, "Healing isn't for today. God *can* heal, but that doesn't mean He always *will*. Sometimes prayers for healing work; sometimes they don't." As a result, Christians must get rid of a lot of doubt and unbelief before they can take hold of healing.

It's different on the mission field. Every time Janet and I visit a place where the Gospel has never been preached, we tell the people Jesus paid the same price for their sins and their sicknesses. The people eagerly receive and get saved and healed at the same time.

Sickness is the price we pay for not understanding the Atonement. But bless God, we're as healed as we're saved. Healing belongs to whosoever will believe. Healing belongs to *you!*

Confession

Healing belongs to me just as much as salvation does.
Jesus is as much my healer as He is my Savior.
I walk in the full benefits of my redemption.

Use Your Authority

And I will give unto thee the keys of the kingdom of heaven: and whatsoever thou shalt bind on earth shall be bound in heaven: and whatsoever thou shalt loose on earth shall be loosed in heaven.

—Matthew 16:19

Many times wrong thinking opens the door to the devil in Christians' lives. They may assume God allows sickness to come. But in reality, it's not God who does it—it's *they themselves. They* don't use the authority Jesus gave them.

In Matthew 16:19, Jesus was talking to Peter just after he had received the revelation that Jesus is the Christ. Another translation of this passage says, "I will give unto thee the keys of the kingdom of heaven: whatever you forbid on earth, Heaven shall forbid, and whatever you allow on earth, Heaven shall allow" (v. 19 RIEU).

You see, Jesus has all authority. But as the Head of the Church, He has given us the same authority He has.

God expects that *you* resist the devil. *You* use the name of Jesus. *You* stand steadfast in the faith. *You* neither give place to the devil. In other words, Jesus is saying, "Whatever you forbid, I'll forbid. Whatever you allow, I'll allow. You make the decision, and I'll back you up."

Authority is like a traffic policeman who doesn't have the physical power to stop a car. But when he holds up his hand, the authority of the city that hired him stands behind him.

So use your God-given authority to shut the door on the devil, and all of heaven will back you up.

Confession

Jesus said what I allow, He'll allow; and what I forbid,
He'll forbid. I refuse to allow sickness in my body.
Body, come in line with God's Word in Jesus' name.

God Will Back You Up

Sometimes we ask, "Why did God allow this illness to come into my life?" But the truth is, *we allowed it.*

It's like driving down a highway at breakneck speed and then telling the policeman who pulls you over, "Sorry, officer, I didn't realize the speed limit wasn't 110 miles an hour." The policeman would *not* say, "Bless your heart. Forgive me, I shouldn't have pulled you over. I didn't know you were ignorant of the law." No, he'd give you a ticket anyway. Ignorance of the law is no excuse.

The same is true in the spiritual realm. You may say, "I didn't know I allowed the devil to keep me from receiving healing." Yes, but you have the Bible which gives you all the answers. Ignorance of the Word is no excuse.

And I will give unto thee the keys of the kingdom of heaven: and whatsoever thou shalt bind on earth shall be bound in heaven: and whatsoever thou shalt loose on earth shall be loosed in heaven.

—Matthew 16:19

Sometimes we don't receive healing because we allow a door to stay open to the devil. Often the open door is the result of wrong thinking, which is usually the result of wrong teaching. Wrong thinking produces wrong believing, and wrong believing produces wrong results.

Bottom line, if you forbid the devil's strategies against you, God stands behind you. If you do nothing, God stands behind you. Whatever you do, God backs you up. So choose wisely.

Confession

My Father has given me authority to choose what to allow or forbid in my life. So I allow only God's thoughts in my mind and divine health in my body.

God Gives Abundant Life–Not Sickness

The thief cometh not, but for to steal, and to kill, and to destroy: I am come that they might have life, and that they might have it more abundantly.

—John 10:10

Do you need healing? Make sure your thinking is in line with God's Word. Wrong thinking is one of the major things that can hinder you from receiving your miracle.

For example, some people think God causes sickness—by sending, commissioning, planning, or allowing it. Therefore, they automatically conclude, "Sickness must be God's will for me. After all, He allowed this sickness to come on me."

But when people say that, in essence they mean, "Yes, I know the devil is the author of sickness, but somehow this sickness is God's will for me. God saw I needed this to teach me something, so He and the devil are somehow working together."

No way. The devil hasn't worked with God for a long time. Long ago he was an archangel named Lucifer, created by God and living in heaven. But sin and iniquity were found in Lucifer, and he was thrown out of God's presence. (Isa. 14:12,14.)

Ever since then, God and the devil have *never* worked together. They are *not* a team. How in the world could they work as a team? Amos 3:3 says, "Can two walk together, except they be agreed?"

The truth is, Satan tries to destroy you, while God sacrificed His only Son to offer you abundant life. Make sure your thinking is in line with God's Word in order to receive that abundant life.

Confession

My Father doesn't put sickness on me. He only gives me life and wants me well. I walk in the abundant life and health my Father has given me.

Refuse To Allow Sickness in Your Life

Sometimes people say, "God allowed the devil to put this sickness on me." No, *they* allowed it. God had no choice in the matter because He will not override people's wills.

Most of us have been guilty of the same thing at one time or another. We allow the devil to put sickness on us because we don't use our God-given authority. God doesn't allow sickness in our lives as a part of His divine plan for us; He only allows sickness when He doesn't have a choice.

Then Peter said, Silver and gold have I none; but such as I have give I thee: In the name of Jesus Christ of Nazareth rise up and walk.

—Acts 3:6

You see, God has bound Himself to His Word. He said, "Whatever you forbid, I'll forbid. All of heaven stands at attention ready to back you up. But if you allow it, I have to allow it. Whatever decision you make, I'll back you up on it." (Matt. 18:19 RIEU.)

Think about it. God doesn't have sickness to give. Remember, He lives in heaven. Do you think you'll see a lot of sick people lying around when you get to heaven? No. There is no sickness and disease up there.

So how would God give us sickness? Would He take a trip to hell and borrow some from the devil? No. God is the One who sent sickness down to hell to begin with through the death, burial, and resurrection of Jesus. And if He didn't want it up in heaven, He sure doesn't want it on His children.

Confession

I refuse everything the devil has to offer.
I won't allow sickness in my body, and all of heaven backs me up.

Set Free by Divine Knowledge

My people are destroyed for lack of knowledge.

—Hosea 4:6

Sometimes we try to discover how we can receive our healing when what we really need to do is find out why we got sick to begin with. If we can find the answer to that question, we can correct the problem and be healed.

Why do Christians get sick? There are many different reasons, but a primary one is a lack of knowledge of God's Word. Isaiah 5:13 says, "Therefore my people are gone into captivity, because they have no knowledge." *The Amplified Bible* says, "Therefore my people go into captivity [to their enemies] without knowing it and because they have no knowledge [of God]."

Many people are bound up and taken captive by the enemy through sickness and disease. Yet they think their physical condition is God's will because they don't have knowledge of His Word. These people say, "I'm sick for the glory of God!" because they don't know that Jesus paid the price for their healing. They don't have knowledge of the Word, so they are taken captive—and they don't even know it.

But when you take hold of the Word in your heart, it transforms your life. You're set free from the notion that God wants you sick for some purpose of His own, and you can receive the healing that rightfully belongs to you as a covenant child of God.

Confession

My God is the God who heals me and
gets glory from my being healthy.
Therefore, I walk in healing and health.

Look in God's "Will" To Find His Will

In order to be healed, we need to be sure of the answers to certain questions: Is it God's will for us to be healed? Does He want us sick for a purpose or to teach us something? Does God have anything to do with disease?

The only way we can find out God's will on any subject is to read the "will" He left for us.

You see, suppose I had a wealthy relative who died and left me not only an inheritance, but also a will explaining what was in the inheritance. I could sit back for years and say, "I wonder what the will says; I wonder what was left to me." Or I could go read the will and find out.

It's the same with God. Jesus provided an inheritance for us because God first appointed Jesus heir of all things. Hebrews 1:2 says God "hath in these last days spoken unto us by his Son, whom he hath appointed heir of all things, by whom also he made the worlds."

The Spirit itself beareth witness with our spirit, that we are the children of God: and if children, then heirs; heirs of God, and joint-heirs with Christ; if so be that we suffer with him, that we may be also glorified together.

—Romans 8:16,17

God also made us joint-heirs with Jesus. *Now, we need to read the will to find out what God's will is.* The New Testament is God's last will and testament, and it will tell us what belongs to us as children of God.

Confession

My Father wrote a will to tell me what is mine
and sealed it with the blood of Jesus.
Healing is part of that inheritance, and it belongs to me now.

God Is a Rewarder

*But without faith
it is impossible
to please him:
for he that cometh
to God must
believe that he is,
and that he is a
rewarder of them
that diligently
seek him.*

—Hebrews 11:6

Do you want to receive God's covenant promise of healing? Then you have to believe that God *is,* and you have to believe He is a *rewarder.* If you don't believe you will receive a reward from Him, you won't.

Most of the time people don't go to God in faith. They may believe that God is, but they aren't sure He is a rewarder. So they say, "Dear God, if it is Your will, please do this for me."

But you can go to God in faith, knowing exactly what His will is because you have His will to read. For example, you never have to say, "I wonder if it's God's will to heal me?" You can just read the Bible and find out. It's His last will and testament to you.

When someone makes out a will, no one else has the right to take away from it or add to it. In the same way, we don't have a right to change God's will to us. All we can do is read what belongs to us and live by it.

So study God's last will and testament until you get these two truths lodged deep in your heart: God is, and God is a rewarder. Then diligently seek Him for your healing, and receive your reward.

Confession

I believe my God is. He is alive, He is powerful, and He is a rewarder.
I live in line with His Word and receive,
all the benefits He has provided for me.

God's Will Be Done in Your Life

Notice what Jesus said: "Thy will be done, as in heaven, so in earth." In other words, God's will on earth is no different than God's will in heaven.

I don't plan to see any sickness when I get to heaven, do you? Of course not! There's no sickness in heaven because sickness cannot exist in the presence of God.

But how do you know what God's will is here on earth? Well, find out what His will is in heaven, and you'll have a pretty good idea. Jesus said, "Thy kingdom come. Thy will be done in earth *as it is in heaven.*"

So if health is God's will in heaven, health is God's will down here on earth too. If He's against sickness there, He's against sickness here.

And he said unto them, When ye pray, say, Our Father which art in heaven, Hallowed be thy name. Thy kingdom come. Thy will be done, as in heaven, so in earth.

—Luke 11:2

God wants you healthy once you're in heaven, and He wants you healthy while you're still here on earth. So let God's kingdom come and His will be done in your life. Receive your healing and walk in divine health.

Confession

Divine health is God's will for me even while I'm here on the earth.
I walk in health because Jesus bore all my sicknesses and pains.
Therefore, in Jesus' name I am healed.

God Wants To Heal All

Is any sick among you? let him call for the elders of the church; and let them pray over him, anointing him with oil in the name of the Lord: and the prayer of faith shall save the sick, and the Lord shall raise him up; and if he have committed sins, they shall be forgiven him.

—James 5:14,15

James was writing to believers, and he asked, "Is there any sick among you?" Notice He didn't say, "If there is any sick among you, let him pray and see if—by some chance—God might want him healed." Nor did James say, "Let him fast and pray for three weeks to see if it's God's will to heal him."

Nothing is said in this Scripture about whether it's God's will or not. And it doesn't say, "The Lord shall raise him up—if he's one of a few destined to get healed because God is in a good mood."

James just tells us, "If there's any sick in the church, let the elders pray for him and anoint him with oil in the name of the Lord." Then James says, "And the prayer of faith *shall* [not *might*] save the sick, and the Lord *shall* raise him up" (v. 15).

God isn't confused or mixed up. If it weren't His will for all to be healed, why would He tell sick people how to get healed? God reveals His will right here in this Scripture, and His perfect will is to heal *all*—anytime and anywhere.

Confession

God has given me several ways to receive healing.
According to His Word, when I ask church elders to anoint
me with oil and pray, the prayer of faith will raise me up.

Healing and the Gospel Are for All

At times I've prayed, "Lord, I laid hands on Brother So-and-so, and he didn't get any better." But notice in this passage God didn't say, "Just go lay hands on the sick, and they will recover." No, He starts out by saying, "Go into all the world and preach the Gospel to every creature." Then He says, "These signs shall follow them that believe...."

We aren't supposed to just go around looking for sick people to lay hands on. They will run away if we do that. First, we have to tell them the good news of the Gospel—that it's God's will to heal them. *Then* we lay hands on them; then they will recover.

We make a mistake rushing to lay hands on people without teaching them to cooperate with the Word. I remember a case like that. People laid hands on a man to pray for him, but the moment they were done, he said, "Well, that sure didn't work." He didn't expect it to work because no one had taught him how it was supposed to work.

And he said unto them, Go ye into all the world, and preach the gospel to every creature. He that believeth and is baptized shall be saved; but he that believeth not shall be damned. And these signs shall follow them that believe; In my name...they shall lay hands on the sick, and they shall recover.

—Mark 16:15-18

If that same man had heard the Gospel first, he could've gotten in agreement with the person praying for him. He could've known for himself that God's will is *healing for all.*

Confession

I'm always ready to give God's Word to someone in need because it will produce faith in me and all who hear it.

Jesus: The Image of the Father

[The Father] hath delivered us from the power of darkness, and hath translated us into the kingdom of his dear Son: in whom we have redemption through his blood, even the forgiveness of sins: who is the image of the invisible God, the firstborn of every creature.

—Colossians 1:13-15

The world has a warped idea of what God is like. People often think God is causing all their problems. They have a mental picture of God sitting up in heaven with a big club waiting for them to make a mistake so He can hit them on the head. In other words, they think God makes them sick, steals their money, or kills their families.

But if you want to know what God is really like, look at Jesus. Jesus gives us a picture of God. In Colossians 1:15, Jesus is called "the image of the invisible God." Jesus Himself said, "If you've seen Me, you've seen the Father." (John 14:9.)

Follow Jesus' earthly ministry to see God's will in action. You see, everything Jesus did (or didn't do) represented God's will.

Jesus led a perfect, sinless life. He never stole, never killed, and never destroyed. He never made anyone sick and never left anyone sick who believed Him to be healed. He never said, "This sickness is here to teach you something, to perfect you, or to make you more pious." He never said, "This sickness is good for you."

Jesus acted out God's will for mankind. He never refused healing to anyone, and He won't refuse healing to *you*.

Confession

Jesus healed everyone who came to Him in faith.
Hebrews 13:8 says Jesus is the same yesterday, today, and forever,
so I come to Him in faith, knowing He will heal me too.

God Wants To Heal All

And ye shall know the truth, and the truth shall make you free.

—John 8:32

People who say, "God doesn't heal anymore," evidently never read the Bible. Hebrews 13:8 says Jesus is the same now as He's ever been. So if Jesus healed while He walked on this earth, He still heals today.

Most people believe it's God's will to heal *some*. But the big question remains, "Is it God's will to heal *all?*" Some say, "Well, that can't be true because Brother So-and-so didn't get healed."

If we go by people's experiences, we may conclude it isn't God's will to heal everyone. But we must gather all the experience, tradition, doctrine, theory, and denominationalism we've ever heard and push it aside. We must look at nothing but God's Word and find out what God has to say.

For example, if you wanted to know my will about something, I hope you wouldn't go ask some guy on the street corner who doesn't know me. There's no telling what that person would say.

Yet, most of us have done that with God. When we've wanted to know God's will, we've sometimes gone to people who don't know Him. They may have given us wild opinions, not having the faintest idea what the Bible says.

To find God's will on a subject, we must go to Jesus, the express image of God. Jesus said, "He that hath seen me hath seen the Father" (John 14:9). He also said, "...The truth shall make you free" (John 8:32). Thank God, the Bible is truth, and it says God heals *all*.

Confession

The truth is God wants to heal me. I've found it in the Word; I know it's God's will. So I believe I receive my healing now.

Look to Jesus To Know the Father

Philip saith unto him, Lord, shew us the Father, and it sufficeth us. Jesus saith unto him, Have I been so long time with you, and yet hast thou not known me, Philip? he that hath seen me hath seen the Father; and how sayest thou then, Shew us the Father? Believest thou not that I am in the Father, and the Father in me? the words that I speak unto you I speak not of myself: but the Father that dwelleth in me, he doeth the works.

—John 14:8-10

Philip had one burning desire—for Jesus to show them the Father. You see, the world didn't understand God. They didn't know what God looked like. Then Jesus came along as love manifested in the flesh and said, "If you want to know what the Father looks like, look at Me. I'll show you what the Father looks like, sounds like, and acts like. I only do that which I see My Father do." (John 5:19.)

Jesus also said in that verse, "The Father in Me does the work. I'm not healing people; *God* is healing them through Me." Therefore, everything Jesus did had to be the will of God. If God didn't supply the power, Jesus couldn't give it out.

Jesus acted out God's will for the human race. And what did Jesus do? He healed *all* who would receive healing in faith. What *didn't* He do? He *never* made people sick or *left* people sick who believed to be healed.

Study the ministry of Jesus, so you'll know for a fact healing is God's will for *all*—for *you.*

Confession

Jesus revealed the Father's desire to heal His people. That means my Father heals me when I come to Him in faith.

Jesus—The Will of God in Action

When Jesus came to Peter's house, Jesus didn't fast and pray to see what the Father wanted Him to do. He knew God's will is healing for *all*. Therefore, it had to be God's will for Peter's mother-in-law to be healed and whole.

You can come to that same conclusion yourself just by studying the Gospels. For example, think about this: How many people did Jesus walk up to and make sick? *None.* How many people did He tell, "This sickness is for the glory of God, so keep it awhile"? *None.* How many times did He say, "I can't heal you"? *Never.* How many people who wanted healing did He turn down? *Not one.* How many times did He say, "Wait until later; I'll do it in My own good time"? *Never.*

And when Jesus was come into Peter's house, he saw his wife's mother laid, and sick of a fever. And he touched her hand, and the fever left her: and she arose, and ministered unto them.

—Matthew 8:14,15

Remember, Jesus' every move in His earthly ministry was the will of God in action. So when we see that Jesus never turned anyone down, that tells us that God never turns anyone down. Jesus never said, "Wait," so God never says, "Wait." Jesus never said, "This sickness is good for you," so God never says, "This sickness is good for you." Jesus did nothing but set people free; therefore, God does nothing but set people free.

Jesus is all the proof we need that God's will is to heal *everyone*.

Confession

Just as Jesus never changes, so also my Father never changes.
Healing was His will then, and healing is His will for me now.
Let Your will be done, Lord!

Hear and Be Healed

And [Jesus] came to Nazareth, where he had been brought up: and, as his custom was, he went into the synagogue on the sabbath day, and stood up for to read. And there was delivered unto him the book of the prophet Esaias. And when he had opened the book, he found the place where it was written, The Spirit of the Lord is upon me, because he hath anointed me to preach the gospel to the poor; he hath sent me to heal the brokenhearted, to preach deliverance to the captives, and recovering of sight to the blind, to set at liberty them that are bruised, to preach the acceptable year of the Lord.

—*Luke 4:16-19*

There's a definite connection between hearing and being healed. You can find several instances in the New Testament where people refused to hear the Word and therefore were not healed.

In Luke 4 Jesus quoted from the book of Isaiah, but the people wouldn't hear it. In fact, verse 28 says, "All they in the synagogue, when they heard these things, were filled with wrath."

If the people had been willing to hear, they would've been filled with faith to receive healing—and all the other benefits of believing in Jesus. But they missed out because they refused to hear.

During Jesus' earthly ministry, we never find Him leaving anyone sick—except people who wouldn't receive from Him. You see, God won't force anything on anyone; He's a gentleman. But when you come to God in faith, He delights to heal you and set you free.

Confession

I choose to hear God's Word and accept His will, which is my healing. I will not allow doubt and unbelief to keep me from receiving from God.

Ask What You Will

If ye abide in me, and my words abide in you, ye shall ask what ye will, and it shall be done unto you.

—John 15:7

From this Scripture we understand it's God's will to heal everyone, because it's God's will to answer prayers. God promises to answer any prayer that lines up with His Word.

We know that healing lines up with God's Word because Psalm 107:20 tells us God sent His Word to heal us. We know healing lines up with His Word because Matthew 9:35 tells us Jesus went through all the cities and villages, teaching, preaching, and healing every sickness and disease among the people. We know healing lines up with His Word because Hebrews 13:8 says Jesus is the same yesterday, today, and forever.

Jesus said, "If you abide in Me, and My words abide in you, you shall ask whatever you will, and it shall be done."

"Lord, what if I will to be healed?" That's good news because God's will is to heal you. And if healing is what you will, too, then you can be sure it shall be done unto you.

Confession

I abide in the Lord Jesus Christ, and His words abide in me.
So I believe I receive my healing today.
By faith, it is done.

Ask and You Shall Receive

And in that day ye shall ask me nothing. Verily, verily, I say unto you, Whatsoever ye shall ask the Father in my name, he will give it you. Hitherto have ye asked nothing in my name: ask, and ye shall receive, that your joy may be full.

—John 16:23,24

One way we know our heavenly Father wants to heal us is by this verse, which tells us that He wants to answer our prayers. Out of all the things He said we could ask for in prayer, Jesus never excluded healing. In fact, He said, "Verily, verily, I say unto you, *whatsoever* ye shall ask the Father in my name, he will give it you." He didn't say, "He will give you whatsoever you ask—unless it's healing."

Jesus said, "Ask, and ye shall receive, that your joy may be full."

"What if I ask for healing?" you may say.

"Ask and ye shall receive, that your joy may be full."

"What if it's a physical need?"

"Ask and ye shall receive, that your joy may be full."

Does God want us healed? He must, because He promised to answer our prayers—including our prayers for healing—when we pray to Him in Jesus' name.

Confession

God's ears are open to my prayer for healing.
I receive what I pray for in Jesus' name,
and I am filled with joy.

Our Creator and Our Healer

As a young man, I had problems with my throat closing up on me. I'd almost panic at times because it became so tight I could hardly swallow.

For I am the Lord that healeth thee.

—Exodus 15:26

Finally I saw an allergist who informed me that I was allergic to weeds, most foods, dust, and other hard-to-avoid allergens. He gave me regular serum injections, and for the first time in years, my throat loosened up. I was supposed to take those injections for life.

Shortly after that I was born again and home from college for the summer leading youth meetings five to seven nights a week. We sang and prayed a lot at the meetings, but we didn't have any real teaching because I was the leader and didn't know anything. I certainly couldn't teach the Word—I didn't even know God could heal.

One day we were all praying when I felt my throat tighten again. Suddenly panic and fear hit me as I realized I left my serum at school. (I didn't know I'd been delivered from fear when I'd gotten saved.) But gradually, a deep realization that God is God began to rise up from my spirit.

Quietly, I said, "Lord, if You're smart and powerful enough to design this body, You sure can fix one defect. Would You do that for me?" Minutes later my throat returned to normal, and it has never tightened up like that again.

My healing came the moment I realized God could heal. That revelation changed my life. God *created* me—surely He could *fix* me.

Confession

My God is the Creator of the universe who upholds all things by the Word of His power. He's the same God who's able and willing to heal me.

Getting Past the Invisible Wall

> *The heart of the prudent getteth knowledge; and the ear of the wise seeketh knowledge.*
>
> *—Proverbs 18:15*

After God healed me of allergies, I went through a real struggle the next time I needed healing. The thought came to me, *Yeah, God's able to heal me, but is He willing?* (I bet you know what that voice in your mind sounds like.)

So the next time I prayed for healing I said, "Lord, I sure would like You to heal me—if You really want to." But I wasn't healed, and I couldn't figure out why. I prayed again, "Lord, here I am. You did it last time; why don't You do it this time?"

I didn't understand that I'd hit an invisible wall because, although I knew God was *able* to heal, I still didn't know He was *willing*.

Then came the thought, *Maybe God wants me sick for a purpose.* I didn't get that thought from a church or a book; it came straight from the source of doubt and unbelief. That thought came to my mind and took root. For years, I had trouble getting rid of that wrong thinking.

Yet, that's the point most Christians have reached in their spiritual walk. They know God is able, but they aren't sure He's willing.

The truth is, your faith will never operate beyond your knowledge of God's will. So root out wrong thinking. Study God's Word until you know it's God's will to heal everyone. Then take God at His Word for your healing.

Confession

My Father wants me well, and I root out every thought otherwise.
God sent His Word to heal me, and I take Him at His Word.

God Is Able and Willing

When I first started hearing the truth of God's Word about healing, I studied the subject with great interest. But whenever symptoms hit my body, my first thought was, *I wonder why God allowed this to happen?* It took me years to get rid of that doubt and unbelief the enemy had planted in me.

When we know God's ability but doubt His willingness, it's like slapping Him in the face. Stop and think about it. Suppose you said to me, "Mark, I have a real problem, and I know you'd help me if you could. But I realize you don't have the capability or the equipment to help me." I'd feel good that you thought I cared enough to help if I could.

And the people, when they knew it, followed him: and he received them, and spake unto them of the kingdom of God, and healed them that had need of healing.

—Luke 9:11

But suppose you said, "Now, Mark, I have a real problem. I know you could help me if you wanted to, but I don't know if you want to." It would hurt my feelings that you found me so uncaring.

How much more, then, does it hurt our Father when we say to Him, "I know You're able, Lord, but I don't know if You're willing"? The worst part is that God's Word tells us He *is* willing, but many of us haven't bothered to search out that truth.

Don't insult God by doubting His willingness to heal you. He's able *and* willing. You have His Word on it.

Confession

I won't insult my Father by doubting His willingness to heal me.
I honor Him by receiving healing today.

"That It Might Be Fulfilled"

When the even was come, they brought unto him many that were possessed with devils: and he cast out the spirits with his word, and healed all that were

—Matthew 8:16

What if God didn't want to heal everyone who came to Jesus? What if God didn't want to heal a few people who slipped into the crowd and received their healing from Jesus before God knew about it?

No, that couldn't happen. You see, for Jesus to heal anyone it had to be God's will because Jesus only did what He saw His Father do. (John 5:19.)

When Jesus walked in to a multitude, He cast out *all* the devils and healed *all* the sick. He never refused one person; He never turned anyone down. He never said, "I'll heal you later; you need to learn a few things before you get healed." Instead, He always said things like, "I will—be thou clean," or "I will—come and be healed."

Jesus always healed *all* who were in faith. Here's why:

> That it might be fulfilled which was spoken by Esaias the prophet, saying, Himself took our infirmities, and bare our sicknesses (Matthew 8:17).

The Bible says Jesus healed in order to fulfill the Scriptures. Every time He healed the multitudes, He proved once more that God's will is healing for *all*.

Confession

Jesus took my infirmities and bore my sicknesses.
I believe He's able and willing to heal me;
therefore, right now I receive my healing by faith.

God Is Willing To Heal

Though physical healing is a great need in the body of Christ today, the greatest hindrance is not knowing that God is willing to heal.

Hosea 4:6 says, "My people are destroyed for lack of knowledge." The marginal note in my Bible says the word *destroyed* literally means "cut off." So that Scripture could be rendered, "For a lack of knowledge people are cut off from the blessings of God."

If we don't know God is willing to heal us, we are cut off from His blessings of healing and health. You see, faith must have a foundation. In order to confidently receive what Jesus purchased and provided for us, we must know it's our Father's desire to give it to us.

God wants us to come boldly to the throne of grace to receive the healing we need. (Heb. 4:16.) That kind of boldness comes only from strong faith—a faith born of knowing the Father's willingness to heal.

And this is the confidence that we have in him, that, if we ask any thing according to his will, he heareth us: and if we know that he hear us, whatsoever we ask, we know that we have the petitions that we desired of him.

—1 John 5:14,15

Confession

I'm confident that God is willing to heal me. Therefore, I'm confident He hears me and gives me the petition of healing I desire.

Healed in Order To Serve

And when Jesus was come into Peter's house, he saw his wife's mother laid, and sick of a fever. And he touched her hand, and the fever left her: and she arose, and ministered unto them.

—Matthew 8:14,15

God lets us know in this Scripture what our motive should be for wanting to be healed. We should want to get healed so God can use us in service to Him, not just so we can go play tennis or golf.

Now, there's nothing wrong with tennis or golf, but our primary motive for desiring healing ought to be because Jesus purchased our healing with His own precious blood and because we want to serve God with all our strength.

When Samuel was sent to anoint David to be king, God said something to Samuel that shows how important right heart motives are to Him: "The Lord seeth not as man seeth; for man looketh on the outward appearance, but the Lord looketh on the heart" (1 Sam. 16:7).

We need to keep our motives right. Wrong motives will keep us out of God's blessings. James 4:3 says, "Ye ask, and receive not, because ye ask amiss [or with wrong motives]."

So keep your motives pure and your heart right, and then believe God for your healing. Faith inspired by right motives for healing and health will quickly move the hand of God.

Confession

My main purpose is to minister to the Lord, putting my hand to the work He gives me to do. I thank God for healing me, so I'm effective and unhindered by pain, sickness, and disease.

Healing–The Children's Bread

God doesn't want His children begging for what already belongs to them. To the woman of Canaan who begged Him to heal her daughter, Jesus said, "It is not meet to take the children's bread, and to cast it to dogs" (Matt. 15:26).

So according to Jesus, healing is the children's bread.

Healing belongs to us. It's part of our redemption, our covenant, our spiritual inheritance. It belongs to us as blood-bought, new creatures in Christ.

I have been young, and now am old; yet have I not seen the righteous forsaken, nor his seed begging bread.

—Psalm 37:25

When a believer begs for healing, God doesn't have the slightest idea why. God says, "Child, healing belongs to you; it's yours. When you accepted Jesus, He became your healer. You don't have to beg."

So get the revelation in your heart that as God's child, healing is your "bread." That's 99 percent of the issue right there.

Confession

As a joint-heir with Jesus Christ, I have a covenant right to receive healing and walk in divine health. I receive my inheritance of healing by faith. Healing belongs to me!

No Longer Just a Promise

According as his divine power hath given unto us all things that pertain unto life and godliness, through the knowledge of him that hath called us to glory and virtue.

—2 Peter 1:3

Under the old covenant, God kept telling Israel about the Messiah and Redeemer, showing them pictures of redemption in types and shadows. Thousands of years passed, and people continued waiting for God's redemptive promises to be fulfilled.

Then Jesus came to earth, fulfilling the will of God through His death, burial, and resurrection. What was a promise is now a fulfilled fact. Now, God says, "I've done My part." The responsibility to act switched from Him to us.

It's like this. If someone said, "I want to give you a book," but sat there doing nothing, you'd wait to receive the book. But if the person said, "I want to give you this book," and then placed the book beside you, it would become your responsibility to pick it up.

You see, in the spiritual realm God *"hath given* unto us all things that pertain unto life and godliness" (2 Peter 1:3). Healing certainly pertains to life and godliness. So if we want the healing God *has already provided,* we have to "pick it up." We don't *wait* for God to heal us—we reach out and take hold of what He's already done. That isn't forcing God's hand—that's saying, "Lord, You did it. I believe it. I take it."

No longer do we look ahead to what God will do someday; we look back to what He did 2000 years ago. Healing is not a promise anymore—it's a fact.

Confession

I'm redeemed and set free!
Sickness and disease are no longer part of me.

Healing Is a Fact

Divine healing belongs to us.

We aren't waiting for God to heal us; God is waiting for us to take the healing that's already ours. God wanted us healed so much that He didn't just promise to heal us; He sent His Son to purchase our healing with His broken body. Therefore, healing is not just a promise—it is a *fact!*

He sent his word, and healed them, and delivered them from their destructions.

—Psalm 107:20

Years ago, I looked at healing as a promise. Then one day I read, "Who his own self bare our sins in his own body on the tree, that we, being dead to sins, should live unto righteousness: by whose stripes *ye were healed*" (1 Peter 2:24). He didn't say you *may* be healed or you *will* be healed. He said, *"Ye were healed"*—past tense. It isn't what God is going to do; it's what He's already done. The day I found that Scripture in the Bible, it turned my life around.

Healing is a fact. As far as God is concerned, His part is done. Now He's waiting for us to do our part—to reach out and take what is already ours.

Confession

I want what the Word says is mine and nothing less.
I want God's best, and that includes healing for my body.
By faith, I reach out and take the healing that is already mine.

Healing Is God's Idea

But my God shall supply all your need according to his riches in glory by Christ Jesus.

—Philippians 4:19

God designed the plan of redemption long before we were ever born. Remember, He called Jesus "the Lamb slain from the foundation of the world" (Rev. 13:8). In His plan of redemption, God provided us with certain benefits—salvation, the infilling of the Holy Ghost, and divine healing.

God gives us these benefits, not because of anything we've done, but because of what He's done through the death, burial, and resurrection of His Son. We're not pushing God to heal us; He chose to do it. Healing was God's idea. We aren't forcing His hand; we're accepting His Word. Our part is to say, "Lord, You said You'd supply every need, so I believe it and receive it."

Make sure you fulfill your part. Don't be like some people who look at God's promise of healing and say, "Well, I don't know if I can go along with that." That's like slapping Jesus in the face. In essence, those people are saying, "Jesus, the Word says You shed Your blood to purchase healing for me, but my religious doctrine says it isn't true. So, I'll take my doctrine instead."

You can't receive healing for your body with that kind of attitude. You must come to the place where it doesn't matter what you've heard or been taught. To receive God's benefits, you must agree with God's Word.

Confession

When I believe God for healing, I'm not forcing God's hand.
Healing is God's idea. He made healing available for me,
and I receive it now in Jesus' name.

The Importance of Hearing the Word

And [Jesus] was teaching in one of the synagogues on the sabbath.

—Luke 13:10

Jesus' teaching ministry was important. In fact, His teaching of the Word is what caused His healing ministry to flow and operate.

Under Jesus' ministry, most people had to hear Him teach the Word to get healed. Luke 5:15 says, "Multitudes came together to hear, and to be healed." That means most people were healed as a result of hearing the Word and then receiving by their own faith.

For example, Jesus said to two blind men, "According to your faith be it unto you" (Matt. 9:29). To a centurion, He said, "As thou hast believed, so be it done unto thee" (Matt. 8:13). Jesus told a leper, "Thy faith hath made thee whole" (Luke 17:19). And to the woman with the issue of blood, Jesus said, "Daughter, thy faith hath made thee whole" (Mark 5:34).

Many Christians are not healed today because they don't take time to listen to the Word of God. They want someone to get them healed so they can get on with life. "Hurry up and lay hands on me so I can get back to what I was doing," some say. Yet, with that kind of attitude it's no wonder these people don't receive healing.

Take the time to hear the Word. Feed your spirit with God's promises of healing. And as you're faithful to *hear* and *hear* and *hear* the Word, your faith will rise up to make you whole.

Confession

I position myself to hear God's Word, and faith rises up
strong within me. As I act on God's Word,
I receive all I need to walk in health.

Hear With Your Spiritual Ears

Let these sayings sink down into your ears: for the Son of man shall be delivered into the hands of men.

—Luke 9:44

There is a direct connection between hearing the Word and being healed. Many people are not being healed because they are either not hearing at all or they are not hearing enough.

Someone may say, "Well, I heard the Word; I know what it says; but it didn't work for me." No. That's not possible. The Word *always* works. Sometimes we fail to receive the benefits of the Word, but the Word never fails. The failure is on our part.

When Jesus told His disciples, "Let these sayings sink down into your ears," He meant that you must hear the Word over and over and over with your spiritual ears—the ears of your inner man—until those truths finally get lodged down on the inside of you. Only then will you be able to receive the benefits of healing that are rightfully yours.

Confession

I will hear and hear and hear the Word until it sinks down into the "ears" of my spirit. The Word always works, and it's working in me now, producing healing and health in my body.

Faith Comes by Hearing

Several years ago, after I'd been walking in health for a number of years, allergy symptoms once again attacked my body. I started waking up in the middle of the night sneezing off and on for hours. So I began declaring, "Thank God, I stand on the Word and believe I'm healed." Nothing happened. Then I said, "I rebuke these symptoms in Jesus' name. Leave my body now." Nothing happened. I asked someone to agree with me for healing; still nothing happened.

Wherefore let him that thinketh he standeth take heed lest he fall.

—1 Corinthians 10:12

I tried everything—pulled every lever, flipped every switch, pushed every button, pulled every knob—but got no better fast. Finally I prayed, "Dear Lord, I know You don't miss it. Show me where I'm missing it, and I'll correct it."

About that time, I was asked to minister on healing for a week in a Bible school. I hadn't taught on healing for about a year and a half, and as a result, I hadn't studied the subject either.

I quickly learned faith cometh by hearing—and goeth by not hearing. In fact, the enemy had used my faith deficit to strap some symptoms on me.

Yet preparing to teach, I spent an entire week studying healing from one to eight hours a day. All week I heard, confessed, and meditated on healing Scriptures.

Toward the end of the week, I asked my wife, Janet, "When did I stop sneezing?" I'd been healed so fast I didn't even know I was healed. And I was so busy enjoying my healing I didn't even notice when the symptoms left. I heard, and I was healed.

Confession

I hear, believe, and confess God's Word.
And it's producing health in my physical body.

Faith–The Product of Hearing the Word

And Jesus went about all Galilee, teaching in their synagogues, and preaching the gospel of the kingdom, and healing all manner of sickness and all manner of disease among the people.

—Matthew 4:23

Did you ever notice in Jesus' ministry that teaching and preaching came before healing? You see, there's a direct connection between hearing and being healed.

In fact, the very best thing you can do if you need healing in your body is to keep *hearing* and *hearing* and *hearing* the Word of God. Hear it with your physical ears so many times that you finally hear it with your spiritual ears.

In Romans 10:10 Paul said, "For with the heart man believeth." Real faith is of the heart—or inner man. You don't believe with your head. The Holy Spirit didn't say through Paul, "With the head man believeth." It's when the Word of God lodges down in your spirit—when the Word is mixed with your "believer"—that faith emerges.

Faith is the product, or the fruit, of your knowledge of God's Word having moved from your mind to your spirit. When you put the Word in your spirit, faith is always the result.

Confession

With my heart, I choose to hear the truth of God's Word.
It's easy to believe God's promises because
I keep hearing and hearing the Word.

The More You Hear, the More You Believe

Years ago I traveled to India with five other ministers to conduct a seminar for native ministers. Six of us taught on different subjects, but I taught on healing for one hour every day for three and a half weeks. Mostly, God dealt with me to teach on the Atonement that Jesus purchased for us on the Cross.

On the first day different ministers asked me to pray for their healing, but the Spirit of God wouldn't allow me to. I told them, "Not yet; we'll do it later." Each day another minister would ask for prayer, and I'd say the same thing. I knew if I prayed for their healing prematurely, they wouldn't receive. They didn't know enough of the Word to have strong faith because they'd only begun to hear about healing.

How then shall they call on him in whom they have not believed? and how shall they believe in him of whom they have not heard? and how shall they hear without a preacher?

—Romans 10:14

On the last day the Lord spoke to my spirit, "It's time to pray, but don't you pray or lay hands on them. They are ministers; let them pray for each other." I obeyed the Lord, and afterward I asked how many received manifestations of healing. Hands went up all over.

After hearing the Word day after day, these ministers could hardly wait for me to finish teaching so they could pray. Their faith had grown strong hearing the Word; they were ready to receive.

The same will happen to you as you hear and hear the Word.

Confession

I take time to hear God's Word on healing and
faith rises in me, producing healing from head to toe.

Activate Jesus' Healing Power With Your Faith

...[Jesus] stood in the plain, and the company of his disciples, and a great multitude of people out of all Judaea and Jerusalem, and from the sea coast of Tyre and Sidon, which came to hear him, and to be healed of their diseases; and they that were vexed with unclean spirits: and they were healed. And the whole multitude sought to touch him: for there went virtue out of him, and healed them all.

—Luke 6:17-19

During Jesus' ministry, people who wanted their lives changed came to hear Him and be healed. Verse 19 reveals what happened when they came: "For there went virtue out of him, and healed them all." You see, the virtue, or power, of God flowed out of Jesus to heal the multitude when the people operated in faith. And when did they operate in faith? After they heard the Word.

Once the people heard, their faith rose up and released the healing power in Jesus. But the power didn't flow out of Him until after the people heard His teaching and drew on it by faith.

If you need healing in your body, you can draw on Jesus' miracle-working power with your faith. However, the first step is to hear what the Word of God says. You must hear it and hear it with your physical ears until you can hear it with your spiritual ears. As the healing virtue flowed out of Jesus then, it still flows out of Him today—activated by faith.

Confession

The same virtue that flowed out of Jesus to heal the multitude heals me now as I hear the Word and draw on His power.

Keep Teaching Others How To Be Healed

Jesus had traveled to His own hometown, and the power of God was present to heal. Jesus was anointed with the Holy Ghost and with power, but still only a few in Nazareth received their healing. Most of them wouldn't receive because their unbelief was so strong. So what was Jesus' solution to that situation? "He went round about the villages, teaching" (v. 6).

When Jesus couldn't get anything else to happen, He taught. Jesus did that all through His ministry. When He encountered the hard places, He'd just lean back and teach. When people weren't receiving their healing, when He couldn't do any mighty works, when no gifts of the Spirit were operating and no one was receiving the anointing, Jesus would teach and teach and teach some more.

And [Jesus] could there do no mighty work, save that he laid his hands upon a few sick folk, and healed them. And he marvelled because of their unbelief. And he went round about the villages, teaching.

—Mark 6:5,6

Jesus is our example. When people won't receive, just keep teaching. That was a major part of Jesus' ministry because when He taught people they were healed. The truth is, the only way to cure unbelief is to keep teaching the Word. Someone will take hold of it because there's a connection between hearing and being healed.

Confession

As the Word becomes life and healing in me,
I can teach others. The healing power of
the Word works in all who hear.

Keep Hearing the Word

My soul, wait thou only upon God; for my expectation is from him.

—Psalm 62:5

Janet and I ministered in a Sunday morning church service, where we told the people, "Come back tonight expecting God to do something. Meditate on the Word. If you need something from God, find out what the Word says about it. If you need healing, find healing Scriptures and meditate on them. Dwell on them. Say them out loud to yourself all afternoon, and then come back tonight expecting."

People came up to us after the service and said, "Just give us a couple of Scriptures, and we'll go home and meditate on them." Others said, "We're going home to pray and listen to the Word all afternoon. We'll come back tonight expecting."

The people did exactly what they said they would do. They went home that afternoon and did their spiritual homework. They schooled themselves in faith—and what a difference it made.

I'm telling you, that night we had church! People were filled with the Holy Spirit and many others healed—all because they took the time to hear the Word.

When you set yourself to continually hear the Word, you build up your faith to be healed, or to be set free from fear, or whatever you need from God's Word. Whatever God promises in His Word will manifest in your life—as long as you keep hearing the Word and building your faith for it.

Confession

The Word of God is stronger than any sickness or disease.
As I hear God's Word, I expect its power to work in
my body, bringing about the healing I desire.

Sow the Word–Reap Healing

Whatever seed you plant, you will reap that kind of harvest. God's entire kingdom works on this principle. Whatever you sow in your heart is what you will reap in your life. So if you sow God's Word on healing, you will reap healing.

Many people are trying to reap a harvest of healing, yet they've never sown a seed. But you see, hearing and healing go hand in hand because "faith cometh by hearing." Whatever we plant on the inside, we will see on the outside. What we are, what we have, and what we look like on the outside is a result of what we have—*or haven't*—put on the inside.

Be not deceived; God is not mocked: for whatsoever a man soweth, that shall he also reap.

—Galatians 6:7

I've noticed whenever symptoms try to attack my body, it's usually when I haven't been putting enough of the Word down on the inside for it to manifest on the outside. So I go back and study the Word.

We made a tape on healing several years ago and received reports from people all over the country who played that tape over and over and were healed. So Janet decided to try it. We were on a plane heading for the Philippines when symptoms attacked her. Janet listened to it over and over again for about four hours. By the time we got to Manila, every symptom was gone. The Word drove symptoms out of her body. That's the connection between hearing and healing.

Confession

Whatever I sow in my life, I reap. So I plant God's Word and reap life, healing, joy, protection, guidance, peace, and safety.

First Hearing, Then Believing

For whosoever shall call upon the name of the Lord shall be saved. How then shall they call on him in whom they have not believed? and how shall they believe in him of whom they have not heard? and how shall they hear without a preacher?

—Romans 10:13,14

Hearing the Word produces belief. You can't call on God unless you believe, and you can't believe unless you hear. That's why hearing and healing go hand in hand. Once you hear, you can believe; and once you believe, you can be healed.

Romans 10:17 says, "So then faith cometh by hearing, and hearing by the word of God." Hearing God's Word causes faith to rise up on the inside. When you release that faith, you get results. That's why Mark 9:23 says, "All things are possible to him that believeth."

God made it easy for you. He said simply to hear and be healed. So if you're having trouble believing God for your healing, don't try to work it up. Go back to the Word and "hear" what He said. Then just keep on hearing until faith rises up on the inside. Healing will be the result!

Confession

As I hear and hear the Word of God,
faith rises up in me to drive every symptom out of my body,
and produces a healing and a cure throughout my entire body.

Call on the Lord in Faith

The word *saved* or *salvation* is actually defined as the sum total of all the blessings bestowed on man by God in Christ through the Holy Spirit. That means salvation also includes healing.

Knowing that, let's word this verse another way: "Whosoever shall call on the name of the Lord shall also be healed."

> *For whosoever shall call upon the name of the Lord shall be saved.*
>
> *—Romans 10:13*

However, to receive the blessing of healing, we must *believe*. Romans 10:14 says, "How then shall they call on him in whom they have not believed?" If we don't believe, either we won't call on God at all, or we won't call on Him in faith.

Many have endeavored to call on God without actually believing. There was a time I did a lot of calling, but not much believing; and therefore, I didn't get any answers. I prayed for two years without seeing results and almost threw away my sign that said, "Prayer Changes Things".

Finally I read Matthew 21:22: "All things, whatsoever ye shall ask in prayer, *believing*, ye shall receive." I had missed that part about believing.

Notice also that Jesus said, *"All things"* you ask in prayer. Well, healing is part of "all things"—and therefore, possible to him who believes.

But you must believe to tap in to God's healing power. You can't call on Him unless you believe, and you can't believe unless you hear. That's why hearing and healing go hand in hand.

Confession

All things are possible to me because I believe.
Whosoever shall call upon the name of the Lord shall be healed.
I hear, I call, I believe—and I am healed.

The Hearing of Faith

*This only would
I learn of you,
Received ye the
Spirit by the works
of the law, or
by the hearing
of faith?*

—*Galatians 3:2*

I once heard a minister say that 99 percent of the problems we have living by faith or receiving from God result from a lack of knowledge. If we're having trouble receiving from God, we need to hear more of God's Word and get more knowledge.

Paul asked, "Received ye the Spirit by the works of the law, or by the hearing of faith?" Well, we didn't receive the Spirit because of any works of the Law, so we know it's by the hearing of faith. When we hear the Word, it builds our faith to receive.

Now look at Galatians 3:5: "He therefore that ministereth to you the Spirit, and worketh miracles among you, doeth he it by the works of the law, or by the hearing of faith?" Again, the hearing of faith produces miracles. Or in other words, we hear and then God works the miracles after we hear.

Why do we have to hear first? We do because when we hear faith rises up in our heart, and faith is the spiritual force that releases God's power.

Confession

Receiving from God is easy. I hear and hear and hear the Word
until I believe it in my heart. Then I speak the Word from my
believing spirit and release power to accomplish healing in my body.

Let Jesus Do a Mighty Work in You

When Jesus was in His own country the people in the synagogue listened to Him, but they really didn't hear Him. They murmured, "Where does Jesus get these things? What wisdom is this?" The people were offended, so we know they didn't really hear Him nor did they allow His words to produce faith. They were listening, but in reality they weren't hearing.

Verse 5 says, [Jesus] "could there do no mighty work, save that he laid his hands upon a few sick folk, and healed them." Think about it. Jesus of Nazareth—God manifested in the flesh, the One anointed with the Holy Ghost and power without limits—*could not* do any mighty works.

The Bible doesn't say Jesus *wouldn't*—it says He *couldn't*. I like the way Brother Kenneth Hagin translated that phrase; he said Jesus laid his hands "upon a few people *with minor ailments.*"

Jesus went in equipped with signs, wonders, and miracles, but only a few people with a cold or the flu were healed. Thank God for the ones who were, but Jesus went to His own home-town to accomplish a whole lot more.

Make sure you *really hear* God's Word and build your faith to receive so Jesus can do a mighty work for you.

Confession

God's power is present to heal me
right now as I hear and believe the Word.

[Jesus]...came into his own country; and his disciples follow him. And when the sabbath day was come, he began to teach in the synagogue: and many hearing him were astonished, saying, From whence hath this man these things? and what wisdom is this which is given unto him, that even such mighty works are wrought by his hands? ...And they were offended at him.

—Mark 6:1-3

Time To Hear Even More

And he could there do no mighty work, save that he laid his hands upon a few sick folk, and healed them. And he marvelled because of their unbelief. And he went round about the villages, teaching.

—Mark 6:5,6

Jesus had been teaching and preaching all over the region where He grew up. But when He came to the part of His message proclaiming God as healer, no one got it. So what did Jesus do? He went back to traveling the region, teaching the Word even more.

That was always the progression of Jesus' ministry: teaching, preaching, and healing. If the people weren't getting healed, Jesus knew their faith wasn't taking hold of the truths he taught. Simply—God's Word had not yet registered on their hearts. So Jesus would back up and start teaching again, feeding them more Word to build their faith.

Notice that Jesus didn't give up on the people. He didn't say, "I throw in the towel. I'm done with you folks. That's it— I'm out of here. I'm going where people are hungry."

Jesus understood when the truths He taught hadn't sufficiently registered in people. But He also knew the minute the truth did register, it would produce healing and wholeness.

If you've endeavored to believe for healing but nothing seems to be happening, maybe the truth of healing has not sufficiently registered to your heart. So back up and hear more of God's Word. And keep hearing until you get so full on the *inside* that healing shows up on the *outside.*

Confession

I am a hearer of God's Word. God's truth of healing registers to my heart more and more each day until healing shows up on my body.

Take a Daily Dose of God's Word

One day Janet and I were talking to a man badly in need of healing, and we advised him: "God's Word is medicine to all your flesh. *Feed on it daily!* If you take God's Word as faithfully as you take other medicines, we guarantee there's no disease that can remain in your body."

The man replied, "Oh, I've been studying the Bible every day doing a thorough study on the book of Revelation."

For [God's words] are life unto those that find them, and health to all their flesh.

—Proverbs 4:22

But the man needed to understand that every seed produces after its own kind. In other words, he needed healing in his body, so the best thing for him to study was healing.

Thank God for the book of Revelation—it will get you ready for heaven. But if you're sick, right now you need to know how to live in victory over sickness on this earth. So if you need healing in your body, feed on healing Scriptures. What you feed on is what you'll have faith for.

And realize even if you fed on healing Scriptures last week, last month, or last year, that Word gave you faith *then.* However, that doesn't mean you will have faith for your answer *today.*

You see, it isn't what you *have* heard; it's what you *are* hearing that counts. Even if you heard healing taught yesterday, a lot of unbelief may have been pumped into your ears since then.

So what are you listening to these days? The answer makes all the difference in your healing.

Confession

When I need healing, I go to God's Word and build healing Scriptures into my spirit. My body is healed as God's Word becomes life to me.

Apply Your Heart to the Word

Bow down thine ear, and hear the words of the wise, and apply thine heart unto my knowledge.

—Proverbs 22:17

Years ago I taught for several days in a camp-meeting and noticed a young woman coming to every service using crutches. She wasn't able to walk without them.

One afternoon I taught the congregation to feed on healing Scriptures when they needed healing. That evening another evangelist preached and called the sick forward for prayer. This woman was the first one to the front. The minister laid hands on her, and the woman was instantly healed. Later she testified, "I suffered with multiple sclerosis and couldn't even walk without crutches. Doctors said my condition would only get worse, but I'd been coming regularly to this church endeavoring to believe God for my healing.

"This afternoon I heard the importance of feeding my faith with healing Scriptures. Until then, I'd been doing all I knew to do, but I hadn't saturated myself with God's Word on healing.

"So I opened my Bible and studied healing Scriptures for hours this afternoon. Suddenly, my heart got so full of Scriptures that I'd been meditating on that faith welled up in me. I came to church tonight and wrote inside my Bible with today's date, 'Healed by the power of God!' I just knew things would change tonight."

Taking hold of a miracle doesn't necessarily work this quickly for everyone, but this woman got so full of the Word it produced unstoppable faith in her.

Many times we wait for God to drop faith on us. But faith *only comes* by hearing God's Word and applying your heart to it.

Confession

As I hear and hear the Word, faith wells up in me
producing healing throughout my body.

Set Your Faith Limits High

Jesus said, "According to your faith be it unto you." I always thought He meant, "If you believe, you'll receive"—and that's true. But there's more to what Jesus meant here than that. He is saying, according to your faith—or according to *what* you believe—be it unto you.

For instance, in Matthew 8:5-10, when the centurion came to Jesus on behalf of his servant, Jesus said, "I'll come and heal him."

But the centurion replied, "I'm not worthy that You should come under my roof. Just speak the word only, and my servant will be healed." What happened? Jesus spoke "and his servant was healed in the selfsame hour" (Matt. 8:13).

In Mark 5, Jairus said to Jesus about his little girl near death, "If You'll just come and lay Your hand upon her, she'll be healed and live." When He arrived at the home, she'd already died. But Jesus threw out all the unbelief, took the child by the hand, and raised her from the dead. (vv. 22-24,35-42.)

And Jesus saith unto them, Believe ye that I am able to do this? They said unto him, Yea, Lord. Then touched he their eyes, saying, According to your faith be it unto you. And their eyes were opened.

—Matthew 9:28-30

Notice in each case, it wasn't just the fact the people believed that brought their miracles—it was *what* they believed. They set their own limits, and Jesus met them at their limits. He'll do the same for you!

Confession

I set my faith to receive all Jesus purchased for me. Healing is one of the benefits provided for me, and I believe I receive it now.

He Sent His Word To Heal You

He sent his word, and healed them, and delivered them from their destructions.

—Psalm 107:20

How did God send His Word to heal us? He gave us sixty-six books of His words—the Bible. As we hear the Word, it starts working inside us to make us completely healed and whole.

When you go all through the Gospels, in most cases you'll find that hearing came before healing. And if it worked that way under Jesus' ministry, it still works that way today.

When you need healing, the best thing you can do is to hear and hear and hear and hear. Keep God's Word going into your ears every way possible. Keep hearing what God says about your healing.

Many people want to go to one particular meeting and miraculously receive healing; they aren't interested in hearing. Sometimes God in His mercy does manifest Himself, and people receive their healing. But most of the time, they have to take time to hear before they are healed.

You see, walking by faith doesn't come from leaving your Bible on the shelf until it's time to dust it off and carry it to church. Faith comes as you get into God's Word. It builds in your spirit as you hear it from the preacher, from teaching tapes and CDs, and especially from out of your own mouth.

God sent His Word, and it heals you. When does it heal you? When you take the time to hear it.

Confession

God sent His Word to heal me, and His Word is life and medicine to all my flesh. I hear His Word and obey it, and I'm delivered from sickness and disease.

Jesus Took Our Place

After Adam's fall, man inherited a load he couldn't carry—a load of death, sin, and sickness. The old covenant provided for man's sins to be covered for a year at a time through the shedding of the blood of bulls and goats. Man could also experience healing in his body through animal sacrifices. But those sacrifices were only temporary and could only cover sins—not wash sins away.

Then Jesus Christ came and took the place for our punishment, dying on the Cross as our substitute. Most people have no problem believing Jesus bore our sins on the Cross so we could stand before God forgiven.

But unfortunately, many Christians believe Jesus left us with our sicknesses, intending to decide on an individual basis who should be healed. These folks believe salvation belongs to everyone, but they think a person can never know who—or if—God will heal.

Well, that may be what some believe, but that's not what the Bible says. Isaiah 53:5 says Jesus "was wounded for our transgressions, bruised for our iniquities: the chastisement of our peace was upon him; and with his stripes *we are* healed." Jesus already took sickness. We have as much right to be healed as we do to be saved.

But Christ being come an high priest of good things to come, by a greater and more perfect tabernacle, not made with hands, that is to say, not of this building; neither by the blood of goats and calves, but by his own blood he entered in once into the holy place, having obtained eternal redemption for us.

—Hebrews 9:11,12

Confession

When I call on Jesus to be my Savior, He also becomes my Healer.
By faith I receive the healing that Jesus bought and paid for.

Two Sides of the Atonement

Bless the Lord, O my soul: and all that is within me, bless his holy name. Bless the Lord, O my soul, and forget not all his benefits: who forgiveth all thine iniquities; who healeth all thy diseases.

—Psalm 103:1-3

This Scripture tells us, "Forget not all his benefits." What are God's benefits? He forgives all our iniquities and heals all our diseases. Now, verse 3 lists these two benefits in the same breath, so to speak, meaning that Jesus provided both when He died on the Cross and was raised from the dead.

Forgiveness of sins and healing go hand in hand: Jesus shed His blood for the remission of sins, and His body was broken for us so we could enjoy physical healing and health. He provided both benefits at once, and there's no place in the Bible that tells us to separate these two sides of the Atonement. Healing belongs to us as much as salvation does.

Confession

When I received Jesus as Savior, healing came in my "benefits package" as well. I don't have to be sick. My healer bore my sicknesses and pains so I wouldn't have to bear them. By His stripes, I am healed.

Healing–Not Just a Divine Afterthought

Did you notice God talks about healing before He talks about salvation? The Scripture says, "Glorify God in your body, and in your spirit." Healing was not a divine afterthought. It was instituted before the new birth.

Look at what Isaiah 53:4-5 says:

> Surely he hath borne our griefs [or sicknesses], and carried our sorrows [or pains]: yet we did esteem him stricken, smitten of God, and afflicted. But he was wounded for our transgressions, he was bruised for our iniquities: the chastisement of our peace was upon him; and with his stripes we are healed.

For ye are bought with a price: therefore glorify God in your body, and in your spirit, which are God's.

—1 Corinthians 6:20

Healing is revealed in verse 4 and salvation in verse 5. Does that mean healing is more important? No, but God knew the body of Christ would have more trouble believing for healing; perhaps that's why He put it first.

Jesus bore stripes on His back before He hung on the Cross, which means He paid the price for our physical health before He paid the price for our new birth. Healing isn't more important, but God wants us to know it's equally as important as salvation. God wants us to have both salvation and healing, and we receive both the same way—by faith.

So study what the Bible says about the Atonement of Jesus, and you'll come to a firm persuasion—an unshakable confidence—that you are as healed as you are saved.

Confession

Jesus paid the price so I could be saved and healed.
Therefore, I live free of sickness. I'm healed, I'm well, I'm whole.

How Many Sick People Does God Want To Heal?

Go ye into all the world, and preach the gospel to every creature. And these signs shall follow them that believe; in my name shall they cast out devils; they shall speak with new tongues; they shall take up serpents; and if they drink any deadly thing, it shall not hurt them; they shall lay hands on the sick, and they shall recover.

—Mark 16:15,17,18

How many sick people is Jesus talking about in verse 18? He's talking about *all* sick people. God wants *all* healed! If God didn't want every sick person healed, Jesus wouldn't have told us to lay hands on them so He could heal them.

And by virtue of the fact this is the last thing Jesus shared with His disciples while on earth, we know how important it is. It's like this. Suppose you were leaving for a long period of time, and you wanted your close friends to remember something important. Wouldn't you make sure the last thing you said to them was the message you really wanted them to remember?

That's just what Jesus did in this Great Commission. Jesus tells us God wants every person saved, healed, and delivered. God doesn't want anyone left out, but He won't force His blessings on anyone either. God is a gentleman, and He only leads as we yield to Him.

Yet God offers mankind all that salvation encompasses and says, "Whosoever will, let him come." He wants every creature to hear the Gospel—and He wants every creature healed.

Confession

Knowing my Father wants me well, I believe I receive healing now in Jesus' name. And when I lay hands on the sick, they surely recover.

Our Divine Commission

It's significant that in this passage of Scripture Jesus didn't say, "When you run across sick people, fast and pray to see if they are among the chosen few God will heal." Nor did He say, "Lay hands on the sick, and they will recover if it's My will." No. Jesus said, "Go find sick people and preach the Gospel to them; then lay hands on them, and they'll recover." This is one of the signs He said would follow all believers.

We should be interested in learning how to operate in faith so we can take hold of our own healing. And, if we're going to be assets to the kingdom of God, we should also be interested in learning how to minister healing to sick people. God has been trying to get that across to the Church for years.

Another thing I want to point out is that Mark 16 doesn't say these signs shall only follow apostles and prophets. No, it clearly states, "These signs shall follow *them that believe.*" Every Christian has a divine commission to preach the Gospel, and the supernatural signs follow all those who believe.

Go ye into all the world, and preach the gospel to every creature. He that believeth and is baptized shall be saved; but he that believeth not shall be damned. And these signs shall follow them that believe; in my name...they shall lay hands on the sick, and they shall recover.

—Mark 16:15-18

So tell sick people God wants to heal them. Lay hands on them, and watch healing come to pass in their lives.

Confession

I gladly tell others the good news that Jesus delivered them from sin and sickness. I lay hands on the sick and watch them recover.

Making Your Point of Contact

Now when the sun was setting, all they that had any sick with divers diseases brought them unto him; and [Jesus] laid his hands on every one of them, and healed them.

—Luke 4:40

Jesus was the will of God in action. He constantly showed people that God wanted them healed.

God wants you healed, and once that truth is lodged in your heart, your next step is to make a point of contact. This "point of contact" refers to the moment you begin to release your faith for your healing. After finding out God's will, you make your petition: "Thank God, I believe I receive my healing. I'm healed by the stripes of Jesus."

A point of contact is made in two ways. One way is through prayer, according to Mark 11:24: "What things soever ye desire, when ye pray, believe that ye receive them, and ye shall have them." Another way is through the laying on of hands: "In my name...they shall lay hands on the sick, and they shall recover" (Mark 16:17,18).

When a person makes his point of contact, at that moment he begins to believe he receives his healing. He may not feel or see it, but he still believes he has received his answer. You may hear him say, "I believe I received when I prayed" or "I believe I received when hands were laid on me."

"Do you feel any different?" someone might ask.

The person in faith will answer, "No, but that doesn't make any difference because I believe I've received!" That's the confession of faith.

Confession

I believe I receive healing through faith. Another way
I receive healing is through the laying on of hands.
Either way, my healing begins at my point of contact.

How To Receive From God

How can we receive all that Jesus bought and paid for through His death, burial, and resurrection? Well, we know faith operates on God's known will. So first we must look into the Word, where we find it's God's perfect will for *every* person to be healed. Next, we make a point of contact, which occurs when we believe we receive.

Imagine a reservoir full of water held back by a dam and a dry valley below. The two represent a "greater" and a "lesser." And if we open the spillgate so contact is made between the two, the greater water would flood into the lesser dry valley.

Therefore I say unto you, What things soever ye desire, when ye pray, believe that ye receive them, and ye shall have them.

—Mark 11:24

In the same way, our point of contact can be likened to "opening the spillgate." The moment we release our faith—the point of contact—the "greater" power in Jesus Christ begins to flow into our "lesser" bodies, whether we feel it or not. God's healing power begins to work in our bodies the very moment we believe.

Anyone can believe when he sees or feels something. But as Christians, we're supposed to believe we receive our healing *before* we see or feel it because we believe the Word.

What else are we supposed to do? We're to *say* what we believe: "I believe I'm healed by Jesus' stripes." Do we feel any different? Not always, but that's all right. Our feelings won't change God's Word, but God's Word will definitely change what we see and feel if we continue in faith.

Confession

By faith I open the spillgate of God's goodness and healing power flows into me as I believe I receive.

The Laying on of Hands

Therefore leaving the principles of the doctrine of Christ, let us go on unto perfection; not laying again the foundation of repentance from dead works, and of faith toward God, of the doctrine of baptisms, and of laying on of hands, and of resurrection of the dead, and of eternal judgment.

—Hebrews 6:1,2

This Scripture outlines the basic, fundamental principles of the doctrines of Christ. Have they passed away? Let's look: "Not laying again the foundation of repentance." Has repentance passed away? No, repentance is still a foundational principle of the doctrine of Christ.

What about "faith toward God"? Is that finished? It can't be, because we are saved by grace through faith. (Eph. 2:8.) If faith has passed away, we're all in trouble.

What about the doctrine of baptisms or the doctrine of the resurrection of the dead? Are baptisms going to continue? Are the dead going to be resurrected? Yes! What about eternal judgment? Has that passed away? No, it's still in the works.

Only one foundational principle remains, and if all the others haven't passed away, then this one hasn't either. Right in the middle of those verses it says, "...not laying again the foundation...of laying on of hands." This is one of the fundamental principles of the doctrines of Christ, and it hasn't passed away. It's still in effect today.

In fact, the Great Commission in Mark 16:18 says, "They [believers] shall lay hands on the sick, and they shall recover." So, if laying on of hands is for today, then healing is still for today as well. It's just that simple.

Confession

God's foundational principles haven't changed. Believers still lay hands on the sick and they still recover. And He's still the God who heals me.

What Was Accomplished on the Cross?

[Jesus] was delivered for our offences, and was raised again for our justification.

—Romans 4:25

Millions of people around the world believe Jesus died on the Cross, but not everyone believes He was raised from the dead. And very few people, even Christians, know what He actually accomplished when He went to the Cross.

Why did Jesus shed His blood? Was it just for forgiveness of sins alone or for even more than that? Jesus was delivered unto death for the payment of our sins. Then He was raised again for our justification so we could live in right standing with God.

When Jesus shed His blood, it was for the forgiveness of our sins. His resurrection from the dead made the new birth available to us. We can now receive Jesus as our Savior and become brand-new creatures on the inside. (2 Cor. 5:17.) And our newly re-created spirits are infused with the nature of God.

Our sins are not just forgiven but *remitted*—totally removed as though they'd never happened. God not only delivers us from our sins, but He also delivers us from the power sin once held over us.

You see, it wouldn't have been enough just to forgive our sins—our nature would still be the same, and we'd still continue to sin. God sent Jesus to deliver us from the power of sin and all its effects, including sickness. Jesus died to pay for our sins, and He was raised from the dead to deliver us from sin and sickness.

Confession

I'm a new creature in Christ. The old sin nature has been removed and holds no more power over me. Now I live free from sin and sickness.

Portraits of Our Redemption

And all things are of God, who hath reconciled us to himself by Jesus Christ, and hath given to us the ministry of reconciliation; to wit, that God was in Christ, reconciling the world unto himself, not imputing their trespasses unto them; and hath committed unto us the word of reconciliation.

—2 Corinthians 5:18,19

God redeemed the world to Himself through Jesus' work on the Cross. That's why John the Baptist referred to Jesus as "the Lamb of God, which taketh away the sin of the world" (John 1:29).

Jesus' work on the Cross is available to anyone and everyone who believes. Therefore, we need to learn what Jesus accomplished on that Cross so we can walk in what belongs to us. If physical healing was a part of what Jesus accomplished, then we can expect divine healing to be our spiritual inheritance.

When we look in the Gospels, we discover what literally happened to Jesus on His way to the Cross: He was beaten. His back was laid open with a whip. He was spat upon, and a crown of thorns was placed on His head. Finally, He was nailed to the Cross, where He hung until He died.

Yet the Gospels don't really tell us what Jesus purchased for us on the Cross. But all through the Old Testament God provided portraits of our redemption—"word pictures" of what Jesus did for us when He went to the Cross.

For the next several days, let's study these vivid pictures of the Cross to gain a greater revelation of our redemption.

Confession

To walk in the fullness of God's blessings, I must know what Jesus did for me on the Cross. My faith grows stronger as I receive a greater revelation of redemption.

Jesus, Our Passover Lamb

Exodus 12 provides one of God's portraits of redemption, a picture of what Jesus did for us in His death, burial, and resurrection.

In the Old Testament, Egypt is a type of sin or bondage—the kingdom we lived in before we were born again. Pharaoh is a type of Satan.

Israel, on the other hand, is a type of the Church. God's man, Moses, is a picture of Jesus arriving on the scene with signs, wonders, and miracles to deliver God's people. Israel's deliverance out of Egyptian bondage into freedom is a type of the new birth.

Finally, the miracle that produced Israel's freedom centered around a lamb—what the Bible calls a Passover lamb. What the Passover lamb in the Old Testament accomplished for the children of Israel through its death is a clear picture of what Jesus accomplished for us on the Cross.

That's why John the Baptist called Jesus the Lamb of God. (John 1:29.) And in Revelation 13:8, Jesus was called "the Lamb slain from the foundation of the world." Jesus is our Passover Lamb, whose death provided a way for those who believe in Him to be saved, delivered, and made whole.

Confession

Jesus is my Passover Lamb who opened the way for me to enter God's family and enjoy my inheritance.

Speak ye unto all the congregation of Israel, saying, In the tenth day of this month they shall take to them every man a lamb, according to the house of their fathers, a lamb for an house: and if the household be too little for the lamb, let him and his neighbour next unto his house take it according to the number of the souls; every man according to his eating shall make your count for the lamb.

—Exodus 12:3,4

Christ, Our Passover

In the tenth day of this month they shall take to them every man a lamb, according to the house of their fathers, a lamb for an house.

...and the whole assembly of the congregation of Israel shall kill it in the evening. And they shall take of the blood, and strike it on the two side posts and on the upper door post of the houses, wherein they shall eat it.

—Exodus 12:3,6,7

In 1 Corinthians 5:7, Jesus Christ is called our Passover: "For even Christ our passover is sacrificed for us." Passover was instituted back in the Old Testament. And if we can find out what Passover did for people back then, we can find out what Jesus, our Passover, did for us in the New Testament.

The children of Israel had been slaves in Egypt for hundreds of years. God told them, "Take a lamb—one per family. Kill the lamb and put the blood on the doorpost. Roast the lamb, eat the flesh, and then get out of Egypt."

So the people obeyed the Lord's instructions. The lamb was slain and the blood applied. And once the atonement was made, the people went free—not only spiritually but also physically.

The Passover lamb is a picture of the new birth. You see, when Jesus, the Lamb of God, was slain on the Cross, the way was opened for us to live free from Satan's dominion. Now the moment we receive Jesus as our Savior and Lord, we are redeemed, saved, and set free from bondage.

Confession

Because of Jesus, the Lamb of God, I'm free from the devil's dominion. I've been removed from the kingdom of darkness and placed in the kingdom of light.

Behold the Lamb of God

When God gave the instructions for the Passover, He gave very specific instructions about the lamb:

Your lamb shall be without blemish, a male of the first year: ye shall take it out from the sheep, or from the goats: and ye shall keep it up until the fourteenth day of the same month: and the whole assembly of the congregation of Israel shall kill it in the evening. (Ex. 12:5,6).

Jesus fit every one of these qualifications. He

The next day John seeth Jesus coming unto him, and saith, Behold the Lamb of God, which taketh away the sin of the world.

—John 1:29

was a Lamb without blemish for He'd never sinned. He was the firstborn in his family, "a male of the first year." There was even a particular time this Lamb had to die: "in the evening." The very hour Jesus died on the Cross was the time when Passover lambs were sacrificed.

Who killed the Passover lamb? "The whole assembly of the congregation of Israel." In Acts 2:23, Peter preached to the Jewish multitude about who was responsible for Jesus' death: "Him, being delivered by the determinate counsel and foreknowledge of God, ye have taken, and by wicked hands have crucified and slain."

Jesus was condemned by the Romans and crucified by Israel, but He laid His life down willingly for you and me. He took *our* sin and *our* sickness upon Himself. He knew it was the only way you and I could be delivered from the bondage of sin and sickness.

Confession

Jesus was the Lamb slain to take away the sin of the whole world.
Yet, Jesus died for *me*. Through Him I receive all the benefits
salvation includes. I'm saved, healed, and delivered!

Covered by the Blood

...They shall take of the blood, and strike it on the two side posts and on the upper door post of the houses....

—Exodus 12:7

God instructed His people to apply the blood of the lamb to the side posts and upper doorposts of their houses. Thus, they would make a type of the Cross and be covered by the blood of the Passover lamb that had been slain for their deliverance.

God was giving His people a portrait of redemption, pointing ahead to the time when Jesus would come and shed His blood at Calvary. God told them, "The blood shall be to you for a token upon the houses where ye are: and when I see the blood, I will pass over you, and the plague shall not be upon you to destroy you, when I smite the land of Egypt" (Ex. 12:13).

That night, death struck the firstborn of every household in Egypt where the blood was not applied. Where the blood was applied, death passed over. Judgment didn't fall on those residing within; instead, they went free. In the same way, when Jesus' blood is applied to us as we make Him our Lord and Savior, final judgment passes over us, and we step into eternal glory.

We know from Hebrews 9:22 that without the shedding of blood, there's no remission of sins. The blood of the lamb was the sacrifice that allowed the Israelites to walk out of Egypt's bondage. And it's the blood of the Lamb of God, Jesus Christ, that enables us to walk free of every demonic bondage—including the bondage of sickness and disease.

Confession

I've applied the blood of the Lamb of God to my life.
Therefore, I'm free from every yoke of bondage, including sickness.

Redeemed–Spirit, Soul, and Body

God gave His people specific instructions about how to eat the Passover lamb. He said, "Put your belts on, put shoes on, and be ready to go." (v. 11.) It's significant that God didn't say, "And thus shall ye eat it, with your loins girded and your wheelchairs, stretchers, crutches, and pills all ready to go. With all your aches and pains go forth."

Among the three million Israelites God was talking to, there had to be plenty who were too sick or old to travel. But the Lord told them *all* to eat and go!

You see, God wasn't satisfied with a partial redemption. He wanted His people to go out—and go out *well*. He wanted them set free from Egyptian bondage, and set free from the bondage of sickness.

What happened when the Israelites applied the blood of the lamb? It spared them from judgment and set them free from bondage. What happened when the Israelites ate the lamb's flesh? They went out *healthy*.

That's why the Passover lamb is a portrait of our full redemption in Christ.

And they shall eat the flesh in that night, roast with fire, and unleavened bread; and with bitter herbs they shall eat it. And thus shall ye eat it; with your loins girded, your shoes on your feet, and your staff in your hand; and ye shall eat it in haste: it is the Lord's passover.

—Exodus 12:8,11

When Adam fell in the Garden of Eden, he fell spirit, soul, and body. When God redeemed man, He redeemed him spirit, soul, and *body*. Jesus died to make us completely whole.

Confession

Now I partake of the Lamb of God and go forth in newness of life, receiving healing as part of my redemption package.

A New and Better Covenant

He brought them forth also with silver and gold: and there was not one feeble person among their tribes.

—Psalm 105:37

God gave us a portrait of the new birth when He delivered Israel from Egypt's bondage. This biblical event is a picture of our coming out of Satan's bondage into new freedom in Jesus Christ.

The way Israel looked when they came out of Egypt is a picture of the way you and I should look the minute we're born again. How did Israel look? Not only that, but Psalm 105:37 says, "He brought them forth also with silver and gold."

The Israelites didn't take silver and gold out of Egypt because they were wealthy. No, they'd been nothing but Egyptian slaves for centuries. God was the source of Israel's sudden wealth. The first thing He did when He brought them out of bondage was to abundantly meet their needs.

God also provided physical health for the Israelites. "There was not one feeble person among their tribes." He brought His people out of Egypt free and healthy.

The Passover opened the way to freedom, healing, and abundance for the Israelites. Now we live under a new and better covenant established on better promises. (Heb. 8:6.) So if God willed healing and health for His people under the old covenant, we can know without a doubt He wills healing and abundance for us under our covenant through Jesus Christ.

Confession

The Lamb of God opened the way to abundantly supply all my needs—spirit, soul, and body. He provided healing for my physical body and peace for my soul. I walk in the fullness of the redemption Jesus purchased for me.

Healing in the Atonement

Numbers 16 provides another portrait of our redemption. Soon after the Israelites were delivered out of Egypt's bondage, they began to worship idols and criticize the men of God in charge. Their muttering and complaining put them on dangerous territory.

A plague hit the multitude and more than 14,000 died. Aaron quickly prepared incense to make atonement before all the people died. He ran into the midst of the congregation to make atonement, and the plague was stopped.

This is a portrait of the Atonement Jesus made for us. You see, when Aaron made atonement for the sin of the Israelites, they were not only forgiven, but the sick were healed. Well, if healing was included in atonement under the old covenant, how much more is healing included in the Atonement Jesus purchased for us?

Confession

Jesus is my Atonement. His sacrifice gives me access to all God's blessings. I receive them now by faith.

...The children of Israel murmured against Moses and against Aaron.... And the Lord spake unto Moses, saying, Get you up from among this congregation, that I may consume them as in a moment....And Moses said unto Aaron, Take a censer, and put fire therein from off the altar, and put on incense, and go quickly unto the congregation, and make an atonement for them: for there is wrath gone out from the Lord; the plague is begun. And Aaron took as Moses commanded, and ran into the midst of the congregation; and, behold, the plague was begun among the people: and he put on incense, and made an atonement for the people. And he stood between the dead and the living; and the plague was stayed. Now they that died in the plague were fourteen thousand and seven hundred.

—Numbers 16:41,44-49

Remember All God Has Done for You

And the soul of the people was much discouraged because of the way.

—Numbers 21:4

As the children of Israel made their way toward the Promised Land, they became discouraged because they were looking at the way—the natural hardships of their journey.

Just think what they could've focused on instead. God had brought them out of Egypt with signs, wonders, and miracles. When they could go no farther because of the Red Sea, God worked another miracle, parting the waters so they could cross on dry ground. When the Egyptian army had tried to pursue them, the two walls of water had closed up again destroying their enemies.

When the Israelites had come to the waters of Marah, where the water was bitter, God had miraculously purified the waters so the people could have water to drink.

God led them with a pillar of cloud by day and a pillar of fire by night. He gave them fresh manna from heaven every night; all they had to do was pick it up. He even gave them water out of a rock. And for the entire forty years they wandered through the desert, their shoes and clothes didn't wear out.

Yet despite all of these things, they became discouraged because they looked at the way. Have we not done the same thing at times?

Encourage yourself today by realizing how much God has already done for you—and how much more He wants to do. It's an instant cure for discouragement.

Confession

Through the blood of Jesus, my Father has delivered me, protected me, provided for me, and healed me. So no matter what I face, I focus my spiritual eyes on my faithful God.

We Choose What We Look At

First Corinthians 10:11 tells us that what happened to Israel was for our admonition. In fact, we can learn a lot by looking at Israel, a type of the Church.

When the Israelites came out of bondage in Egypt, they headed toward the Promised Land. Now, the Promised Land is not a picture of heaven. (It had giants to overcome, and heaven doesn't.) The Promised Land is actually a picture of the abundant life God has for us while we're here on earth.

Yet as Numbers 21:4 says, the Israelites marched through the wilderness becoming much discouraged because of the way. They were just like the rest of us and had a tendency to become discouraged when things got tough.

And they journeyed from mount Hor by the way of the Red sea, to compass the land of Edom: and the soul of the people was much discouraged because of the way.

—Numbers 21:4

It's easy to find natural circumstances that will discourage us if we look at them. For example, focusing on symptoms of pain or sickness in our bodies can be very disheartening.

But we choose what we're going to look at. Will we set our eyes on the circumstances we face or on our great God and His ability to take us to our promised land of abundant life?

The Bible says, "According as his divine power *hath given* unto us *all* things that pertain unto life and godliness..." (2 Peter 1:3). Everything God has, is, and can do has been made available to us as we look to Him.

Confession

I keep my eyes on Jesus and His Word. He is greater than any problem or sickness that could ever come against me.

Keep Your Mouth Out of Trouble

And the soul of the people was much discouraged because of the way. And the people spake against God, and against Moses, Wherefore have ye brought us up out of Egypt to die in the wilderness? for there is no bread, neither is there any water; and our soul loatheth this light bread.

—Numbers 21:4,5

When the Israelites got discouraged, the first thing they did was open their mouths. If you continue reading in Numbers, you'll notice they got into big trouble by muttering and complaining.

When some people are discouraged, the first One they want to accuse is God. "God, why did You send me this trouble? Why did this disease come on me? God, this is all Your fault!"

Others get mad at preachers when things don't seem to work out right. That's what happened in the wilderness; the people came against the two men who had delivered them.

God had protected the children of Israel every step of the way, yet they were still discouraged and complained, "We're going to die out here because we don't have any bread or water." They forgot that God had already given them fresh food from heaven and water from a rock! Then they admitted the real problem: They just didn't like the light bread God gave them. Let their behavior be a lesson to us.

No matter how long it might take for your healing to manifest, don't let discouragement get you in trouble. Remember, God has already provided healing for you so use your mouth to praise Him.

Confession

Even in trying situations, I watch my words and refuse to blame God.
He's the One who heals and delivers me.

Don't Step out of God's Protection

After the Israelites complained against Moses and God, an army of fiery serpents crawled into the camp and began biting them. The Isaac Leeser translation says, "The Lord *let loose* fiery serpents."[1]

There's a big difference between *sending* and *letting loose*. Remember, the Israelites were in the wilderness full of snakes. So the miracle was not that the snakes started biting them, but that three million people had lived in the wilderness *not having been* bitten until then!

And the Lord sent fiery serpents among the people, and they bit the people; and much people of Israel died.

—Numbers 21:6

God had supernaturally protected His people and kept the snakes out. But when they broke their covenant through rebellion and complaining, God withdrew His merciful protection. Only then were they bitten. The people got into trouble spiritually when they sinned. Consequently, the serpents were able to enter the camp, and the people got into trouble physically as well.

"Therefore the people came to Moses, and said, We have sinned, for we have spoken against the Lord, and against thee; pray unto the Lord, that he take away the serpents from us. And Moses prayed for the people" (v. 7). Isn't it amazing how quickly the people got revelation that they had sinned. One minute they complained about Moses, but the next minute they wanted him to pray for them.

Moses could've said, "No way—you got what you had coming!" But instead he prayed for them. And God not only forgave His people of their sin, but He also healed them of their deadly wounds.

Confession

When I miss it, I run to my Father for forgiveness.
I walk daily with Him as my Savior, Healer, and Protector.

Behold Jesus and Live

...The Lord said unto Moses, Make thee a fiery serpent, and set it upon a pole: and it shall come to pass, that every one that is bitten, when he looketh upon it, shall live. And Moses made a serpent of brass, and put it upon a pole, and it came to pass, that if a serpent had bitten any man, when he beheld the serpent of brass, he lived.

—Numbers 21:8,9

God told Moses to put a brass serpent on a pole, and whoever looked at the serpent would live. Why? Well, the serpent is a type of Jesus Christ, and brass is a type of judgment. Once again, the Israelites were looking at a portrait of redemption—a vivid picture of Atonement.

Some might ask, "How can a serpent be a type of Jesus?" Ever since the Garden of Eden, a serpent has been a sign of sin.

Jesus never sinned in His life. But when He hung on the Cross, He *became sin* for us. At that moment, God had to turn His back on His Son because all the sins and sicknesses of the world were nailed to Jesus' body on the Cross. Judgment fell on Him instead of on us.

When Moses held up that serpent, he was showing a picture of Jesus who would someday hang on the Cross as the Atonement for all mankind.

So when the children of Israel *looked ahead* to what Jesus would do, they were forgiven and healed. And God didn't turn anyone down: *"Every one* that is bitten, when he looks will live." (v. 8.)

Now, we can *look back* in faith to the forgiveness and healing Jesus already purchased for us. Behold Jesus and live!

Confession

I behold Jesus and receive forgiveness and healing today.

In Exchange for a Look Receive Life

When the Israelites were bitten by snakes in the wilderness, God offered them *life for a look!*

Just because the bronze serpent was placed on the pole didn't mean the people would automatically be healed. God said, "Every one that is bitten, when he *looketh* upon it, shall live" (Num. 21:8). The answer was held up before the Israelites, but they had to *look* at it.

After all, God didn't say, "Once you put the serpent on a pole, take a quick glance and head for home." No, according to *The Amplified Bible,* God said, "If you want to live, you'll have to *attentively, expectantly and with a steady and absorbing gaze look to the answer.*"

In essence, God was telling the Israelites, "You cannot look at the biting snakes and the serpent on the pole at the same time. You must choose whether you gaze at the problem or the answer. But if you want to live, you have to look to My answer."

And Moses made a serpent of bronze and put it on a pole, and if a serpent had bitten any man, when he looked to the serpent of bronze [attentively, expectantly, with a steady and absorbing gaze], he lived.

—Numbers 21:9, AMP

Healing was theirs for the taking as they looked at the serpent on the pole. The same is true for us today as we attentively, expectantly, with a steady and absorbing gaze fix our eyes on Jesus who "took our infirmities and bore our sicknesses." (Matt. 8:17.)

Confession

When symptoms of pain and sickness attack me, I *look* to Jesus.
He causes me to triumph in every situation as I *look* to Him.

The Divine Exchange

For he hath made [Jesus] to be sin for us, who knew no sin; that we might be made the righteousness of God in him.

—2 Corinthians 5:21

When the Israelites were bitten by snakes, they needed three answers: forgiveness for complaining, deliverance from the snakes, and healing of their wounds. However, God gave them only one answer: the serpent on a pole.

How were the people forgiven, healed, and delivered by looking at a picture of sin and sickness? Jesus Himself gives the answer in John 3:14: "And as Moses lifted up the serpent in the wilderness, even so must the Son of man be lifted up." Jesus was saying, "That serpent on the pole is a picture of Me on the Cross."

When Jesus went to the Cross, a divine exchange took place. He became what we were and gave us what He is. Jesus became our substitute. He'd never sinned, but He became our sin. He was never sick Himself, but He took on our sickness. In exchange, Jesus gave us His right standing with God and His divine health.

So when the Israelites in the wilderness looked at a symbolic image of Jesus Christ going to the Cross, they were forgiven, healed, and delivered. When Jesus went to the Cross, He forgave our sins, purchased healing for us, and delivered us from the power of darkness. Then He was raised from the dead so we could become born again, new creatures in Him.

When we look to Jesus and receive Him as Savior, everything He did for us on the Cross becomes ours.

Confession

Jesus took sin and sickness and gave me righteousness,
health, and eternal life. He paid for all these benefits
and freely gives them to me when I ask in faith.

Jesus, Our Scapegoat

The Isaac Leeser translation of Isaiah 53:4 tells us Jesus took on our sicknesses and pains as our substitute so you and I wouldn't have to carry them: "But only our diseases did he bear himself, and our pains he carried."[1]

But notice that in the *King James Version* Isaiah used the words *borne* and *carried.* Those same words are used in the book of Leviticus when referring to the role of the scapegoat. This scapegoat gives us another Old Testament portrait of redemption.

When Israel sinned, that sin had to be judged. But God didn't want the people to suffer judgment; He wanted them to receive mercy. So He told them to find a spotless, perfect goat and have Aaron the priest lay hands on it and confess the sins of the nation over it. The judgment belonging to Israel then fell on that scapegoat. In other words, God allowed the sins of the people to be transferred to the goat, and the goat bore them and carried them away.

Jesus was our ultimate Scapegoat when He hung on the Cross, taking the judgment and punishment we deserved so we could walk free from sin and sickness.

Confession

Jesus is my Substitute; He bore my sin and sickness so I wouldn't have to. Now, because of Jesus, I'm healed and whole.

And Aaron shall lay both his hands upon the head of the live goat, and confess over him all the iniquities of the children of Israel, and all their transgressions in all their sins, putting them upon the head of the goat, and shall send him away by the hand of a fit man into the wilderness: and the goat shall bear upon him all their iniquities unto a land not inhabited....

—Leviticus 16:21,22

91

The Year of Jubilee

And ye shall hallow the fiftieth year, and proclaim liberty throughout all the land unto all the inhabitants thereof: it shall be a jubilee unto you; and ye shall return every man unto his possession, and ye shall return every man unto his family.

—Leviticus 25:10

Another portrait of our redemption is found in this Scripture in Leviticus. While talking to Moses on Mount Sinai, God established the Year of Jubilee. According to the instructions He gave to Moses, every fiftieth year would be a special time of setting people free from debt and servitude. (vv. 8-10.)

Yet, this wasn't meant to be just an old covenant blessing. When Jesus was just beginning His earthly ministry He said, "The Spirit of the Lord is upon me, because he hath anointed me to preach the gospel to the poor...to set at liberty them that are bruised, to preach the acceptable year of the Lord" (Luke 4:18,19). Right then, Jesus told us that part of His commission was to preach the acceptable year of the Lord, or the Year of Jubilee.

Jesus came to establish the new covenant through His death, burial, and resurrection. So, apparently, the Year of Jubilee was not only meant to be an Old Testament blessing, but also a New Testament blessing. The Old Testament Year of Jubilee was simply a picture of what Jesus Christ would one day do for us when He came to this earth—wipe out our debt of sin and set us free.

Confession

Jesus is my Jubilee. He bought me back from the power of darkness and translated me into the kingdom of God. Praise God, He has made available everything I could ever need for an abundant life on this earth.

Sounding the Jubilee Trumpet

In the fiftieth year the Israelites celebrated the Day of Atonement, when animal sacrifices were made to atone for the people's sins. After atonement was made, the trumpet of Jubilee was sounded. It signaled freedom far and wide.

Every man went back to his own possessions. If he had debts, they were forgiven. If he'd been forced to sell property to pay debts, the property was returned. If he'd been sold as a servant or slave, he was set free.

The Year of Jubilee, then, was the year of forgiveness, freedom, and restoration to one's original position—a remarkable portrait of our new covenant redemption in Christ.

Today, as part of the body of Christ, we are sounding the trumpets by preaching and teaching the Word of God and telling others the good news of Jesus' Atonement for them.

Thank God, Jesus came and atoned us once and for all. Every one of the Old Testament animal sacrifices was simply a picture of when Jesus would someday die on the Cross for us. Jesus wiped out our debt and liberated us from every bondage of the enemy.

Confession

I'm a trumpet in my Father's hands.
I proclaim liberty to the captives, and
I tell of Jesus' power to heal and deliver
from every bondage of the enemy.

Then shalt thou cause the trumpet of jubilee to sound on the tenth day of the seventh month, in the day of atonement shall ye make the trumpet sound throughout all your land. And ye shall hallow the fiftieth year, and proclaim liberty throughout all the land unto all the inhabitants thereof: it shall be a jubilee unto you; and ye shall return every man unto his possession, and ye shall return every man unto his family.

—Leviticus 25:9,10

Returned to Our Original Possession

And ye shall hallow the fiftieth year, and proclaim liberty throughout all the land unto all the inhabitants thereof: it shall be a jubilee unto you; and ye shall return every man unto his possession, and ye shall return every man unto his family.

—Leviticus 25:10

In the Year of Jubilee every man was to return to his original possessions. Likewise, we're supposed to return to man's original state—to all Adam possessed in the Garden of Eden before he lost everything.

So what was our original possession? When we know that, we'll know what God wants us to return to.

In 1 Corinthians 15:45, God makes a comparison between the first Adam and the last Adam: "The first man Adam was made a living soul; the last Adam was made a quickening spirit." The first Adam disobeyed God and got mankind in trouble.

The last Adam was Jesus Christ who made atonement for us when He died on the Cross and God raised Him from the dead. By laying down His life, Jesus enabled us to return to the original possession Adam had before the Fall, a family relationship with God. Adam was even called the son of God. (Luke 3:38.) But when he sinned in the Garden, he broke that relationship.

So what do we return to? We return to our relationship with God. That's why 1 John 3:1 says, "Behold, what manner of love the Father hath bestowed upon us, that we should be called the sons of God." When we receive Jesus, our Jubilee, He sets us free to become the sons of God.

Confession

When I was born again, Jesus—my Jubilee—gave me back a relationship with my Father. I'm privileged to be called a son or daughter of God.

Adam's Blessings Restored to Us

And ye shall return every man unto his possession.

—Leviticus 25:10

What did Adam have before the Fall? He enjoyed relationship and fellowship with God. Adam walked and talked with God in the cool of the day. But after he fell God came looking for him, calling, "Adam where are you?" (Gen. 3:9.)

"I hid myself," (v. 10) Adam answered because their fellowship had been broken.

What about our fellowship with God? Well, because of Jesus' death, burial, and resurrection we can be restored right back to our original position in God the very minute we're born again.

God invites His children to "come boldly unto the throne of grace" (Heb. 4:16). We can talk to God not just as servants or friends, but as sons and daughters. We're brought back into the fellowship Adam lost.

Adam also possessed supernatural intelligence and memory before the Fall. Think about it. God brought every living creature to Adam who named them all. (Gen. 2:19,20.) Even more remarkable, Adam remembered every one of their names. When you're born again, that same capacity for supernatural intelligence is returned to you.

There's more. God wanted to make sure Adam was abundantly taken care of, so when He saw it wasn't good for Adam to be alone, God formed Eve. And He also showed Adam where all the gold was buried. (Gen. 2:11.)

God wants to meet our needs as well, which is why He sent Jesus to the Cross for you and me. Now, once again, God's sons and daughters can enjoy fellowship with the Father, a sound mind, and every need abundantly met.

Confession

God has restored to me all Adam possessed before he sinned in the Garden. I have fellowship with God, a sound mind, and everything I need.

Our Day of Atonement

And ye shall return every man unto his possession, and ye shall return every man unto his family.

—Leviticus 25:10

Just as the Year of Jubilee enabled the Israelites to return to their original possessions, salvation through Jesus enables us to return to the original position Adam enjoyed with God.

In that original state, Adam was healthy. No sickness or disease existed in his body because no sickness or disease existed on earth.

If God had wanted man sick, He would've created sickness. But God never said, "Let there be cancer or colds and flu." Instead, the Bible tells us God sent His Word to heal us. (Ps. 107:20.) Matthew 8:17 says, "Himself took our infirmities, and bare our sicknesses." Referring to Jesus, 1 Peter 2:24 says, "By whose stripes ye were healed."

Adam enjoyed divine health and every need met before he sinned. All he had to do was obey God's command to stay away from the Tree of the Knowledge of Good and Evil. But when the serpent said, "Go ahead and eat from it," Adam disobeyed God and chose a new master. (Gen. 3:4-6.) At that moment, he lost all the blessings that had been his to enjoy.

From that point on, Adam and his descendants were plagued with hate, murder, poverty, and sickness.

Yet, thank God, our day of atonement finally came. Jesus became the sacrificial Lamb of God, who takes away the sin of the world. (John 1:29.) The last Adam purchased back everything the first Adam lost. Now, through Jesus, we can come into the family of God fully restored.

Confession

Jesus restored me to all the benefits God originally planned for mankind. Because of Jesus, I walk in divine health with all my needs met—spirit, soul, and body.

Receiving Your Petition by Faith

This Scripture promises if you pray in faith according to God's will, you can have whatever you ask for. God Himself has promised He will hear *you* and answer *you*.

Your part is to pray according to God's will and to pray in faith.

How can you pray according to God's will? That's easy. God's Word is His will, and from cover to cover, the Bible proclaims healing legally belongs to you.

The prayer of faith is how you take hold of your healing. You see, all prayers must be prayed in faith because faith is the currency that receives from heaven.

You pray in faith by believing you receive your answer at the very moment you pray—even in the face of symptoms and circumstances. Mark 11:24 says, "...What things soever ye desire, *when ye pray, believe that ye receive* them...."

And this is the confidence that we have in him, that, if we ask any thing according to his will, he heareth us: and if we know that he hear us, whatsoever we ask, we know that we have the petitions that we desired of him.

—1 John 5:14,15

Notice you don't keep requesting your petition over and over again. Think about it. Why would you ask again, if you really believe you *have* received? In fact, 20th century apostle of faith Smith Wigglesworth said if you pray for something seven times, the first six were in unbelief.

So meditate on Scriptures that cover your case until your heart is filled with God's will. Then lock onto your petition in faith and watch God deliver your answer.

Confession

I fill my heart with God's will on healing and pray in faith to receive.
Thank You, Father, for hearing me and granting my petition.

Jesus Paid for Physical Healing

Who his own self bare our sins in his own body on the tree, that we, being dead to sins, should live unto righteousness: by whose stripes ye were healed.

—1 Peter 2:24

This Scripture is a New Testament portrait of redemption—a picture of what Jesus did for you and me.

While teaching on this verse one day I made the comment, "This Scripture proves healing belongs to anyone who's saved because it covers both sides of redemption in one verse."

A person attending the meeting spoke up saying, "Apparently, you think this Scripture refers to physical healing, but it's talking about spiritual healing."

Before I realized what happened, I heard these words come out my mouth: "When you were saved, what happened in your spirit?"

"God took out the heart of stone and put in a heart of flesh," he replied. "He gave me a new spirit."

"Why did you have to be born again?" I asked.

"Because I was spiritually dead," he said.

"Why would you need spiritual healing then?" I asked. "You can't heal something that's dead—it has to be reborn."

You see, when we're spiritually dead, we don't need to get spiritually healed. That won't do the job. We must be born again. The Bible says, "Therefore if any man be in Christ, he is a new creature: old things are passed away; behold, all things are become new" (2 Cor. 5:17). God gives us brand-new spirits that don't need healing—only our physical bodies do.

So live in the fullness of your redemption—your spirit reborn and your body healed by the power of God.

Confession

Jesus' sacrifice was more than enough to save and heal.
I have a brand-new spirit and a healed body because of Jesus.

His Death for Our Life

What is the Atonement? It's the redemptive work Jesus accomplished when He went to the Cross as our Substitute and paid the price for our sins with His blood. He was also chastised for our peace and broken in His body for our physical healing. (Isa. 53:5.)

For God so loved the world, that he gave his only begotten Son, that whosoever believeth in him should not perish, but have everlasting life.

—John 3:16

The Atonement is the most basic of all Christian truths—the very essence of what we believe. It isn't complicated theology or church doctrine. Atonement is His death for our life.

If you don't understand and believe Jesus Christ shed His blood for your sins and was raised again from the dead so you could be born again, His death won't do you any good. Likewise, if you don't understand and believe Jesus bore stripes on His back for your physical healing, His broken body won't do you any good.

It all boils down to what you understand. Faith can't operate where the will of God isn't known; neither can the will of God be known about a subject if you have no knowledge. In other words, the only part of the Atonement that will work for you is the part you understand and believe.

Spend time in God's Word understanding and believing all that Jesus accomplished in the Atonement so you're able to take full advantage of what Jesus purchased for you.

Confession

I believe Jesus Christ shed His blood for my sins.
I believe He bore stripes for my physical healing.
By faith I take full advantage of the benefits He paid for.

A Promissory Note on Redemption

That it might be fulfilled which was spoken by Esaias the prophet, saying, Himself took our infirmities, and bare our sicknesses.

—Matthew 8:17

Do you realize Jesus healed people before He ever went to the Cross?

At the Cross, healing was provided as part of God's redemption plan, but Jesus proved redemption beforehand by giving people part of it on a promissory note. Every time He forgave people of their sins, in essence He was saying, "I'll pay for it later." Every time He healed the multitudes, He was saying, "I'll pay for it later."

Jesus knew those sicknesses and diseases would be on His own back in a short period of time, but He still let His compassion flow out. He wanted to prove to the world that redemption, freedom, peace, and healing belong to every single person.

Jesus didn't turn anyone down. Matthew 8:16 says, "When the even was come, they brought unto him many that were possessed with devils: and he cast out the spirits with his word, and healed all that were sick." The people brought the sick, and He healed all who came to Him for help.

Jesus didn't question who the sick people were or where they came from. If redemption belonged to all mankind, it had to be clearly shown that it was available to every person. So to all who came to Him in faith, Jesus delivered a promissory note on God's redemption plan—a promise He would pay for later.

Confession

Jesus' own life was a demonstration of God's will.
I know God wants me well because Jesus healed all who
came to Him and paid the price to make healing available to me.

Split the Atonement in Two?

In the past, many in the body of Christ have tried to split the Atonement down the middle. Then they've tried to separate the two halves. They say, "Thank God, salvation is for anyone, any time. Second Peter 3:9 says, 'The Lord is...not willing that any should perish, but that all should come to repentance.' So whoever wants to be saved may freely come."

"However," they continue, "healing is not for today." Or they say, "God can heal, but He normally doesn't. He heals some, but He doesn't heal everyone." Or perhaps they rationalize, "God has replaced healing with doctors and hospitals."

But he was wounded for our transgressions, he was bruised for our iniquities: the chastisement of our peace was upon him; and with his stripes we are healed.

—Isaiah 53:5

But no one has a right to split the Atonement down the middle. Jesus paid the price for us spirit, soul, and body.

One half of the Atonement is the forgiveness of sin; the other half of the Atonement is healing for the physical body. Jesus Christ not only paid the price for our sins and iniquities, but at the same time He also paid the price for our sicknesses and diseases. When the body of Christ grabs hold of that revelation, the sick will be healed, the weak will be made strong, and the healthy will stay well.

Confession

Jesus wants me saved and healthy, so He purchased
my salvation and healing with His own death on the Cross.
His body was broken for me; His blood was shed for me.
And I gladly receive the salvation and healing He provided.

Forever Redeemed

In whom we have redemption through his blood, the forgiveness of sins, according to the riches of his grace.

—Ephesians 1:7

When Jesus shed His blood on the Cross He *redeemed* us, which means "to purchase or buy back."[1]

For example, years ago stores offered green stamps as an incentive to buy groceries in their store. After collecting and filling several books of stamps you could visit a "redemption center." The center was stocked with all kinds of nice gifts: radios, stereos, camping supplies, and so forth. But you couldn't buy those items with money; you had to redeem them with green stamps.

Likewise, Jesus redeemed us with His own blood. You see, when Adam sinned mankind fell into a state of spiritual death, or separation from God. Along with sin came sickness, poverty, fear, and failure.

Man was in the grips of sin under Satan's control, but God wanted to buy him back. Silver and gold couldn't do it. Only one price was enough to buy man back—sinless, spotless blood.

So God sent His only begotten Son to be our sacrifice. Jesus took on flesh and walked sinless among us as "the Lamb of God, which taketh away the sin of the world" (John 1:29). Then He shed His perfect, spotless blood on the Cross, redeeming us from Satan's dominion.

Now, all we have to do is believe in our hearts and confess with our mouths that Jesus is our Lord. (Rom. 10:9,10.) At that moment, we're translated out of the kingdom of darkness into the kingdom of light—forever redeemed.

Confession

I'm redeemed from Satan's control. Sickness no longer has jurisdiction over me. Divine health is a benefit of my Father's kingdom, and I walk in all the benefits Jesus purchased for me.

Jesus Bore the Punishment We Deserved

When Jesus finished the earthly ministry God had given Him, He was about thirty-three years old. Only one thing was left to do. Jesus, the Son of God, had to die on the Cross. Just imagine. Jesus—who never sinned, never made a mistake in His life, and never hurt anyone but instead helped everyone—had to die to pay the ultimate price for you and me.

In whom we have redemption through his blood, even the forgiveness of sins.

—Colossians 1:14

The cross was a death reserved for criminals. If anyone belonged on that cross, it was you and me—not Jesus.

The Bible says, "All have sinned, and come short of the glory of God" (Rom. 3:23). We were the ones who sinned, made mistakes, and hurt people; we deserved to go to the place of judgment. But Jesus took our place. He is "the Lamb of God, which taketh away the sin of the world" (John 1:29).

The Bible says, "Without shedding of blood [there] is no remission" (Heb. 9:22). Someone had to die for us. We deserved death, but Jesus took our death on Himself so we can walk in newness of life.

Confession

Jesus, my Savior, redeemed me. With the price of His own blood,
He became the way for me to be reconciled to the Father.
He took my spiritual death and my sicknesses so
I could have His eternal life and health.

We're Already Delivered

Who hath delivered us from the power of darkness, and hath translated us into the kingdom of his dear Son.

—Colossians 1:13

When Jesus redeemed us, He delivered us from the power of darkness. That means every Christian is *already delivered*, even though some Christians still run around trying to get delivered.

For instance, one evening a lady came over to me in a meeting and said, "I need to be delivered."

"Ma'am, you came to the right place," I replied. "I have good news for you!" Her eyes lit up. Then I asked, "Do you have a Bible?"

She gave me a wary look and said, "Yes."

I told her to open to Colossians 1:13 and read it, which she did: "Who hath delivered us from the power of darkness, and hath translated us into the kingdom of his dear Son."

I instructed the woman to read the first part again several times: "Who hath delivered us from the power of darkness...." I could tell she was getting angry with me. Then I said, "Well, did Jesus deliver us from the power of darkness or not? Either the Bible is true or it isn't."

"I know the Bible says that," she replied, "but you're not getting rid of me that easy! I want help! I want something that works."

"Ma'am, you'll never find anything that works any better," I said.

Christians who run around trying to get delivered ought to read the Bible. Then they'd realize they've *already been delivered!* Start each day off praising and thanking God for delivering you, and there isn't a devil in hell who will stick around.

Confession

Thank God, I'm free! My God delivered me from the power of darkness, and sin and sickness no longer have control over me.

He Already Paid the Price

Jesus went to the Cross and shed His blood for you and me. Through His death, burial, and resurrection He forgave our sins, redeemed us, delivered us from the power of darkness, and enabled us to become partakers of God's inheritance.

Yet most Christians have had little understanding of what redemption really is all about. They will say, "Well, redemption is when Jesus redeemed me from sin."

That's true, but there's so much more! Thank God, we've been redeemed from every single curse in the Old Testament—that includes sickness. Jesus didn't do away with any blessings in the Old Testament; He just added to them to create a new and better covenant.

Giving thanks unto the Father, which hath made us meet to be partakers of the inheritance of the saints in light.

—Colossians 1:12

Look at Isaiah 53:5: "But he was wounded for our transgressions, he was bruised for our iniquities: the chastisement of our peace was upon him; and with his stripes we are healed." Jesus not only redeemed us from our sins, but He also redeemed us from torment and oppression so we could have peace. He redeemed us from sickness so we could have health.

God's report says we were forgiven, delivered, and healed. Now we can just reach out in faith to receive any of these covenant blessings. They all belong to us because Jesus already paid the price.

Confession

I'm free from sin and all its effects—worry, anxiety,
fear, sickness, and pain. God's inheritance
blesses me—spirit, soul, and body.

Saved and Healed

Being justified freely by his grace through the redemption that is in Christ Jesus.

—Romans 3:24

Once believers receive a revelation of the redemption Jesus purchased on the Cross, it changes them. Nothing can stop them anymore. I'm not talking about a mental assent to the truth. I'm talking about people who say from their hearts, "Yes, that's the truth, and the truth is setting me free!"

Consider how a person is adopted into God's family. The minute a person finds out Jesus' blood was shed for the forgiveness of his sins, he can confess Jesus as his Savior, and not a devil in hell can stop him from getting born again. Peace and fellowship with God are available to anyone who receives Jesus in faith.

The same thing happens in the area of healing when people discover the truth that healing is included in the Atonement. Miracles abound when people act on that revelation. And, in fact, as believers proclaim that Jesus redeemed mankind from both sin and sickness, people jump up to get saved and healed at the same time!

As believers, we must be sure to establish the truth in our hearts that just as Jesus' blood was shed for us, just as much as His body was broken for us. Then we will not only be saved, but we will also rise up healed.

Confession

Jesus gave Himself as the sacrifice for my total redemption
from the kingdom of darkness. Therefore, I receive healing
from the Father as freely as I received salvation.

Redeemed From the Curse of the Law

Christ hath redeemed us from the curse of the law, being made a curse for us: for it is written, Cursed is every one that hangeth on a tree: That the blessing of Abraham might come on the Gentiles through Jesus Christ; that we might receive the promise of the Spirit through faith.

—Galatians 3:13,14

Jesus has redeemed us from the curse of the Law, which is outlined in Deuteronomy 28:15-68. The Lord told the children of Israel if they didn't obey Him, all the terrible curses listed in this passage would come upon them.

Spiritual death is a part of the curse—so are poverty and every kind of sickness and disease. Verse 61 says, "Also every sickness, and every plague, which is not written in the book of this law, them will the Lord bring upon thee."

But Galatians 3:13-14 tells us the good news: Believers have been redeemed from the curse of the Law through the death, burial, and resurrection of Jesus. That curse doesn't exist anymore for the believer. Deuteronomy 28:15-68 doesn't apply to God's children because Jesus took that curse upon Himself when He went to the Cross. That's the Good News!

In Deuteronomy 28:1-14, the Lord gives us the blessing of Abraham. That blessing includes divine health. We've been redeemed from the curse of every sickness and every plague—even those not mentioned in the Law. That means we've been redeemed from cancer, arthritis, colds, and flu. If we can name it, praise God, we've been redeemed from it!

Confession

When I received Jesus as my Savior, He freed me from the curse of the Law. Jesus took the curse upon Himself as my substitute, and now I'm redeemed from every disease. I walk in divine health.

Don't Carry the Devil's Burden

But Christ being come an high priest of good things to come, by a greater and more perfect tabernacle, not made with hands, that is to say, not of this building; neither by the blood of goats and calves, but by his own blood he entered in once into the holy place, having obtained eternal redemption for us.

—Hebrews 9:11, 12

Some people think Jesus came to help us carry our burdens. "Oh, Lord," they pray, "if You could just help me bear this disease until the end, I'd sure appreciate it. Maybe if You carry half, I could carry the other half."

Yet, these people don't realize what actually took place in redemption. They may understand Jesus took their sins to the Cross and wiped their slate free of sin. They may even realize God doesn't want them to take the condemnation for those sins back on themselves again.

But people must also realize Jesus completed a full redemption for them. Not only did He take on Himself their sin, but He bore their sickness and disease as well.

Just as we've known God doesn't want us to live in sin, we must know God doesn't want us to live in sickness either. Jesus paid the price to redeem us from *both* sin *and* sickness. *He already carried it all for us!* So Jesus doesn't want us carrying the burden of our sicknesses any more than He wants us carrying the burden of our sins. Sin and sickness belong in the devil's kingdom, but we're now citizens of the kingdom of light.

Confession

I'm redeemed from the curse of the Law. I refuse to carry the burden of sickness because Jesus already bore my sicknesses and carried my pains. By His stripes, I'm healed!

The Same Price

Who does redemption belong to? It belongs to "whosoever" will call on the name of the Lord Jesus Christ.

It's said all through the Bible. God is "not willing that any should perish, but that all should come to repentance" (2 Peter 3:9). Jesus said in John 6:37, "Him that cometh to me I will in no wise cast out." And John 1:12 tells us, "As many as received him, to them gave he power to become the sons of God."

And it shall come to pass, that whosoever shall call on the name of the Lord shall be saved.

—Acts 2:21

Jesus died on the Cross for every person. Anyone who believes in Him can freely come into God's family through His blood. But not only did He provide salvation for all mankind; He also provided peace of mind and physical healing to anyone who will receive it. He paid the same price for it all.

That means because of Jesus' resurrection, your spirit can be born again. And you can also enjoy peace of mind and a healthy body. First you receive the Healer; then you receive His healing touch, though sometimes God supernaturally heals the lost to get their attention.

You see, salvation results from accepting the spiritual side of redemption. Then it's up to you to walk in the soulish and physical sides of Jesus' redemptive work.

Jesus has already provided all of it for you.

Confession

I'm redeemed for I've called on the name of the Lord. I'm healed. I'm peaceful. And I'm so grateful for all my Lord has done for me.

Healing Is Simple

And Jesus went about all the cities and villages, teaching in their synagogues, and preaching the gospel of the kingdom, and healing every sickness and every disease among the people.

—Matthew 9:35

God's Word is simple and easy to understand. He didn't make it complicated because He didn't want anyone left out of His blessings.

Yet some people are deceived into thinking it's hard to receive from God, especially in the area of divine healing. They beg, plead, cry, bawl, and squall to be healed yet to no avail.

However, it's easy to receive healing. Why would it be hard to obtain something that already belongs to us? Jesus purchased healing for us with the stripes on His back. We just have to reach out and take what's already ours!

The only reason it's seemed difficult to receive healing is that we've lacked a thorough understanding of Jesus' work on the Cross. Thank God, what Jesus provided for us in the Atonement is simple to receive. Think about it: Was it difficult to get saved? No, we simply found out God loved us, believed in our hearts Jesus was raised from the dead, and confessed Him as our Savior.

Healing is received the very same way. We find out healing is God's will for us, believe in our hearts we receive our healing, and confess Jesus as our Healer. It's as simple as that.

We're healed by faith just as we're saved by faith. As we learn to appropriate what already belongs to us, we'll walk in blessings far beyond what we can ask or think.

Confession

Healing is simple: God wants me well! I know Jesus' body was broken so I could have His health, so right now I believe I receive my healing.

Confess, Believe, Receive

It's so easy to receive from God. God made it easy. He purchased everything we could ever need and then told us, "Just take it."

Someone may say, "But believing God for healing is so hard." Wait! Do you know you're saved? Doesn't that mean you've already believed for the biggest miracle there is?

One day you said, "Lord, I believe in my heart Jesus was raised from the dead for me. I receive Him as my Savior, and I'm a new creature in Christ!"

You didn't labor and strain and stand on the Word of God for years to get saved. Neither do you get up every morning to see if you still feel saved. You *know* you're saved, because the Bible tells you so!

If thou shalt confess with thy mouth the Lord Jesus, and shalt believe in thine heart that God hath raised him from the dead, thou shalt be saved.

—Romans 10:9

Well, if getting saved is the biggest miracle, would a lesser miracle such as healing be more difficult to receive? *No!* We receive salvation and healing exactly the same way; they're both part of redemption.

You'll be amazed at your results if you simply receive healing by faith the same way you once received salvation. Just say, "Lord, I believe by Jesus' stripes I'm healed, and I receive You as my Healer now. I count it done in Jesus' name!"

Don't check to see if you feel healed—you aren't healed because you feel better. You're healed because the Bible says so. And if you hold fast to your faith, your healing will come to pass.

Confession

I confess from a believing heart that Jesus is my Savior—
and my Healer. I receive healing now by the stripes of Jesus.

Head Faith vs. Heart Faith

Wherefore, sirs, be of good cheer: for I believe God, that it shall be even as it was told me.

—Acts 27:25

How can we know if we're really in *heart* faith and not *head* faith or mental assent? That's an important question. We have to learn how to locate ourselves in faith so we can effectively receive from God.

Head faith says, "I believe the Word, but look at the size of this problem." Or, "I believe I'm healed, but I feel so sick. And, hey, did you hear what the doctor said?"

Head faith is really "billygoat" faith—it likes to *"but."* "I believe the Bible, *but...."* "I believe for healing, *but...."*

On the other hand, heart faith says, "I see the problems or symptoms, but no matter, the Bible is my final authority. It will be as God's Word promises me."

Heart faith fixes its attention on the Word and always finishes with this statement: "I believe God no matter what it looks or feels like."

Faith doesn't deny symptoms or circumstances, nor buries its head in the sand and hopes problems go away. Faith faces problems head on and says, "It may look bad, but I have inside information. I'm coming through this as an overcomer in Jesus Christ!"

In a boat about to sink during a storm Paul said, "I believe God, that it shall be even as it was told me" (Acts 27:25). We must say the same thing. Sure—the storms of life come to all, and there's no denying it. Yet, we put our faith in something bigger, better, and higher: God's Word.

Confession

My faith rests in God's Word that's greater than symptoms or circumstances. Therefore, I'm of good cheer no matter what I feel or see!

The Rest of Faith

Does this sound familiar? You're facing a situation where everything looks, sounds, and feels bad. There seems to be no way out. But for some reason, you can't work up a good worry about it. "Don't you know how serious this is?" people ask. But you walk around with this silly grin on your face, saying, "I just can't seem to get concerned. Everything will be all right."

"How do you know it will be all right?" they ask.

"I just know."

That's called the *rest of faith*. Things look bad on the outside, but on the inside you sense only a velvety, peaceful rest.

Hebrews 4:3 talks about the rest of faith: "We which have believed do enter into rest." Now, God isn't talking here about physical or mental rest. Even when your mind gives you fits, a quiet peace prevails deep down inside.

For unto us was the gospel preached, as well as unto them: but the word preached did not profit them, not being mixed with faith in them that heard it. For we which have believed do enter into rest.

—Hebrews 4:2,3

Consider this second scenario: You're in a situation that looks, sounds, and feels bad, and you're endeavoring to believe God. You pray, "Oh, God, this better work!" You scrunch your face and say, "God, I'm trying to believe, but if You don't come through, I'm sunk!" That is definitely *not* the rest of faith.

What's the difference between the first and second responses? The difference is in *what* you believe.

So if you need healing in your body, put your faith in God and His Word and enter into rest.

Confession

I've entered into rest believing God's Word. I'm confident
I'm healed, for I know my God has already won my victory.

Enter Into Rest

For only we who believe God can enter into his place of rest.

—Hebrews 4:3 TLB

When you're in a difficult situation and you need a miracle, locate what you believe. Do you believe what God's Word says? Or do you believe what people or circumstances say?

Hebrews 4:3 says, "We which have believed do enter into rest." Belief produces rest, and what you hear determines what you believe.

So if you see you haven't entered into the rest of faith, don't waste your time feeling condemned, discouraged, or upset about it. Just realize your belief isn't strong enough yet to produce rest.

What do you do? Find out what God's Word says about your situation. Search for Scriptures that cover your case. Feed on the Word at every opportunity because hearing produces faith.

Listen to good healing tapes again and again. Read good books on healing, such as *Christ the Healer* by F. F. Bosworth. Don't just read the books once and set them down; read them from cover to cover several times until you're full of the Word on healing. Then out of the abundance of your heart, your mouth will speak. (Matt. 12:34.) You'll find yourself saying, "It's so good to be healed!"

And when someone asks, "Do you feel better? Are the symptoms gone?" you'll say, "I haven't checked yet, but I know I'm healed because the Bible says so. God says healing is mine, and I have whatever God says!"

Remember, hearing produces faith, faith produces rest, and the rest of faith produces *results!*

Confession

God's Word is firmly lodged down in my heart, and I enter into rest. God's Word is greater inside me than what I see with my natural eye. It's so good to be healed.

Manifestations of the Spirit

*But the
manifestation of
the Spirit is given
to every man to
profit withal. For
to one is given by
the Spirit the word
of wisdom; to
another the word
of knowledge by
the same Spirit; to
another faith by
the same Spirit; to
another the gifts of
healing by the
same Spirit; to
another the
working of
miracles; to
another prophecy;
to another
discerning of
spirits; to another
divers kinds of
tongues; to another
the interpretation
of tongues.*

*—1 Corinthians
12:7-10*

This is a list of the nine gifts, or manifestations, of the Spirit. Some have thought this passage of Scripture only refers to natural abilities God gives people. But God calls them supernatural manifestations of the Spirit, or sudden actions of the Holy Ghost.

Notice that healing is among this list of spiritual gifts. The phrase "gifts of healing" refers to supernatural manifestations of the Holy Ghost to produce physical healings in the physical body. God works many kinds of miracles on the earth, but this Scripture proves He performs healing miracles.

Now look at verse 11: "But all these worketh that one and the selfsame Spirit, dividing to every man severally as he will." We might wish we could control the gifts of the Spirit, but we don't. They operate as God wills. The gifts are given to the Church, but the manifestations are controlled by the Holy Ghost.

In fact, we don't know how, when, or for whom the gifts will manifest. But we can be assured that "the manifestation of the Spirit is given to every man to profit withal" (v. 7).

Confession

Because of His goodness and mercy,
God manifests His power through the nine
gifts of the Spirit. Thank God for gifts of
healing manifesting still today.

The Sovereign Side of God

Thus saith the Lord the King of Israel, and his redeemer the Lord of hosts; I am the first, and I am the last; and beside me there is no God.Is there a God beside me? yea, there is no God; I know not any.

—Isaiah 44:6,8

Let's talk about the sovereign side of God. God is the sovereign Creator of the universe, the God of heaven and earth. He can work miracles within the boundaries of His Word any time and any place He wants to—even without our approval.

Just think about your own life. Have you ever received something from God you weren't believing for? You probably have more times than you can count.

Most of us wouldn't have lived this long if God hadn't sovereignly done some things for us along the way. His love goes a long way.

For instance, look at Saul of Tarsus on the road to Damascus. He was on his way to persecute even more Christians when "suddenly there shined round about him a light from heaven" (Acts 9:3). Jesus appeared to Saul that day on the road to Damascus, and Saul was born again.

I wasn't saved that way. I heard the Gospel preached, believed it, and confessed Jesus as Lord. I never saw a bright light from heaven.

But God has left Himself room to sovereignly intervene in a person's life, as He did with Saul. Why did God intervene with Saul? I don't know, but it sure paid off because the apostle Paul wrote half the New Testament.

Confession

Sometimes my Father moves in miraculous or unusual ways, but
I don't have to wait for that to happen. I can go to God any time
and receive by faith whatever He's promised in His Word.

The Father's Love

God performs miracles in two different ways: By sovereignly initiating a miracle *at His will*, or initiating a miracle *at our will* in response to our faith. For the next few days, we'll see this principle illustrated in Jesus' story of the prodigal son.

This is the account of the younger son who left his father's house to indulge in sin. Eventually, he realized the pleasures of sin weren't worth the price he was paying. He decided he'd be better off back in his father's house if only a servant. But his father received him with open arms and sovereignly went out of his way to prove his love. (vv. 22-24.)

This is really a picture of our loving heavenly Father who also welcomes back into fellowship His repentant children. Often God will sovereignly perform miracles to show them how much He loves them.

Confession

I'm grateful when God performs
sovereign miracles in my life,
but I can always depend on Him to
perform His Word as I walk by faith.

A certain man had two sons; And the younger of them said to his father, Father, give me the portion of goods that falleth to me. And he divided unto them his living. And not many days after the younger son gathered all together, and took his journey into a far country, and there wasted his substance with riotous living. And when he came to himself, he said.... I will arise and go to my father, and will say unto him, Father, I have sinned against heaven, and before thee.

And he arose, and came to his father. But when he was yet a great way off, his father saw him, and had compassion, and ran, and fell on his neck, and kissed him.

—Luke 15:11-13,17,18,20

The Elder Son's Inheritance

Now his elder son was in the field: and as he came and drew nigh to the house, he heard musick and dancing. And he was angry, and would not go in: therefore came his father out, and entreated him. And he answering said to his father, Lo, these many years do I serve thee, neither transgressed I at any time thy commandment: and yet thou never gavest me a kid, that I might make merry with my friends: but as soon as this thy son was come, which hath devoured thy living with harlots, thou hast killed for him the fatted calf. And he said unto him, Son, thou art ever with me, and all that I have is thine....

—*Luke 15:25,28-31*

The elder son was upset. He'd stayed home with the father and worked while his younger brother wasted his inheritance through riotous living. Now his brother returned home, and his father proved his love by clothing him luxuriously and killing the fatted calf for a feast in his honor. (vv. 22,23.)

Sometimes Christians feel like that elder son. They see God miraculously heal a backslider who doesn't have an ounce of faith. This proves to the backslider that God loves him. But sometimes believers get upset and say, "Why did God heal that person? I've never backslidden, but He didn't heal me."

In essence, this is what the older son said. He'd been faithful, yet there was no big celebration in his honor. But the elder son could have whatever he desired any time. His father told him, "Son, all I have belongs to you!"

Your heavenly Father is saying the same thing to you.

Confession

Because I'm a child of God,
everything my Father has is mine.
Healing is mine, and by faith, I accept it now.

Everything God Has Is Yours

"All that I have is thine." This is what God says to His faithful children. So often believers ask, "God, why don't You work a miracle for me?" But God responds, "Child, you are with Me. Everything I have is yours. Healing is yours. Don't wait for Me to sovereignly step out and do something for you. Come get it any time you want. Receive it by faith!"

So often we've wanted God to do something special for us, but He expects more out of us as His children. He didn't say, "The just shall live by the gifts of the Spirit or the sovereignty of God." He said, "The just shall live by faith" (Rom. 1:17).

We must find in the Word what belongs to us through God's plan of redemption, then take hold of it with the hand of faith. Everything He has is ours—it belongs to us.

And he said unto him, Son, thou art ever with me, and all that I have is thine. It was meet that we should make merry, and be glad: for this thy brother was dead, and is alive again; and was lost, and is found.

—Luke 15:31,32

Confession

Everything my Father has is mine. He has provided everything I could ever need. So I receive my needs met now in Jesus' name.

God Limits Himself to His Word

I will worship toward thy holy temple, and praise thy name for thy lovingkindness and for thy truth: for thou hast magnified thy word above all thy name.

—Psalm 138:2

I've heard people say, "God is sovereign so He can make you sick if He wants to." But God gave us His Word, which says He is our healer, and promises He'd never go outside its boundaries.

I've heard other people say, "I know what His Word says, but God is still God and He can do anything He wants." In other words, they're saying, "God's Word is one thing, but He is God. He has a title that enables Him to do anything He wants."

But the Word says, "Thou hast magnified thy word above all thy name." God is the sovereign God of the universe, but He has elevated His Word above His name. He has limited Himself within the boundaries of His Word.

God is saying He can sovereignly manifest anything promised in His Word through signs, wonders, miracles, and gifts of the Holy Spirit, but He cannot sovereignly steal, kill, and destroy. That's the work of the devil. (John 10:10.) By the decree of His own Word, God is a merciful, loving Father who has only good gifts to give. (James 1:17.)

Confession

My God is my healer, and He has magnified
His Word above His own holy name. According
to that Word, I believe healing is mine now.

Learning To Walk by Faith

We are well equipped to walk in the blessings of God. Therefore, after we've had time to grow spiritually, God usually doesn't move on our behalf with sovereign miracles or manifestations of the Holy Spirit that require no faith on our part.

You see, God holds us responsible to learn how to believe His Word. He expects us to switch over from the natural realm and begin operating in the faith realm.

When I started to hear and apply the truth of God's Word, it changed my life. I started receiving answers to my prayers according to my own faith.

You see, the Word sets our doctrines straight. God won't force His truth on us. But if we're willing to learn, He will show us how to rightly divide His Word. (2 Tim. 2:15.) His truth will set us straight and put us on a new course to victory.

As ye have therefore received Christ Jesus the Lord, so walk ye in him: Rooted and built up in him, and stablished in the faith, as ye have been taught, abounding therein with thanksgiving.

—Colossians 2:6,7

Confession

I spend time with my heavenly Father and grow up in Him.
I walk by faith, depending on Him to perform His Word
in my life. It's my privilege to walk by faith.

Initiating Your Miracle

How shall we escape, if we neglect so great salvation; which at the first began to be spoken by the Lord, and was confirmed unto us by them that heard him; God also bearing them witness, both with signs and wonders, and with divers miracles, and gifts of the Holy Ghost, according to his own will?

—Hebrews 2:3,4

Sometimes people get healed out of the clear blue. It doesn't look as if they did a thing to receive their healing. They weren't standing in faith; they were just healed.

I heard about one fellow who walked past a church meeting and decided to go in and get a drink of water. Interestingly enough, he was drunk at the time. And even more interesting is the fact that as he left and walked down the street, he suddenly realized he'd been healed. He returned to the meeting and was saved!

That man wasn't believing for his healing. He wasn't in faith, and he didn't expect anything. He just got healed according to God's own will and mercy.

Yet, we can move over into the realm of faith to receive answers any time we need them. When we exercise our faith in God's Word, we release the same power and get the same results as when God moves sovereignly. We don't have to wait to see if God passes by with a miracle because "we walk by faith, not by sight" (2 Cor. 5:7). God expects us to use faith to initiate our own miracle.

Reach out by faith and take hold of whatever you need from God's Word. It belongs to you!

Confession

My God is good to me and shows me in His Word how to receive the blessings He's provided. I receive by faith the healing I desire.

God Is True to His Word

When we talk about God's sovereignty, we aren't talking about the religious world's viewpoint of sovereignty. Religious people who don't know the Word say, "God is a sovereign God. If He wants you healed, you'll get healed. If He wants you sick, you'll stay sick. If He wants you prosperous, He'll take care of you financially. But God may want you sick and broke. Whatever will be, will be."

God is not a man, that he should lie; neither the son of man, that he should repent.

—Numbers 23:19

According to that way of thinking, it wouldn't do you any good to believe God's Word because you'll still get whatever God wants you to have. That faulty religious thinking believes God will take your money, steal your health, and knock you in the head three or four times a week to keep you in line. They believe that's just the kind of mood God is in most of the time.

Yet one thing is certain—religious people who think that way don't know God or His Word.

No, when we say God does something sovereignly, we simply mean God does something according to His Word at His own discretion. He initiates it. But God cannot sovereignly do anything outside His Word because He's bound Himself to His Word.

Titus 1:2 and Hebrews 6:18 say God cannot lie or fail to keep His Word. So just as surely as you can trust that "whosoever shall call upon the name of the Lord shall be saved" (Rom. 10:13), you can believe "by [Jesus'] stripes ye were healed" (1 Peter 2:24).

Confession

God's says I'm healed by the stripes Jesus bore. That healing word is truth in my life because I believe it and act upon it.

Follow the Holy Ghost

And I, brethren, when I came to you, came not with excellency of speech or of wisdom, declaring unto you the testimony of God.

And my speech and my preaching was not with enticing words of man's wisdom, but in demonstration of the Spirit and of power: that your faith should not stand in the wisdom of men, but in the power of God.

—1 Corinthians 2:1,4,5

Sometimes God wants to demonstrate His love and compassion for us. He knows we'll retain and understand a greater percentage of what we both hear and see.

God will also go out of His way to demonstrate to us that the Holy Ghost flows in many different directions. You see, in John 7:37-38, Jesus likens the Holy Spirit to a river of living water: "If any man thirst, let him come unto me, and drink. He that believeth on me, as the Scripture hath said, out of his belly shall flow rivers of living water."

Just as no two rivers are alike, neither are any two flows of the Holy Spirit alike. Sometimes God will almost give us a spiritual "jerk," demonstrating His power in a new way just to show us that He is a God of variety. We need every one of His different directions because we are creatures of habit who get into ruts easily.

Someone once said, "A rut is nothing but a grave with both ends kicked out of it." We want to make sure we don't get into a rut. The best way to do that is to follow the Holy Ghost, because He's never in a rut.

Confession

My God moves in many different ways as He leads me into healing and whatever else I need. I stay sensitive to His Spirit so that wherever He leads, I follow His flow.

Build Your Spiritual Muscles

Nay, in all these things we are more than conquerors through him that loved us.

—Romans 8:37

Though you're not of this world, you still live in this world so tests, trials, and temptations are bound to come your way.

Many people think, *Tests and trials come to make me strong.* Some have even written songs with that message. These folks may even have been taught that sickness and disease come to teach them lessons or make them more pious.

But the truth is, sickness, tests, trials, and temptations will never make you strong. If they did, you'd be Mr. or Mrs. Universe by now. No, it's what you do with tests and trials that makes the difference.

Think in terms of weight lifting. A weight lifter wants to develop his muscles, but he'll never reach that goal unless he actually lifts weights. He certainly won't turn into Charles Atlas sitting in an easy chair reading weight lifting books and thinking, *I'm strong! I'm strong!* And when he lies on the workout bench, the 100-pound weight lying across his chest won't help his muscles gain strength unless he lifts up the weight and starts pushing it away.

The same is true with tests and trials. You won't be strong in faith unless you exercise your spiritual muscles. Every time you push problems away in Jesus' name you gain strength. Strong faith only comes by exercising the faith you have against something that's contrary to God's Word.

So when problems arise we can say, "Glory to God, here's one more opportunity to develop my faith muscles and prove God's Word works!"

Confession

I develop faith muscles by using God's Word when problems come against me. The Word works for me because I work the Word.

Let Patience Have Her Perfect Work

My brethren, count it all joy when ye fall into divers temptations; knowing this, that the trying of your faith worketh patience. But let patience have her perfect work, that ye may be perfect and entire, wanting nothing.

—James 1:2-4

Notice James didn't say, "Let those tests and trials have their perfect work." He said, "Let patience have her perfect work...."

You see, tests and trials don't perfect you. It's what you do with them that counts. You're not perfected because a bunch of problems come along. You're perfected because you stick with the Word of God in the midst of those problems and patiently endure. That's when patience has its perfect work.

Patience is consistent endurance. When you walk in patience, you aren't up and down like a yo-yo. You base everything on God's Word. You don't get up in the morning and ask yourself how you feel. You get up in the morning and tell yourself how you feel according to God's Word.

I've seen people grow as a result of using their faith against tests and trials. And I've seen other people go under when they faced the same tests and trials. It's what people do with their problems that makes the difference.

Faith thrives in the midst of a trial. That doesn't mean we enjoy the trial, but we don't shrink from it either. We just dig our heels in and say, "I don't care what it looks like, seems like, sounds like, or feels like. I believe what God's Word says."

Confession

My faith thrives in a trial. When symptoms come, I tell my body,
"You're healed because Jesus bore your sickness." After all,
I'm not the sick trying to get healed. I'm the healed staying well.

Conquer Sickness With Your Faith

A few years back my father decided he didn't want to get "soft," so he started lifting weights. As Dad worked out every morning, he became stronger and stronger. He'd say, "I don't like lifting these weights, but I'm going to conquer them. If it takes the rest of my life, I'm going to conquer them."

It's the same way with tests and trials. You can either let them plant themselves in your life and put pressure on you, or you can use your faith muscles to push those trials out of your life. You can decide, "Bless God, I'm going after those tests and trials, and I'm going to conquer them."

Now thanks be unto God, which always causeth us to triumph in Christ, and maketh manifest the savour of his knowledge by us in every place.

—2 Corinthians 2:14

I remember when it used to take me two weeks to get rid of a cold. But I didn't sit back and say, "Well, I'm going to learn from this cold." (I don't know what you could learn from a cold anyway—except that you don't want another one!) I kept using my faith muscles to push off those cold symptoms. After a while, the symptoms only lasted one week instead of two. Then they lasted three days instead of a week. Soon the cold symptoms just started falling off before they could attach to my body.

And the more you push off the enemy's attacks—symptoms, tests, trials, temptations—the stronger your faith muscles will get and the quicker problems will leave.

Confession

God's Word is full of truths that empower me to push off symptoms, tests, and trials that come my way. I walk in victory!

Come Out of the Trial Stronger

Fight the good fight of faith, lay hold on eternal life, whereunto thou art also called, and hast professed a good profession before many witnesses.

—1 Timothy 6:12

Someone once said to me, "I thought when a person operated in faith, he wouldn't have any problems." No, that's what faith is for—to help you overcome the enemy when he attacks you with problems.

A man said to another minister, "I want you to pray I'll never have any more trouble with the devil."

"Do you want me to pray you'll die?" the minister answered.

You see, you can count on the enemy bringing tests and trials your way. He will try to steal from, kill, and destroy you. (John 10:10.) As long as we live down here, we're going to have trouble with the devil.

He tries to stir up negative circumstances, symptoms, thoughts, imaginations, and trials. He does anything he can to discourage us and make us quit. I'm not preaching doom and gloom; I'm just saying we may as well face the fact that life on earth won't be "a bed of roses."

Nevertheless, we aren't supposed to bury our heads in the sand or run in fear and cry, "Oh, God, what do I do now?"

No, when the devil comes to harrass us we need to get silly grins on our faces and say, "Glory to God! Here's one more chance for me to flex my faith muscle. I'll throw this problem back in the devil's face with God's Word and come out of this even stronger than I went in."

Confession

I always overcome with God's Word. I won't be discouraged, I won't fear, I won't quit. By faith, I come out of every test even stronger.

God's Kind of Life

The thief cometh not, but for to steal, and to kill, and to destroy: I am come that they might have life, and that they might have it more abundantly.

—John 10:10

Where does sickness come from? I was taught for years that sickness was sent from God to teach us and make us pious and more "Christ-like."

However, if we look in the Word, we definitely see that sickness comes from the enemy—not from God. Jesus certainly didn't get Christ-like through sickness and disease, so I don't know why we would either. Sickness is a satanic force. God called it a curse in Deuteronomy 28:59-61. In Luke 13:16, Jesus called it a bondage. And by the inspiration of the Holy Ghost, Peter called it satanic oppression in Acts 10:38.

God doesn't like sickness; He's totally and completely against it. He has done, and is still doing, everything in His power to get healing and health to His children.

The devil is the one who steals, kills, and destroys. Sickness steals money, families, homes—it steals everything it can steal.

Jesus said, "I have come that you might have life and have it more abundantly" (John 10:10). The word *life* in the Greek is "zoe," and it refers to life as God has it.[1] Jesus was saying, "I have come that you might have the life of God."

Was God ever sick? No! Sickness doesn't come from God; otherwise, Jesus would've included it in His "abundant life" package. No, Jesus didn't come to bind us in chains of bondage. He came to set us free!

Confession

Jesus gives me abundant life—life as God has it. God doesn't get sick, so I don't allow sickness to stay in my body. Divine health belongs to me.

Fill Your Mind With the Word

For this purpose the Son of God was manifested, that he might destroy the works of the devil.

—1 John 3:8

Where does sickness come from? We have to understand its source so we can can get rid of it.

Let's look at the reason Jesus came to earth. First John 3:8 says He came "to destroy the works of the devil." What are those works Jesus came to destroy? Sin, poverty, sickness, and disease.

I know people who are just beginning to walk by faith. But even though they are learning to believe and confess the truth of God's Word, they still have that old, doubt-filled thought following them around: *God may want me sick for a purpose. This sickness may be sent from God to teach me something.*

But as long as you think that way, you won't be healed. Your faith will never operate beyond your knowledge of God's will. You have to know healing is God's will before you can believe for it.

So feed your spirit on healing Scriptures that tell you God wants you healthy and whole. Fill your mind with the Word so those old, doubt-filled thoughts can't even find their way back in.

Then steadfastly cling to God's Word in faith, and it will bring healing and health to your whole body.

Confession

It's God's will for me to be healed and live in health.
Sickness doesn't come from God, and He doesn't use
sickness to teach me. Jesus destroyed the works
of the devil, so I live free of sickness and disease.

Don't Be Double-Minded

When disease attacks our bodies, everything in us wants to be free of it. It's uncomfortable. It is "dis-ease," and we automatically want to get rid of it as quickly as we can.

But if we think sickness is from God for any reason—whether we think it's commissioned by Him, sent by Him, or allowed by Him—we're in trouble. We become double-minded. One side of our mind thinks, *I don't want this.* But the other side thinks, *If God wants me to have this sickness, it must be good for me so I should keep it.*

If sickness is a blessing from God, we should never be found fighting against it. We shouldn't fight it with medical science, with prayer, with the laying on of hands, or with anything else. If our sickness is from God, we should keep it and pray for more for the rest of the family.

He that wavereth is like a wave of the sea driven with the wind and tossed. For let not that man think that he shall receive any thing of the Lord. A double minded man is unstable in all his ways.

—James 1:6-8

But sickness is not from God! And as God's children, redeemed by the blood of Jesus, we shouldn't have any part of it.

So don't be double-minded about it—refuse to accept sickness when it comes. If symptoms attack your body, attack those symptoms with the Word of God. You are God's child, and you don't have to keep one thing that doesn't come from Him.

Confession

I'm single-minded in all my ways.
I know God's will for me is healing and health.
Sickness has no place in me, and I refuse to let it stay.

Does Sickness Come From God?

He sent his word, and healed them, and delivered them from their destructions.

—Psalm 107:20

If sickness or disease comes from God, how does He give it to us? Does He reach out and touch us, giving it to us by His own hand?

Jesus was the express image of God—the will of God in action. He said, "If you've seen Me, you've seen the Father." (John 14:9.) So if it were true that God gave us sickness by His hand, then Jesus would have given sickness to people instead of taking it away from them.

But when Jesus touched people, they were healed. He lived on this earth thirty-three-and-a-half years and ministered for three-and-a-half of those years. In all that time, Jesus never gave sickness or disease to anyone. He acted out the will of God, taking sickness away from people.

Well, then, does God give us sickness by His Word? Does He speak it on us? No, Psalm 107:20 says, "He sent his word, and healed them." So God doesn't put sickness on us with His hands nor by His Word.

Where would God get sickness to put on us anyway? He doesn't have sickness in heaven. And when sickness entered this earth through the fall of man, Jesus paid the price to send it to the depths of hell, where it belongs.

So there's only one conclusion to make: God doesn't have any sickness to give us because sickness and disease are not from God.

Confession

Father, let Your will be done in my life as it is in heaven. Since there's no sickness in heaven, there should be no sickness in me. I receive God's healing power at work in my body now in Jesus' name.

The God Who Never Changes

Every good and perfect gift comes from God who never changes. So when we find out something is good and perfect, we know it comes from God. And if it isn't good or perfect, we know it doesn't come from above.

What about sickness? Well, if sickness were from God, it would have to be good. But we know sickness isn't good because it steals, kills, and destroys. Clearly, sickness doesn't come from God.

And it never has. In fact, I like the last part of verse 17, where James describes God as "the Father of lights, with whom is no variableness, neither shadow of turning." God never changes. This verse says He doesn't even have a shadow of turning. There's not even a trace of change in God.

> *Do not err, my beloved brethren. Every good gift and every perfect gift is from above, and cometh down from the Father of lights, with whom is no variableness, neither shadow of turning.*
>
> *—James 1:16,17*

Jesus doesn't change either. He's the express image of the Father, and He's the same yesterday, today, and forever. (Heb. 13:8.) And Acts 10:38 says Jesus "went about doing good, and healing all that were oppressed of the devil; for God was with him."

God didn't send sickness and disease to the earth in the beginning; He didn't send sickness and disease during Jesus' earthly walk, and He doesn't send sickness and disease to the earth today. Rather, God delivered us from sickness and disease when He sent the living Word, Jesus Christ.

Confession

God never changes. He sent His Word to heal His people under
the old covenant, and He sends His Word to heal me today.
By faith, God's healing power is at work in me.

Was Sickness Part of God's Creation?

And God saw every thing that he had made, and, behold, it was very good. And the evening and the morning were the sixth day.

—Genesis 1:31

God finished Creation and said, "That's it. I'm through!" His finished creation displayed His perfect will for Adam and all his descendants. That was the way He wanted everything to be.

But what was not in God's creation on that sixth day? Well, you'll never find a Scripture that says, "On such-and-such a day, God created sickness and disease." You'll never read, "And God said, 'Let there be cancer! Let there be pneumonia!'" No, God looked at His creation, and "behold, it was very good" (Gen. 1:31). That means sickness and disease were absent in the original creation.

When Adam sinned and fell spiritually in the Garden of Eden, he chose a new master to serve. And at that moment, Satan became the god of this world with a long-term lease on creation.

When Satan entered into his new domain, he brought all his goods with him—sickness, fear, poverty, depression, oppression, death, and everything else that's evil. Someone once said, "Sickness is the foul offspring of its father, Satan, and its mother, sin."

You don't find sickness and disease anywhere in the Bible until after Satan became the god of this world. Then you find sickness running rampant throughout the earth.

Satan is the author of sickness, but through the redemptive work of Jesus on the Cross, life can become "very good" once again.

Confession

Sickness doesn't come from God. Satan is the father of all diseases, but I've been delivered from his kingdom. I walk in health and healing because my Father wants me well.

Healing Is Good

The Bible doesn't say, "God anointed Jesus of Nazareth with the Holy Ghost and power: who went about making people sick everywhere He went." No, Jesus went about doing good. What "good" did Jesus do? Acts 10:38 says He "went about doing good, and healing." Whom did He heal? Those who were oppressed.

Who oppressed them? The devil. That's plain. God tells us plain and simple in this Scripture where sickness and disease come from—the devil.

God also tells us what "good" is: Good is *healing.* Sickness isn't good, because Jesus healed those who were sick and oppressed of the devil. "Good" is setting people free from sickness and disease.

> *God anointed Jesus of Nazareth with the Holy Ghost and with power: who went about doing good, and healing all that were oppressed of the devil; for God was with him.*
>
> *—Acts 10:38*

Sickness isn't a blessing from God. It's a curse, a satanic oppression, and a bondage the enemy uses to slow us down or stop us from preaching the Gospel to all the world.

God wants us well so we can fulfill the Great Commission. He wants us not only to preach the Gospel, but also to lay hands on the sick to set them free. (Mark 16:18.) Why? Because sickness is bad, and healing is *good!*

Confession

My Father says healing is good. He willingly heals me.
And as I lay hands on the sick, God's power causes them to recover.

Rightly Discerning Jesus' Body

But let a man examine himself, and so let him eat of that bread, and drink of that cup. For he that eateth and drinketh unworthily, eateth and drinketh damnation to himself, not discerning the Lord's body. For this cause many are weak and sickly among you, and many sleep.

—1 Corinthians 11:28-30

Writing to the believers at the Corinthian church, Paul says, "Many in the church are weak, sickly, and sleeping."

What does Paul mean? Some definitions will help us understand. The word *weak* indicates being without strength, infirmed, feeble, impotent, diseased, and sick. A *sickly* person is one whose strength has failed through disease. Paul is talking about physical problems in this Scripture. And when he refers to those who are *sleeping,* he's talking about the "sleep" of death.

So Paul is actually saying in this verse, "For this reason, many are physically sick and even dying early."

What is the reason Paul refers to? In discussing the Lord's Supper in verse 29, he says, "For he that eateth and drinketh unworthily, eateth and drinketh damnation to himself, not discerning the Lord's body." Weymouth's translation says, "...if he fails to estimate the body right." Wuest's translation says, "...if he does not properly evaluate the body." *The Living Bible* puts it this way: "...not thinking about the body of Christ and what it means." Finally, *The Modern Language Bible* says, "...without due appreciation of the body."

This is the only place in the Bible where Paul says, *"For this cause* many are weak and sickly among you, and many sleep." Apparently, it's important to understand how to rightly discern, evaluate, and appreciate the body.

Confession

I rightly discern Jesus' body, broken for my physical healing.
I appreciate and appropriate the healing Jesus purchased for me.

Don't Judge Others

One way we can look at Paul's warning about "not discerning the Lord's body" is as it refers to our discernment of others in the body of Christ.

Some Christians say, "We have more revelation than anyone else in the body of Christ. If you aren't one of us, you don't have anything." These people want to criticize others and put themselves on a level above everyone else. That's a bad position to be in. A church like that is not rightly discerning the body of Christ and will be full of sick people who don't receive their healing.

Those of us who have received the fullness of the Holy Spirit have to be careful about this kind of prideful attitude. We aren't on a level above anyone else. We only have more responsibility. You see, when we understand what God's Word says about healing, faith, and confession, the way is opened for us to receive more benefits.

For he that eateth and drinketh unworthily, eateth and drinketh damnation to himself, not discerning the Lord's body. For this cause many are weak and sickly among you, and many sleep.

—1 Corinthians 11:29,30

We need to walk in love toward fellow Christians who haven't received as much revelation of the Word as we have. When we look down on other believers, we do not rightly discern the body of Christ. Judging others will always give us trouble because everyone in the body of Christ is important.

Confession

Jesus' blood was shed and His body was broken for all people. Each person is important to the Lord. I will not judge another in the body of Christ. I will pray and intercede so we all may be healed.

Understand Why Jesus' Body Was Broken

For he that eateth and drinketh unworthily, eateth and drinketh damnation to himself, not discerning the Lord's body. For this cause many are weak and sickly among you, and many sleep.

—1 Corinthians 11:29,30

Let's look at another meaning of the phrase "not discerning the Lord's body." In Communion, the cup is the symbol of Jesus' blood, which was shed for our sins. We've preached about the blood of Jesus for years, and most people have a revelation of it.

Yet a person who takes Communion without understanding the purpose of the blood may think, *I don't know why Jesus went to the Cross or believe His blood has anything to do with me.*

What blessings will such a person receive? Someone who doesn't understand or believe in the blood of Jesus can't partake of salvation. He is walking in spiritual death because he doesn't know why Jesus shed His blood.

In the same way, the Communion bread is the symbol of Jesus' body, which was broken for us. But many Christians haven't been taught the body of Jesus was broken for their physical health. Therefore, they remain sick.

A person can partake of the symbol of Jesus' broken body in Communion for years and still say, "I don't believe healing is for today." If people don't understand, believe, and act on the truth that Jesus' body was broken for their physical healing, then Jesus' redemptive work won't help them. Don't make that mistake. Believe Jesus' body was broken for you, and enjoy walking in good health.

Confession

Jesus' body was broken for my physical healing
just as surely as His blood was shed for my sins.
I rightly discern His body, so I walk in divine health.

Choose God's Higher Thoughts

People say, "I believe God wants to use sickness to teach me." But is that in the Bible?

All of us have probably held theories and beliefs at one time that messed up our thinking. Perhaps Satan's biggest lie is that sickness is from God. When we fall for that lie, we stop resisting the devil's attacks on our bodies and open the door for him to strap sickness on us. Then we wonder why we can't get rid of it.

We might receive temporary relief from sickness if people pray for us, but often the symptoms return. We won't find permanent relief until we make sure the door giving the enemy access is closed and locked. How do we lock the door? By getting a strong revelation that healing is God's will.

You see, we open the door to sickness through wrong thinking. Wrong thinking produces wrong believing, and wrong believing produces wrong speaking. When all those factors work together, we experience only bad results.

When faced with symptoms we should immediately say, "The Bible is God talking to me. What does God think? What does the Bible say?"

We should think God's thoughts because they're higher than ours. (Isa. 55:9.) God wrote down His thoughts and ways for us in sixty-six books called the Bible, where He makes it clear healing is His will.

For my thoughts are not your thoughts, neither are your ways my ways, saith the Lord. For as the heavens are higher than the earth, so are my ways higher than your ways, and my thoughts than your thoughts.

—Isaiah 55:8,9

Confession

I don't allow the devil's doubt and unbelief to keep me
from receiving my healing. I choose God's higher
thoughts and ways that produce healing in me.

Act Like the Word Is True

Giving thanks unto the Father, which hath made us meet to be partakers of the inheritance of the saints in light: who hath delivered us from the power of darkness, and hath translated us into the kingdom of his dear Son.

—Colossians 1:12,13

Why do people get sick? Well, we know why people in the world get sick: Their father, the devil, gives sickness to them. But what about Christians? Our Father God doesn't have any sickness to give to us, and we don't have to take it from the devil anymore. We've been delivered from darkness.

But because of a lack of knowledge, Christians often don't realize sickness comes from the devil and don't resist symptoms when they show up. Or they may think God has some purpose in the sickness so they keep it.

When these Christians start feeling symptoms, they just say in resignation, "I guess I'm sick." They don't know the enemy is trying to cause them problems and keep them from obeying God. They're ignorant of the devil's efforts to hinder them from fulfilling the Great Commission. Therefore, they don't resist the devil. When symptoms come, they "sign for the package" and get sick.

Amazingly enough, another major reason many Christians are sick is that they haven't obeyed James 4:7: "Submit yourselves therefore to God. Resist the devil, and he will flee from you."

If you're going to live in divine health as God intended, you must know sickness comes from the devil. When symptoms come, resist them in Jesus' name. Then act like God's Word is true—because it is.

Confession

I'm delivered from the power of darkness. I submit to God and resist the devil, and the devil has to go and take his symptoms with him.

Be a Person of Your Word

You cannot separate yourself from your word, for you are only as good as your word.

I heard one minister say, "Sometimes a person's faith doesn't work because his word is no good." After hearing this probably 100 times, I finally realized if our word isn't any good, our faith will never work.

Out of the abundance of the heart the mouth speaketh.

—Matthew 12:34

Sometimes people aren't used to believing their own words. If they don't believe their words in certain natural areas of their lives, they'll have a hard time believing their words when they're standing in faith for something.

Faith is believing that what you say according to the Word will come to pass. Mark 11:23 says, "For verily I say unto you, that whosoever shall say unto this mountain, Be thou removed, and be thou cast into the sea; and shall not doubt in his heart, but shall believe that those things which he saith shall come to pass; he shall have whatsoever he saith."

If you're going to be a person of faith whose faith works, you have to be a person of your word. Stick to your word. Keep your word. Honor your word. Watch over your word.

As you do, people will begin saying, "I'm telling you, if that person says something, you can just count on it coming to pass. You can count on him to back up his word." When you gain a reputation like that, your faith will skyrocket.

Confession

My words create God's realities in my life. I watch my words carefully and speak only truth and life. As I walk in faith according to God's Word, I shall have whatever I say. So right now I say, by Jesus' stripes, I'm healed!

The Miracle at the Pool of Bethesda

Now there is at Jerusalem by the sheep market a pool, which is called in the Hebrew tongue Bethesda, having five porches. In these lay a great multitude of impotent folk, of blind, halt, withered, waiting for the moving of the water. For an angel went down at a certain season into the pool, and troubled the water: whosoever then first after the troubling of the water stepped in was made whole of whatsoever disease he had.

—John 5:2-4

This account gives us a picture of God's sovereign side. Five sheds full of people sat by that pool not knowing when the angel was coming or who would be healed. And afterward, the rest of the people would have to sit and wait for the next time the angel came to trouble the water.

Let's look at verses 5-9:

> And a certain man was there, which had an infirmity thirty and eight years. When Jesus saw him lie...he saith...Wilt thou be made whole?

> The impotent man answered him, Sir, I have no man, when the water is troubled, to put me into the pool....

> Jesus saith unto him, Rise, take up thy bed, and walk. And immediately the man was made whole....

Obviously, the impotent man wasn't healed on his own faith. And he wasn't healed on Jesus' faith. Jesus never once said in the Bible, "My faith made you whole." If Jesus' faith had healed that man, He would've healed everyone else there too.

The truth is, God sovereignly healed this man. Why? I don't know; that's God's business, but He knows what He's doing.

Confession

God heals sovereignly as He wills, but He made a way for me to receive healing by faith any time. I exercise that faith and receive healing now.

Keep a Watch on Your Words

The Living Bible puts it this way: "When Jesus saw him and knew how long he had been ill, he asked, 'Would you like to get well?'"

"'I can't,' the sick man said...."

Just as we can locate this man's faith by his words, we can locate our faith by our words.

You see, many of us have been taught a great deal about faith and confession (or saying what the Word says) and can "talk a good talk." It's

[Jesus] saith unto him, Wilt thou be made whole? The impotent man answered him, Sir I have no man.

—John 5:6,7

easy to keep a good confession when things are going well. But when no one is listening and the pressure is on, we may discover some adjustments we need to make.

When many of us first heard the teaching, "You can have what you say," we were dangerous. We'd say, "Don't say that!" to people who had no idea what we were talking about. Hopefully we've learned better by now. We don't need to be "confession monitors" for other people; we can stay busy just checking up on ourselves.

When you get in a tight spot while standing in faith, you may speak words of doubt. Don't let that put you under condemnation. Don't say, "Oh, dear God, I thought I was in faith, but now I've completely blown it by speaking unbelief!" No, all isn't lost. Just make the adjustment, and feed in the Word. In fact, get full of the Word, for "out of the abundance of the heart the mouth speaketh" (Matt. 12:34).

Confession

My words control my life. I can have what I say, and I say I'm healed.
God's Word in me drives out sickness and disease.

Don't Wait for the Water To Move

When Jesus saw him lie, and knew that he had been now a long time in that case, he saith unto him, Wilt thou be made whole?

—John 5:6

Notice Jesus went to this pool where a multitude of sick people gathered waiting for the water to be troubled. The first person who stepped in would be healed, though everyone else had to wait for the next visitation. And they'd wait and wait and wait....

The situation was like a person who decides to stand in a field waiting for lightning to strike. Maybe it will strike; maybe it won't—no guarantees.

Unfortunately, many Christians are in that same state of wishful thinking. They'd like healing to hit them, but they haven't done their part to take hold of it by faith.

"Wilt thou be made whole?" That's a good question.

Some Christians would protest, "But if healing were for today, everyone would be healed." No, not everyone even wants healing. Some folks would rather stay sick. For example, Janet and I know a lady who's been sick for thirty-five years, and she's become accustomed to it. If some people were healed, they wouldn't have anything to talk about or get any attention.

I don't mean that unkindly, but that kind of situation is a reproach to the body of Christ. We ought to love people and give them the attention they need so they don't have to be sick to receive it.

We also need to examine ourselves. Are we "waiting for the water to move"? Or are we doing our part to receive healing by faith?

Confession

I don't use sickness to get attention, and I don't wait for the "water to move." Healing is mine, and I receive it now by faith.

Put Your Trust in Jesus, Not Man

Jesus walked directly to the man and asked, "Is it your will to be healed?"

The man replied, "But I have no man...."

That was the man's first problem—he looked to man. He was saying, "I'd like to be healed, but I'm too slow. I've been here too long. I don't have any friends. No one helps me, so I can't be healed."

Apparently, some of the sick around the pool were prosperous enough to hire help. When the water was troubled, the hired man would pick up the sick person and run to put him in the pool. But evidently this crippled man didn't have any money.

We must not make the mistake this man did by keeping our eyes on lack. We have a man—the Man Jesus—and in Him there is no lack. If we focus on what we don't have, we miss our answer when it's before us.

When you look to man, you'll always be disappointed. Some believers even go to a specific healing evangelist to heal them. But regardless of the anointing someone operates in, no man is a healer. Jesus alone is the Healer. Jesus is all you need!

And a certain man was there, which had an infirmity thirty and eight years. When Jesus saw him lie, and knew that he had been now a long time in that case, he saith unto him, Wilt thou be made whole?

The impotent man answered him, Sir, I have no man, when the water is troubled, to put me into the pool: but while I am coming, another steppeth down before me.

—John 5:5-8

Confession

I focus my spiritual eyes on Jesus who has no lack.
No man is my healer—Jesus is my Healer.

When God Is Moving, Enter In

Now there is at Jerusalem by the sheep market a pool, which is called in the Hebrew tongue Bethesda, having five porches. In these lay a great multitude of impotent folk, of blind, halt, withered, waiting for the moving of the water.

—John 5:2,3

Let's talk about the Holy Ghost. This incident occurs, of course, under the old covenant, but moving waters are always a type of the flow of the Spirit of God—the move of the Holy Ghost. When sick people come into the flow of the Holy Ghost, that is the easiest time for them to be healed.

Many times as we endeavor to receive our healing, we do all we know to do. We hear the Word of God, act on the Word, hold fast to our confession of faith, and stand fast. (Heb. 4:14; 10:23.)

The best thing to do at that point is to get into the move of the Holy Ghost. Wherever God is moving, whether it's in our prayer closets or in a church service, we must do everything we can to enter in. It's much easier to receive the manifestation of what we're believing for when we're in the flow of the Spirit.

You see, the Holy Ghost is the One who causes our answers to come. He's the One who confirms the Word. I like what someone said: "When the Holy Ghost starts moving, your manifestation will catch up with your confession."

Confession

I know my Father wants me well, so I enter into
the flow of His Spirit when He's showing Himself strong.
I take every opportunity for the Holy Ghost to move in my life.

Take God at His Word

The Roman centurion had great faith because he understood Jesus' words had authority over sickness and disease. The centurion was willing to believe the words of Jesus and act on them.

The centurion didn't say, "Jesus, I need You to come to my house." He said, "Just speak the Word, Jesus, and I'll take that Word and act on it!" In verse 13, Jesus responded to the centurion's faith: "Go thy way; and as thou hast believed, so be it done unto thee. And his servant was healed in the selfsame hour."

That's what God expects us to do. He doesn't expect us to wait for some special manifestation, even though that may happen at times. God expects us to simply take Him at His Word, believe we receive His promises, and boldly act on them in faith.

Confession

Jesus responds to faith. The servant was healed because the centurion believed the words Jesus spoke. I'm healed because I believe God's healing promises are at work in me.

And when Jesus was entered into Capernaum, there came unto him a centurion, beseeching him, and saying, Lord, my servant lieth at home sick of the palsy, grievously tormented.

And Jesus saith unto him, I will come and heal him.

The centurion answered and said, Lord, I am not worthy that thou shouldest come under my roof: but speak the word only, and my servant shall be healed. For I am a man under authority....

When Jesus heard it, he marvelled, and said to them that followed, Verily I say unto you, I have not found so great faith, no, not in Israel.

—Matthew 8:5-10

You Can Do Something About the Devil

And when Jesus was entered into Capernaum, there came unto him a centurion, beseeching him, and saying, Lord, my servant lieth at home sick of the palsy, grievously tormented.

And Jesus saith unto him, I will come and heal him.

The centurion answered and said, Lord, I am not worthy that thou shouldest come under my roof: but speak the word only, and my servant shall be healed. For I am a man under authority.

—Matthew 8:5-9

There's a connection between understanding authority and having great faith. Sometimes a believer's faith doesn't operate because he doesn't understand his authority. When the believer starts to receive from God, the devil steals from him, and he doesn't realize he can stop the devil in his tracks.

So we must develop an understanding of the authority God has given us. Authority is not our own power or strength. The best term to explain authority is "delegated power." You see, Jesus delegated authority to us: "Verily I say unto you, Whatsoever ye shall bind on earth shall be bound in heaven: and whatsoever ye shall loose on earth shall be loosed in heaven" (Matt. 18:18). In other words, what we forbid is forbidden, and what we allow is allowed.

Jesus is the Head of the Church. We're His body on this earth with the right to use the authority vested in His name. The body has the same authority as the Head.

God is waiting for us to give orders to the enemy so He can legally enforce them. We're the ones with the authority to do something about the devil.

Confession

Jesus has spoken healing to me through His Word, and I have authority to stop the devil from hindering me. Healing is mine in Jesus' name.

Jesus' Will Is the Father's Will

When the centurion asked Jesus to come heal his servant, Jesus responded, "I will." Jesus was saying, "My will is to heal him because I do My Father's will. And the Father's will is to heal everyone who allows Him to. Therefore, I will come heal him."

Jesus didn't know the centurion's servant well, and He wasn't even in the location of the servant. But Jesus knew the will of the Father.

Then the centurion said, "You don't need to come to my house, Lord; I'm not really worthy of that. But if You will just speak the word, my servant will be healed." Jesus commended the centurion for his faith and sent him home. When the centurion got home, he found his servant healed and set free.

Healing the servant was God's will. Jesus had probably never seen the centurion or the servant before. But Jesus knew the will of the Father—healing for all!

And when Jesus was entered into Capernaum, there came unto him a centurion, beseeching him, and saying, Lord, my servant lieth at home sick of the palsy, grievously tormented.

And Jesus saith unto him, I will come and heal him.

—Matthew 8:5-7

Confession

Like the centurion,
I believe in the power and authority of Jesus' words.
I know God's will is for me to be healed and walk in health.
So I ask in faith for my healing, and I believe I receive my answer.

A Crippled Man Walks

And [throughout Lycaonia] they preached the gospel. And there sat a certain man at Lystra, impotent in his feet, being a cripple from his mother's womb, who never had walked: the same heard Paul speak: who stedfastly beholding him, and perceiving that he had faith to be healed, said with a loud voice, Stand upright on thy feet. And he leaped and walked.

—Acts 14:7-10

Paul and Barnabas were preaching the Gospel, the Good News, in the cities of Lycaonia. Good news to a sinner is that he can be saved, good news to a poor man is that his needs can be met, and good news to a sick man is that he can be healed.

As they preached in Lystra, a crippled man who had never walked sat in the crowd. Suddenly, something radically changed his condition. What was it that changed the course of his life? "The same heard Paul speak." The man heard the Gospel. Healing had to be part of the Gospel Paul and Barnabas were preaching. How do we know? Because Romans 10:17 says faith cometh by hearing and hearing the Word of God. Therefore, the man had to hear on healing to have faith for healing. (Rom. 10:17.)

Then, while he heard, Paul "stedfastly beholding him, and perceiving that he had faith to be healed, said with a loud voice, Stand upright on thy feet. And he leaped and walked."

A miracle happened that day, but the first step he took that set a new course in his life was to *hear.* He tapped into the connection between hearing and healing.

Confession

Hearing God's Word produces faith in me. Therefore, as I continually hear the Word, I walk in divine health, peace, and abundance.

A Miracle Received Through Faith

That crippled man had never taken a step in his life. Then suddenly, he was up leaping and praising God. How did that happen? He received through faith. Where did he get his faith? "The same heard Paul speak." What did Paul speak? Verse 7 says, "And there they preached the gospel." So the man put his faith in the Gospel message and received a miraculous healing.

You hear some people say, "Well, Brother, we don't preach healing around here; we just preach the Gospel." That's amazing. When Paul preached the Gospel, people had faith to be healed. A person can't preach the whole Gospel without preaching healing.

Let me ask: Did Paul perceive that someday the man would get faith? No, Paul perceived the man had faith right then. The man hadn't taken a step yet, but he had faith to be healed. However, his faith didn't work until he acted on it.

Just as God healed this man, we can know for a fact it's God's will to heal *every* person *every* time of *every* disease. We have God's Word on it.

And there they preached the gospel. And there sat a certain man at Lystra, impotent in his feet, being a cripple from his mother's womb, who never had walked: the same heard Paul speak: who stedfastly beholding him, and perceiving that he had faith to be healed, said with a loud voice, Stand upright on thy feet. And he leaped and walked.

—Acts 14:7-10

Confession

I hear the full Gospel of salvation and healing, and faith rises in me to be healed. I act on my faith in God's Word, and it produces what I desire. God's Word works!

God Is Willing To Heal

And, behold, there came a leper and worshipped him, saying, Lord, if thou wilt, thou canst make me clean.

And Jesus put forth his hand, and touched him, saying, I will; be thou clean. And immediately his leprosy was cleansed.

—Matthew 8:2,3

This leper is the only person in the New Testament to question God's will to heal. This man is also the first in the four Gospels whom Jesus heals. So the first thing God does through Jesus is to clear up the question: Is it God's will to heal?

A major obstacle between Christians and miracles today is they know God is able to heal, but they don't know if He's willing. Many pray, "Lord, heal this person, if it be Thy will."

Under the Levitical law, a leper was unclean and had to live in the wilderness away from civilization. This particular leper, however, had apparently heard that Jesus was healing people and took risks to get well.

The leper fell before Jesus and said, "Lord, if it's Your will, make me clean." He came to Jesus desiring to be healed. But desire wasn't enough. The leper didn't receive anything until Jesus cleared up the question of His willingness.

One translation of verse 3 says, "Jesus stretched out his hand and placed it on the leper saying, 'Of course I want to. Be clean!'" (PHILLIPS).

When Jesus answered the leper and said, "I will, I want to," Jesus was giving that same answer to all mankind—including you. God is able and willing to heal you. He wants to!

Confession

With two words, "I will," Jesus showed me beyond
a doubt that God's will for me is divine health.
According to Your will, Lord, I accept my healing.

It's God's Will To Heal You

The average Christian is in the same position as this leper was. He believes God is *able* to heal, but he doesn't know whether or not it's God's *will* to heal.

The leper knew the ability of Jesus. He came and said, "Lord, if You will, You can make me clean." I've heard the same thing from people in prayer lines. They stand there praying, "Oh, Lord, I know You're able to heal me."

But knowing God is able isn't enough; it's just a starting point. Knowing God's ability is about 25 percent of the answer. The other 75 percent is knowing His will.

The one hindrance standing between the leper and his miracle was revealed in his statement: "If thou wilt, thou canst make me clean." The same is true for people all over the world. If you asked if they're convinced it's God's will to heal them, they'd probably answer, "I sure hope so." That's strong hope—not faith.

Faith always begins where God's will is known. "I know God heals some," you may say. But only when you know it's God's will to heal *you*, do *you* reach the beginning point of faith.

And there came a leper to him, beseeching him, and kneeling down to him, and saying unto him, If thou wilt, thou canst make me clean.

And Jesus, moved with compassion, put forth his hand, and touched him, and saith unto him, I will; be thou clean. And as soon as he had spoken, immediately the leprosy departed from him, and he was cleansed.

—Mark 1:40-42

Confession

I know without a doubt it's my Father's will to heal me. I have confident assurance that He desires my healing even more than I do. Healing is mine now!

Taking the "If" Out of Healing

And Jesus put forth his hand, and touched him, saying, I will; be thou clean. And immediately his leprosy was cleansed.

—Matthew 8:3

What did Jesus do when this leper said, "I know You're able to heal me, Lord, but I don't know if You're willing"? Did Jesus say, "Now, Brother, I'll have to fast and pray first to see if it's God's will to heal you"? No, Jesus answered the question for all mankind right there. He turned to that man and said, "I will; be thou clean."

In other words, Jesus was saying, "Why in the world would you doubt a thing like that? If I'm able, surely I'm willing."

We shouldn't have any question in our hearts about God's will to heal. Jesus certainly didn't. He didn't hesitate when the leper said to Him, "If You will." Immediately Jesus turned to the man and said, "Of course, I will. That's part of My commission. That's part of the reason I came. Of course it's My will for you to be whole."

Jesus took the "if" right out of the healing issue. He didn't have to beg, plead, or spend three days finding God's will about healing. He just automatically said, "I will heal you." Why? Because Jesus was the will of God in action.

Jesus didn't say, "I heal on My own." He said, "The Father that dwelleth in me, he doeth the works" (John 14:10). Therefore, for Jesus to heal the leper, it had to be God's will because it was the Father, dwelling inside Jesus, who did the work.

Confession

God's Word has built an unshakable confidence in me
that God wants me healthy. So I boldly say, "I am healed."
And the Holy Spirit in me does the work.

God's Compassion To Heal

"Moved with compassion," Jesus touched the leper. This may have been the first time in years that someone touched this man. No one wanted to touch him. He wasn't even supposed to come near people.

And Jesus, moved with compassion, put forth his hand, and touched him.

—Mark 1:41

In Luke 17:12, ten lepers cried to Jesus from afar because it was illegal to approach him. If a leper came within 100 paces of a healthy person, he had to get out of the way and call out, "Unclean! Unclean!" Still, Jesus heard the lepers call to Him and told them to go show themselves to the priest, and they were healed as they went. (v. 14.)

Yet this one leper in Mark 1 came close to Jesus. Though he could've been stoned for being there, he had the tenacity of someone who wanted healing so badly he was willing to take a risk for it.

The leper fell down before Jesus and said, "Lord, if You will, You can make me clean." Jesus immediately settled that question. Moved with compassion, He put forth His hand and touched the leper, saying, "I will; be thou clean."

You see, God's ability shows His power, but His willingness shows His compassion. In the Word, God's compassion is magnified above His power. The Bible says, "God is love" (1 John 4:8), but it never says, "God is power."

So trust your heavenly Father's love for you. As you come to Him in faith, His compassion will flow freely to heal you and make you whole.

Confession

God's love and compassion reach out to me and heal me
of every sickness and disease. He's able and willing
to make me whole. So I am whole.

"I Will"

And, behold, there came a leper and worshipped him, saying, Lord, if thou wilt, thou canst make me clean.

And Jesus put forth his hand, and touched him, saying, I will; be thou clean. And immediately his leprosy was cleansed.

—Matthew 8:2,3

Jesus did two things when He was moved with compassion: He touched the leper, *and* He said something to him.

I always thought the moment Jesus touched someone, that person was healed. But this man's leprosy didn't depart until Jesus said something. Apparently, His words were as important as His touch.

What did Jesus say to the leper? "Be thou clean." He gave the command for the leprosy to depart. But He also said something else—the phrase most Christians are looking for—"I will."

Notice Jesus didn't say, "I won't" or "Later." He didn't say, "This disease is good for you" or "You deserve this" or "God sent this leprosy to teach you something."

Jesus didn't have to fast and pray to find out God's will. He just said, "I will." He knew God's will. He also knew one of His purposes for coming to earth was to destroy all the works of the devil (1 John 3:8), including sickness and disease. Part of Jesus' commission was to heal the sick, cleanse the lepers, raise the dead, cast out devils, and bring deliverance to all mankind.

God never told Jesus to just seek out a few here and there who needed healing. Jesus was sent to heal all. So when the leper said, "If You will," Jesus responded, "Of course I will! God's will is healing for all mankind!"

Confession

My Father sent Jesus to destroy the works of the devil,
including sickness. Sickness isn't God's plan for me.
Therefore, by faith I receive healing.

Step Out on the Word

Here was a man who had been blind from birth. Jesus walked over to him, spit in the dirt, made clay of the spittle, smeared the clay on the man's eyes, and said, "Go, wash in the pool of Siloam."

That man could've said, "What do You mean, 'go wash in the pool of Siloam'? Look, Jesus, I don't need a bath—I need my sight! What is mud going to do? Everyone will laugh at me. I'm waiting for You to work a miracle here."

Instead, He obeyed what Jesus told him to do with no feeling and no manifestation. Every symptom was still there; he was still blind. The only difference was he now had mud in his eyes.

But Jesus said, "Go," and the man went. Jesus gave him an opportunity to walk by faith, and the blind man took off on the Word of God alone. That was his faith in operation. He went, he washed, and he came again seeing. But he had to step out on the word Jesus spoke before he saw results—and that's how he got results.

Find out what God has said about your situation, and then step out on that Word. Let your faith release God's power in your life.

And as Jesus passed by, he saw a man which was blind from his birth.

[Jesus] spat on the ground, and made clay of the spittle, and he anointed the eyes of the blind man with the clay, and said unto him, Go, wash in the pool of Siloam...He went his way therefore, and washed, and came seeing.

—John 9:1,6,7

Confession

I take God at His Word, even when I'm not able to see my answer. Jesus says I'm healed, so I am.

Jesus Is the Healer

And when they were come to the multitude, there came to him a certain man, kneeling down to him, and saying, Lord, have mercy on my son: for he is lunatick, and sore vexed: for ofttimes he falleth into the fire, and oft into the water. And I brought him to thy disciples, and they could not cure him.

Then Jesus answered and said, O faithless and perverse generation, how long shall I be with you? how long shall I suffer you? bring him hither to me. And Jesus rebuked the devil; and he departed out of him: and the child was cured from that very hour.

—Matthew 17:14-18

Some people have said, "I've been to every preacher in the country, and I couldn't get healed. It must not be God's will to heal me." Yet the father in this account could've come to that same conclusion. After all, he'd taken his son to Jesus' own personal trainees, but the boy still wasn't healed.

However, instead of concluding it wasn't God's will to heal his son, the father took the boy to Jesus and explained, "I brought my son to Your disciples, and they couldn't heal him."

Jesus didn't turn to the man and say, "Well, it must not be the will of God then." He said, "Bring the boy to Me." Jesus was the will of God in action, and He revealed God's will by setting him free. At that moment, Jesus was also revealing God's willingness to heal you and me today.

Are you ready to go free?

Confession

Jesus is the will of God in action, and He's revealed God's will to me. I know God wants me free from sickness. Thank You, Father, for Your healing power at work in me.

Call On the Mercy of God

In this passage a man brought his son to Jesus' disciples asking them to deliver his son from seizures. After the disciples' unsuccessful attempt to help the boy, they took him to Jesus. Then the father said to Jesus, "Your disciples couldn't do anything. If You can do anything, have *compassion on us and help us.*"

The man called on the compassion—or the mercy—of God. In other words, He called on the very nature of God. God is the God of mercy; He's the God of compassion.

In Matthew 20:30, two blind men cried out, "Have mercy on us, O Lord, thou son of David." The disciples and the people in the crowd tried to quiet them down, but they kept crying, "Have mercy on us, O Lord...."

Jesus didn't say, "Do you want your healing?" He just asked, "What would you have Me do?" You see, the blind men in Matthew 20 and the father in Mark 9 called on God's nature. So Jesus responded, "I'm at your disposal. Whatever you need is yours because you've called on the nature of God. I'm here to meet your needs." And He's ready to meet your needs as well.

Confession

My God is full of mercy and compassion.
I call upon His compassion and
mercy and by faith receive my healing.

And one of the multitude answered and said, Master, I have brought unto thee my son, which hath a dumb spirit; and wheresoever he taketh him, he teareth him: and he foameth, and gnasheth with his teeth, and pineth away: and I spake to thy disciples that they should cast him out; and they could not.

But if thou canst do any thing, have compassion on us, and help us.

—Mark 9:17,18,22

A Withered Hand Becomes Whole

And it came to pass also on another sabbath, that he entered into the synagogue and taught: and there was a man whose right hand was withered. And the scribes and Pharisees watched him, whether he would heal on the sabbath day; that they might find an accusation against him.

But he knew their thoughts, and said to the man which had the withered hand, Rise up, and stand forth in the midst. And he arose and stood forth. Then Jesus said unto them, I will ask you one thing; Is it lawful on the sabbath days to do good, or to do evil? To save life, or to destroy it?

And looking round about upon them all, he said unto the man, Stretch forth thy hand. And he did so: and his hand was restored whole as the other. And they were filled with madness....

—*Luke 6:6-11*

The scribes and Pharisees watched closely to see whether Jesus would heal on the Sabbath. They wanted to accuse Jesus of breaking the law.

But Jesus was looking for a way to show the goodness of God, the Lord of the Sabbath. Jesus called the man with the withered hand forward saying, "Stretch forth thy hand." Immediately it was restored, which made the religious leaders angry.

You see, while the scribes and Pharisees associated doing good with obeying man-made Sabbath traditions, Jesus associated doing good with healing and saving life.

Acts 10:38 says Jesus "went about doing good...." What good? "...*healing* all that were oppressed of the devil; for God was with him." Obviously, healing is good in God's sight.

Confession

Jesus healed all who came to Him in faith, and He's still the same today. It's good in His sight when by faith I receive my healing.

The Making of a Miracle

"Stretch forth your hand," Jesus instructed the man with the withered hand. When he did, a miracle occurred. However, that miracle didn't just fall on the man—*the man's faith produced it.* How do we know that? Well, Jesus told a man with a *withered* hand to stretch it. If that man had not been in faith he might have said, "What do You mean, stretch it forth? That's why I'm here—it doesn't stretch! I'm waiting for You to heal me so I can stretch it!"

But this man's faith was in operation. You see, real faith does what it can do and then attempts to do what it cannot do.

So when Jesus said, "Stretch out your hand," the man stretched it out. A person can't stretch a hand that doesn't stretch, so the man wouldn't even have tried to stretch his hand if he weren't expecting results.

Why did the man expect results? He was in faith. How did he get in faith? Verse 6 says Jesus "entered into the synagogue and taught." The man heard Jesus teach.

And it came to pass also on another sabbath, that he entered into the synagogue and taught: and there was a man whose right hand was withered.

And looking round about upon them all, he said unto the man, Stretch forth thy hand. And he did so: and his hand was restored whole as the other.

—Luke 6:6,10

That's the way most miracles happened in Jesus' ministry. People heard Jesus teach, faith arose, and they were healed. And the same will be true for you.

Confession

Faith comes by hearing, and hearing by the Word of God. I hear the Word on healing, act on it, and confidently receive my healing.

Partaking of the Ministry of Jesus

And again he entered into Capernaum after some days; and it was noised that he was in the house. And straightway many were gathered together, insomuch that there was no room to receive them, no, not so much as about the door: and he preached the word unto them.

And they come unto him, bringing one sick of the palsy, which was borne of four. And when they could not come nigh unto him for the press, they uncovered the roof where he was: and when they had broken it up, they let down the bed wherein the sick of the palsy lay.

When Jesus saw their faith, he said unto the sick of the palsy, Son, thy sins be forgiven thee.

—Mark 2:1-5

Notice verse 1 says, "And again he entered into Capernaum." The word *again* indicates Jesus must have been there before. Mark 1 mentions the first time He went to Capernaum many sick were healed, many devils were cast out, and Jesus performed miracles all over the city. So when Jesus returned, word got around. Soon the house where He stayed was packed to overflowing.

That's the way it's supposed to happen. As more and more people are healed and set free through the preaching of the Word, churches won't have buildings big enough to hold all the people. Word gets out when Jesus shows up!

We're about to see Jesus' ministry go forth through the Church as never before. Of course, Jesus had the Spirit without measure, whereas each believer has the anointing by measure. But as the body of Christ rises up in unity, that same powerful anointing is sweeping the earth again.

Confession

When Jesus preached, miracles happened. The Holy Spirit teaches me that same living Word, which produces miracles in my life.

Hearing and Miracles Go Hand in Hand

Jesus always gave the people something to believe—He preached the Word to them. He didn't tiptoe from town to town, healing a leper here and a blind man there, and then teaching on the Beatitudes for a while. There was a method to what Jesus did.

About 70 percent of the time in His ministry, Jesus either stated or implied that people were healed on *their own faith.*

Where did people get their faith? Did God lean over the balcony of heaven and zap them with a faith gun? No, they obtained faith the same way we do today: "Faith cometh by hearing, and hearing by the word of God" (Rom. 10:17).

Matthew 4:23 says, "And Jesus went about all Galilee, teaching in their synagogues, and preaching the gospel of the kingdom, and healing all manner of sickness and all manner of disease among the people." Healing came *after* teaching and preaching.

And again he entered into Capernaum after some days...and straightway many were gathered together, insomuch that there was no room to receive them, no, not so much as about the door: and he preached the word unto them.

—Mark 2:1,2

Jesus had to teach the people the Word so they'd have faith to be healed. When they heard the Word, faith arose; then as Jesus instructed them to act on their faith, they were healed.

So often today, people aren't healed because they haven't taken time to hear God's Word. They want a miracle, but they don't want to hear.

Don't make that mistake! Diligently feed on God's Word knowing that hearing and miracles go hand in hand.

Confession

Faith comes when I hear God's Word. I meditate upon the Word, and my faith grows to receive the miracle I need.

God's Power To Heal

And it came to pass on a certain day, as he was teaching, that there were Pharisees and doctors of the law sitting by, which were come out of every town of Galilee, and Judaea, and Jerusalem: and the power of the Lord was present to heal them.

—Luke 5:17

This verse says, "The power of the Lord was present to heal them." Who is *"them"*? The Pharisees and doctors of the law. Was it God's will to heal them? Absolutely. God wouldn't have sent His power if He hadn't wanted them healed. God isn't confused, and He doesn't waste His power.

How many were healed? One man lowered through the roof. But to the best of our knowledge, not one Pharisee or doctor of the law received healing.

Yet Jesus said, "My meat is to do My Father's will." (John 4:34.) So it must have been God's will for Jesus to go to Capernaum and teach the Word. It also must have been God's will for the Pharisees and doctors of the law to be healed because God sent His power. When God's power is present, anyone who will receive by faith can be healed.

But if that's true, why are so many of us not healed? Our problem hasn't been a lack of power, but a lack of knowledge. God gave us the power when He gave the Holy Spirit. We just haven't known how to tap in.

So learn to receive from God. Get the revelation of His will, act on it, and hold fast to your confession that God's power is working in you, effecting a healing and a cure.

Confession

God's power is available to me through the Word. I tap into His power by believing, confessing, and acting on the Word.

Don't Just Listen–Hear

The power of the Lord was present to heal the Pharisees and doctors of the law, but not one of them was healed. The Bible says Jesus was teaching, but how many present were actually hearing?

Someone may say, "Well, all of them must have been hearing; they were sitting right there in the same room with Jesus."

Not necessarily so! Did you know you can be listening without hearing? I know that from experience. I've been in numerous conversations with my wife, Janet, where she suddenly stopped talking and said, "Mark, you haven't heard a word I've said."

"I've been listening!" I always protest. But then I think, *Have I really been listening?* Although I can remember what Janet said five minutes earlier, my mind has been on something else. I've been listening; I know she's been talking, but I didn't *hear* what she said. So yes, it's possible to listen and still not hear a thing.

And it came to pass on a certain day, as he was teaching, that there were Pharisees and doctors of the law sitting by, which were come out of every town of Galilee, and Judea, and Jerusalem: and the power of the Lord was present to heal them.

—Luke 5:17

Yet the Bible never said a word about the scribes, Pharisees, and doctors of the law hearing. In fact, those religious leaders weren't listening so faith could grow in their hearts; they were listening to accuse Jesus. Despite their wrong reason, God still sent His power to heal them. All they had to do was receive by faith.

Confession

I don't just listen; I hear the Word of God concerning healing.
Then faith rises up in my heart to receive, and I'm healed.

Get Tired of Being Sick

And they come unto him, bringing one sick of the palsy, which was borne of four.

—Mark 2:3

This man who had palsy, or paralysis, found four friends to pick him up and carry him to Jesus. But notice the way verse 3 is worded: "And they come unto him, bringing one sick of the palsy." The man was sick of the palsy—sick with it and sick of it. He was tired of the whole mess.

I don't blame him. That's actually a good state of mind to be in. People will go after their healing when they're sick of being sick. They've had it; they're finished with it; they're tired of being sick. No more.

Janet and I were in a service where a man greatly used of God in the gifts of the Spirit was ministering in a healing line. At one point, he called a woman to the front and told her, "The Spirit of God is showing me right now exactly what is wrong with you." Then he proceeded to tell her exactly what her problem was.

The woman replied, "No, that's not it—and beside, I can live with it!" She probably will, too, bless her heart. She wasn't sick of being sick yet.

But this man in Mark 2 was. He was sick and tired of the palsy. So when Jesus spoke out his miracle, he was ready to receive. (vv. 11,12.)

Things happen when we get tired of being overrun by the devil. That's when we jump out in faith and refuse to give up until we receive the miracle we need.

Confession

I refuse to put up with sickness or pain in my
body because God's Word is medicine to my flesh.

Determined Faith

During Jesus' first visit to Capernaum (Mark 1:21-34) the entire city gathered around the house where He stayed, and Jesus healed and delivered many.

This time the place filled up again, but with a crowd of religious leaders who didn't come for miracles. They came to catch Jesus saying something wrong so they could accuse Him. They resisted everything He said.

So the first time Jesus visited Capernaum, people came to be healed. The second time, many came to *stop* folks from being healed.

Sometimes doubt and unbelief are so strong in a place it's difficult for anyone to receive from God. That was the situation here. God's power was present in the midst of a room packed with people, but there was so much unbelief no one was receiving healing.

What did Jesus do? Luke 5:17 tells us Jesus continued teaching. That was always His solution to unbelief. Suddenly, four men came carrying a stretcher. The place was so full of people not getting healed the one who wanted healing couldn't squeeze in. So the sick man's determined friends tore off the roof of the house and lowered the man to Jesus. When Jesus saw their faith, He healed him on the spot.

And they come unto him, bringing one sick of the palsy...borne of four. And when they could not come nigh unto him for the press, they uncovered the roof where he was: and when they had broken it up, they let down the bed wherein the sick of the palsy lay.

When Jesus saw their faith, he said unto the sick of the palsy, Son, thy sins be forgiven thee.

—Mark 2:3-5

Confession

Those who won't receive from God won't stop me from receiving.
I will enjoy salvation, healing, and every other blessing God's provided.

Bring Them to Jesus

And they come unto him, bringing one sick of the palsy, which was borne of four. And when they could not come nigh unto him for the press, they uncovered the roof where he was: and when they had broken it up, they let down the bed wherein the sick of the palsy lay.

—Mark 2:3,4

I can't prove this, but I wouldn't be surprised if those four men were among those healed the last time Jesus was in town. They seemed so convinced if they got their friend to Jesus he'd be healed.

They were so convinced, they took the roof apart to get the paralyzed man before Jesus. And they didn't say, "Lord, heal him, if it be Thy will." No, these four men were sure Jesus would heal their friend.

Matthew 8:16 talks about others who brought the sick to Jesus: "When the even was come, *they brought unto him* many that were possessed with devils: and he cast out the spirits with his word, and healed all that were sick." That phrase *"they brought unto him"* is used several times in the Gospels. (Matt. 9:32; Mark 1:32.)

Ever wonder who "they" were? Did Jesus have healing teams? No, "they" are people who find folks in need and bring them to Jesus. The truth is, "they" are the body of believers! People say, "What if I invite someone to church, and God doesn't do anything spectacular?" Yes, but what if He does? Either way, people we bring to church will still hear the Word.

Fulfill your part of "they" and bring folks who need miracles to Jesus.

Confession

I'll be a "they"! I've experienced the healing power of Jesus, and
I know without a doubt when I bring others to Him, they'll be healed.

Faith Won't Quit

This passage illustrates one of the differences between faith and hope. Four men carried this man to where Jesus was, but the building was so full they couldn't get in.

Now, hope would've said, "Well, we tried, but we couldn't get our friend to Jesus. We might as well go home." Hope will go just so far and quit. It says, "I tried that faith business, but it didn't work." Then hope throws in the towel.

But faith won't quit! It has tenacity. Faith digs in its heels and says, "I know whom I have believed, and am persuaded that he is able to keep that which I have committed unto him against that day" (2 Tim. 1:12). It says, "Healing belongs to me; I won't go without it!"

The four men were certainly in faith. They tore a hole in the roof big enough to lower their friend on a stretcher. Up till then, Jesus hadn't yet seen a spark of faith. But now He was seeing faith come through the roof and healed the man.

No one likes tests and trials, but faith thrives on them. Our heads may give us trouble in hard times. But if we're really in faith, we won't quit.

Confession

Jesus paid for my healing, and I have it by faith regardless of feelings or circumstances.

And they come unto him, bringing one sick of the palsy, which was borne of four. And when they could not come nigh unto him for the press, they uncovered the roof where he was: and when they had broken it up, they let down the bed wherein the sick of the palsy lay.

When Jesus saw their faith, he said unto the sick of the palsy, Son, thy sins be forgiven thee.

—Mark 2:3-5

Forgiveness and Healing–A Package Deal

When Jesus saw their faith, he said unto the sick of the palsy, Son, thy sins be forgiven thee.

But there were certain of the scribes sitting there, and reasoning in their hearts, Why doth this man thus speak blasphemies? who can forgive sins but God only?

—Mark 2:5-7

The paralyzed man needed to be healed, but Jesus didn't say, "Get up and walk." Instead, He told the man his sins were forgiven. That presented a problem to the religious leaders sitting there in that house. They didn't believe that Jesus was God manifest in the flesh, so they didn't believe He could forgive sins.

But Jesus was proving something to us through this incident. He was making the point that forgiveness and healing go hand in hand. When we receive one, the other belongs to us as well.

Mark 2:8 says, "Jesus perceived in his spirit that they so reasoned within themselves." Then Jesus asked the religious leaders, "Which is easier to say: 'Your sins are forgiven,' or 'Take up your bed and walk'?"

That didn't make sense to me for a long time. Then I saw it. It's so simple. Jesus was saying, "It doesn't matter which one I say. If I say, 'Get up and walk' that means you're forgiven. If I say, 'You're forgiven,' that means 'Get up and walk.' The two always go together. Once you have one, the other automatically belongs to you. It's a package deal!"

Confession

I'm forgiven! I'm healed! Healing belongs to me
as surely as forgiveness does. Both are included in
my covenant with my heavenly Father.

Healing Comes With Forgiveness

Jesus wasn't known for being a diplomat. He wasn't on the earth to please man; He was here to please God. He really didn't care what men thought, as long as He was pleasing to God. So, knowing full well He'd be in trouble with the religious leaders, Jesus looked at the paralyzed man and said, "Son, your sins are forgiven."

When Jesus saw their faith, he said unto the sick of the palsy, Son, thy sins be forgiven thee.

—Mark 2:5

All through the Bible, forgiveness of sin and physical healing have always been a package deal. Jesus wasn't trying to make those religious leaders angry; He was trying to prove a point to them. So Jesus gave them an illustrated sermon. He preached, and then He demonstrated His point. He said, "If I say you're forgiven, it means you're also healed."

Back then, people thought Jesus could heal but not forgive sins. Today most people believe Jesus can forgive sins but not heal. The truth is, during Jesus' ministry on earth He could do both, and today He can do both. He never turns anyone down for either forgiveness or healing.

Some people ask, "If I'm sick in my body, does that mean I'm not forgiven of my sins?" No, if you've made Jesus Lord of your life, then healing belongs to you whether you know it or not. So reach out and take hold of the blessing that's rightfully yours.

Confession

God has provided forgiveness for my sins and healing
for my physical body. As surely as I know
He wants me forgiven, I know He wants me well.

Healing–Proof of Jesus' Power To Forgive

> *Whether is it easier to say to the sick of the palsy, Thy sins be forgiven thee; or to say, Arise, and take up thy bed, and walk? But that ye may know that the Son of man hath power on earth to forgive sins....*
>
> *—Mark 2:9,10*

How could Jesus prove to the religious leaders that the paralyzed man's sins were forgiven? Jesus knew exactly how to do it.

Speaking to the whole group as well, Jesus told the paralyzed man, "Arise, and take up thy bed, and go thy way into thine house. And immediately he arose, took up the bed, and went forth before them all; insomuch that they were all amazed" (vv. 11,12).

Jesus said, "I'll prove to you I have power to forgive sins: I'll tell this man to get up and walk, and he will do it!" He did, and they were all shocked.

If the religious leaders had been as knowledgeable about Scriptures as they were traditions, they would've jumped up and exclaimed, "Jesus is the Messiah! The One we're looking for!" Remember, these were the Old Testament scholars. They should've known that every time God gave them a picture of the Messiah's crucifixion in the Old Testament, two things happened: People were forgiven of their sins and healed of their diseases.

How's that help us? Well, if forgiveness and healing were a package deal under the old covenant, how much more do they belong to us today under a new and better covenant. (Heb. 8:6.)

Confession

If healing and forgiveness were connected under the old covenant, how much more they belong to me under a new and better covenant. I'm both healed and forgiven.

Two Inseparable Blessings

Forgiveness of sins in the new birth belongs to everyone. But we've tried to make healing a different matter, saying, "You never know whom God will heal." We've taken what God put together at the Cross and tried to make them two different subjects.

Yet, forgiveness and healing cannot be taken apart. They're not two different subjects. Healing is nothing more than the new birth affecting the human body. Certainly, sin takes a toll on the body. You've probably looked at someone and thought, *Boy, that person has lived a tough life.* You were noticing the person's sinful lifestyle had an adverse effect on his physical appearance.

Whether is it easier to say to the sick of the palsy, Thy sins be forgiven thee; or to say, Arise, and take up thy bed, and walk?

—Mark 2:9

Well, if sin can have an effect, righteousness can have an effect as well. When the new birth, which takes place in the inner man, works its way to the outer man, the results are strength, healing, and health.

You may ask, "Why haven't strength, healing, and health worked their way to my outer man before now?" Well, perhaps you haven't been thinking, believing, and talking in line with God's Word.

Yet whom does God want healed? Anyone who is forgiven. Who is forgiven? Anyone who has received Jesus as Savior. Healing belongs to every believer because forgiveness and healing always go hand in hand.

Confession

God's Word says both forgiveness and healing are available
to me through the new birth. I believe the Word,
so I walk in the fullness of all its benefits.

A Gentile Woman's Great Faith

*A woman of Canaan...
cried...saying, Have
mercy on me, O Lord,
thou Son of David; my
daughter is grievously
vexed with a devil. But he
answered her not a word.*

*And his disciples came
and besought him,
saying, Send her away;
for she crieth after us.*

*But he answered and
said, I am not sent but
unto the lost sheep of the
house of Israel.*

*Then came she and
worshipped him, saying,
Lord, help me.*

*But he answered and
said, It is not meet to take
the children's bread, and
to cast it to dogs.*

*And she said, Truth, Lord:
yet the dogs eat of the
crumbs which fall from
their masters' table.*

*Then Jesus answered and
said unto her, O woman,
great is thy faith: be it
unto thee even as thou
wilt. And her daughter
was made whole from
that very hour.*

—Matthew 15:22-28

If anyone had a right to give up, this woman did. Her daughter desperately needed to be set free of an evil spirit. But this woman was a Syrophenician, a Gentile, and didn't have a covenant with God.

Even so, she came to Jesus crying out for help. At first, Jesus ignored her. Then He turned to His disciples and said, "I'm not sent to help her anyway. I'm sent to the lost sheep of Israel."

I used to read this Scripture passage and think, *Why did Jesus harass that poor woman?* But Jesus wasn't harassing her; He was locating her faith. Jesus knew if the woman had faith, she could get results even without a legal covenant with God.

This woman did have real faith that held on. And as a result, her daughter was made whole.

Confession

My covenant with God includes healing.
And I will never give up.

What Is "Great Faith"?

Then Jesus answered and said unto her, O woman, great is thy faith: be it unto thee even as thou wilt. And her daughter was made whole from that very hour.

—Matthew 15:28

Jesus said the Syrophenician woman had great faith. If she had faith under the old covenant, we surely ought to have faith under the new covenant. What made this woman's faith great? She put so much confidence in Jesus' Word that she came for healing for her daughter—and didn't even bring the daughter with her! In essence, she said to Jesus, "You just say the word, and my daughter will be healed."

In Matthew 8:6-8, a Roman centurion displayed that kind of great faith. He came to Jesus and said, "My servant is at home sick."

Jesus answered, "I will come and heal him."

The centurion said, "No, I'm not worthy that You should come under my roof. If You'll just speak the Word, my servant will be healed."

Many people in the Bible operated in faith: the ten lepers (Luke 17:12-19), the nobleman at Capernaum whose son was sick (John 4:46-53) and, of course, Abraham (Rom. 4:19). They all operated in faith, saying, "Whatever You say, Lord, we'll believe it. We take You at Your Word. We don't need goose bumps; we don't need burning bushes. You say it, and we'll go our way believing."

Great faith always takes God at His Word. That's why, in Mark 11:24, Jesus said, "When you pray, believe the answer has been granted to you, and you will have it."

Confession

The written Word is God's word to me today. I believe, I receive, and I go my way praising and thanking God for my answer. I have great faith because I take God at His word.

It Pays To Persevere

Then came she and worshipped him, saying, Lord, help me.

But he answered and said, It is not meet to take the children's bread, and to cast it to dogs.

And she said, Truth, Lord: yet the dogs eat of the crumbs which fall from their masters' table.

Then Jesus answered and said unto her, O woman, great is thy faith....

—Matthew 15:25-28

Most of us would have given up, but not this woman. At first Jesus ignored her; then He said to His disciples, "I'm not even sent to help her." Still, she worshipped Him and asked for help. This Gentile mother just wouldn't leave Jesus alone.

Then Jesus told her it wasn't right to take the children's bread and give it to dogs. Think about it. Jesus called her a dog. Most of us would've gone home angry. But what she really said was, "Lord, I don't need the whole loaf. Give that to the children, although most of them won't take it. Just give me a crumb. I know what Your bread will do."

You may have thought she responded that way because of her humble attitude. But it wasn't a matter of humility to her; she was talking about how powerful Jesus' bread is. She was saying, "Call me anything You want to, but heal my daughter anyway."

Then Jesus told her, "With faith like that, you can have anything you want!" Jesus had taken this woman to the limits, and she'd passed the test. He knew her faith would turn His power loose, and it did.

It paid off for the woman to hang on—it paid off with her daughter's healing.

Confession

I hang on to God's Word with tenacity until my healing manifests.
I won't give up because God's Word works.

Healing–The Children's Bread

The Syrophenician woman wanted healing for her daughter. Jesus called healing "the children's bread." If healing was the children's bread back then, it's still the children's bread today.

Who were the children back then? The lost sheep of the house of Israel. Who are the children today? These Scriptures tell us:

> The Spirit itself beareth witness with our spirit, that we are the children of God.

Romans 8:16

But [Jesus] answered and said, It is not meet to take the children's bread, and to cast it to dogs.

—Matthew 15:26

Behold, what manner of love the Father hath bestowed upon us, that we should be called the sons of God....

1 John 3:1

But as many as received him, to them gave he power to become the sons of God, even to them that believe on his name.

John 1:12

We are the children! Healing is our bread! We have been grafted into God's family through the shed blood of Jesus Christ. Through the new birth, we are now new creatures in Christ, the children of God.

Psalm 37:25 says, "I have been young, and now am old; yet have I not seen the righteous forsaken, nor his seed begging bread." We don't have to beg for bread, because the bread belongs to us through Jesus Christ. It's part of our redemption, our covenant, our inheritance in Christ. God doesn't want us begging for healing, because healing belongs to us.

Confession

Jesus called healing the children's bread. I qualify for that bread, for I'm a child of God. I don't beg for healing; I receive it now because it already belongs to me.

"Be It Unto Thee as Thou Wilt"

Then Jesus answered and said unto her, O woman, great is thy faith: be it unto thee even as thou wilt. And her daughter was made whole from that very hour.

—Matthew 15:28

Did Jesus say, "Oh, woman, great is thy faith. Be it unto thee as God wills"? No, He said, "Be it unto thee even *as thou wilt.*" You see, this woman's will was involved.

Sometimes people don't set their wills into action as they try to get healed—they only hope and pray their faith works. And if they don't receive their healing in a certain time frame, they let loose of their faith rather than holding fast.

But this woman set her will in motion, and she wouldn't consider anything less than healing.

She came to Jesus and said, "My daughter is grievously vexed with a devil." Jesus didn't speak a word to her. She fell down and worshiped Him, and He said, "It's not right to take the children's bread and cast it to dogs."

But the Syrophenician woman said, "Well, even the dogs get the crumbs that fall off their masters' tables." She called Jesus her Master. And she wouldn't let anything defeat her; she was going after healing for her daughter no matter what it took.

We need to realize that God has provided healing for us, and make a bold stance of faith. We need to set our wills in action by saying, "Healing is mine, and I'm not quitting until it's manifested." When we get that stubborn and tenacious in our faith, we'll see results.

Confession

A high price was paid for my healing, and
I refuse to go without it. I know what is mine,
and by faith I won't quit until it manifests.

The Touch of Faith

Jesus was walking through the crowd, and everyone was pushing toward Him. Yet no one was being healed—no miracles were occurring, and no power was flowing out of Him.

Suddenly Jesus felt power surge out of Him. (v. 30.) He stopped and said, "Who touched My clothes?" His disciples replied, "What do You mean? Everyone is touching You!" But Jesus recognized a different touch. It wasn't a physical touch He sensed; it was the touch of faith.

Why was this woman the only one healed in the crowd? Jesus answered that question in verse 34: "And he said unto her, Daughter, thy faith hath made thee whole; go in peace, and be whole of thy plague."

The rest of the crowd apparently came wondering what would happen and thinking, *Well, I'll give this Jesus fellow a try.* But this woman had come in faith. She knew exactly what would happen when she touched the hem of Jesus' garment—exactly what she had believed. She came believing—and, therefore, she received.

Confession

I'm thoroughly convinced I can touch Jesus with my faith just as the woman with the issue of blood did. My faith draws that same healing power out of Him now, and healing is what I receive.

And a certain woman, which had an issue of blood twelve years, and had suffered many things of many physicians, and had spent all that she had, and was nothing bettered, but rather grew worse, when she had heard of Jesus, came in the press behind, and touched his garment. For she said, If I may touch but his clothes, I shall be whole.

And straightway the fountain of her blood was dried up; and she felt in her body that she was healed of that plague.

—Mark 5:25-29

Our Faith Releases God's Power

And Jesus, immediately knowing in himself that virtue had gone out of him, turned him about in the press, and said, Who touched my clothes?

And he said unto her, Daughter, thy faith hath made thee whole; go in peace, and be whole of thy plague.

—Mark 5:30,34

Jesus didn't walk up to this woman with the issue of blood and say, "God has sovereignly chosen to make you well." No, the woman crept up behind Jesus in the crowd, touched the hem of His garment, and literally took hold of her healing. In fact, her great faith drew so much healing power out of Jesus that it stopped Him in His tracks.

Jesus asked, "Who touched Me?" I'm sure everyone thought His question was a little strange because everyone was trying to touch Him. His disciples exclaimed, "The multitude is thronging You! How can You ask, 'Who touched Me?'"

Then Jesus looked around to find the person who had touched Him in faith. The woman returned to Him, trembling with fear, and told Him what had happened to her. Jesus didn't rebuke her; instead, He praised her faith.

You see, the woman's faith released Jesus' power. And if faith released His power 2000 years ago, our faith can still release His power today.

Confession

God's power heals all who come to Him in faith.
My faith releases His healing power in my life.
My faith and His power make me whole.

You Can Believe for Your Miracle

If this woman's faith made her whole, our faith can make us whole.

Some folks say, "Oh, but it was easier for her. Jesus was standing right there." No, not a chance. You see, this woman wasn't born again. The new birth wasn't available until the death, burial, and resurrection of Jesus.

Therefore, the woman was under the old covenant. She wasn't alive unto God. She wasn't filled with the Holy Ghost. She wasn't a temple of the living God. Her redemption hadn't been purchased yet.

And he said unto her, Daughter, thy faith hath made thee whole; go in peace, and be whole of thy plague.

—Mark 5:34

This woman received her blessings on a promissory note. In other words, Jesus said, "I'll heal you now and pay for it later on the Cross."

Some say, "Yes, but it was still easy for her to believe for her healing because Jesus was standing there." Well, where is Jesus today? He said, "My Father and I will come and make our abode with you. Where two or more are gathered in My name, there I am in their midst." (John 14:23; Matt. 18:20.)

Jesus lives on the inside of every born-again believer through the presence of the Holy Spirit. That means we're wall-to-wall filled with His presence. How does it get any better than that? We should not only be able to do the same things this woman did, but it should also be easier. We're full of the life, nature, and ability of God. We're part of God's family—faith sons and daughters of a faith God. We *can believe* for miracles!

Confession

I'm a faith son or daughter of a faith God.
I can and do believe I receive my healing.

Our Faith Plus God's Power Equals Healing

And Jesus, immediately knowing in himself that virtue had gone out of him, turned him about in the press, and said, Who touched my clothes?

And he said unto her, Daughter, thy faith hath made thee whole; go in peace, and be whole of thy plague.

—Mark 5:30,34

What was it that made this woman whole? The Bible says Jesus knew "virtue," or power, had gone out of Him at the same time the woman felt in her body she was healed of the issue of blood. (vv. 29,30.) But then Jesus said, "Daughter, your faith made you whole." So which was it? Did Jesus' power heal her, or was it her faith?

It was a combination of the two. If Jesus had said, "Daughter, My power has healed you," everyone in the crowd could've asked, "Why didn't Your power heal me? I need a miracle too."

Jesus answered that question before it was even asked. He said, "Daughter, your faith made you whole." Then everyone knew why she'd gotten healed and they hadn't.

Jesus' healing power would've gone into anyone in that crowd who reached out in faith. But no faith was involved when the others touched Jesus. Therefore, God's power wasn't released on their behalf, and the woman was the only one healed.

Even today we need a combination of faith and power. It's our faith that releases God's power to perform miracles in our lives. God's power is always available to His children—it's just a matter of learning how to tap in to that divine source of power by faith.

Confession

The woman with the issue of blood released God's power with her faith. By faith I release that same power in my life. God's power is making me whole.

Make Your Miracle Happen

There are three kinds of people in the world: those who watch things happen, those who make things happen, and those who wonder what is happening.

Likewise, we have three kinds of people in the body of Christ. We have folks who wonder what's happening most of the time. Then, we have believers who watch things happen. In other words, they watch folks get healed and receive miracles and think, *Man, I wish God would do something like that for me.*

But then there's the third kind of Christian.

When she had heard of Jesus, came in the press behind, and touched his garment. For she said, If I may touch but his clothes, I shall be whole.

—Mark 5:27,28

These believers are the bunch who make things happen. That's the group I want to be part of. I don't want to wait for anything to happen; I want to be out there making it happen.

"That's pushing God," some folks say. No, we don't push or control God. No one does. We just act on what He's already said in His Word.

This woman with the issue of blood didn't wonder what was happening or wait for something to happen. She made something happen *with her faith.* She didn't say, "I wish Jesus would come to my house." No, she went to find Him.

Many in the crowd touched Jesus, but power didn't flow into any of them. But this woman didn't touch Him with her hand only—*she touched Jesus with her faith.* Reach out in faith for your miracle!

Confession

I'm as convinced as this woman that God wants me well.
I reach out now with the hand of faith and receive my miracle.

Change the Course of Your Life

And a certain woman, which had an issue of blood twelve years...when she had heard of Jesus....

—Mark 5:25,27

The woman with the issue of blood had been sick for a very long time. She'd seen every doctor in the country and spent everything she had trying to get better. She desired healing with all her heart, but nothing had helped; she'd only grown worse.

What was the first step this woman took that totally changed her condition? What did she do that set her on a new course toward healing? Mark 5:27 gives us the answer: "When she had *heard*...."

Nothing happened in this woman's life until she heard. That may sound like a small thing, but hearing is the biggest factor in changing the course of a person's life. All through the Bible, we find a direct correlation between hearing and healing.

What did she hear? "When she had heard of Jesus...." In John 1:1, Jesus is called the Word. So when the Bible says, "She had heard of Jesus," it could just as well say, "She heard the Word." Psalm 107:20 says, "He sent his word, and healed them...."

Jesus doesn't dwell among us today in the flesh, but we still have the written Word. As we set ourselves to continually hear the Word, our faith will grow. That's the first step to changing the course of our lives.

Confession

The power in God's written Word heals me as
I hear it, believe it, and act upon it in faith.

Get Tenacious in Your Faith

This woman had tenacity—she was stubborn. And we have to be stubborn if we're going to walk in God's best. That doesn't mean we're to be stubborn with other people, but we must be stubborn in our stand on God's Word.

Now, tenacity could also be defined as *"resistance to flow."* Many people "flow" with whatever word or wind of doctrine comes along. They say, "The Word says I'm healed, but the doctors tell me there's no hope." These people are double-minded, flowing back and forth between God's promises and man's opinions.

But this woman got tenacious about her healing. She heard of Jesus and decided to trust Him. She'd been to every doctor in the country, and they'd probably pronounced her incurable. She didn't have any natural hope left.

And a certain woman, which had an issue of blood twelve years, and had suffered many things of many physicians, and had spent all that she had, and was nothing bettered, but rather grew worse.

—Mark 5:25,26

So she decided to flow against natural circumstances. It wasn't easy to do because she was sick, tired, and broke. Beside that, she had to flow against a multitude of people crowding around Jesus until she finally reached Him.

The flow of the natural realm was telling her, "Give up, lady. This won't work. You've tried everything. Remember, the doctor said you can't make it." But the woman got stubborn—and the woman got healed.

Thank God for good doctors, but the Word of God is an even higher authority. We need to get stubborn about holding fast to that anointed Word—no matter what circumstances look like.

Confession

I'm stubborn about standing on God's Word.
Circumstances don't move me. I walk by faith—and not sight.

Take a Stand

And a certain woman, which had an issue of blood twelve years...came in the press behind, and touched his garment.

—Mark 5:25,27

The more you consider this woman with the issue of blood, the more you understand she had to be a stubborn woman. Under Jewish law she was considered unclean, which meant when she came out in public she risked being stoned. As if that weren't bad enough, notice whom Jesus was walking with at the time: "And, behold, there cometh one of the rulers of the synagogue, Jairus by name" (v. 22).

Jesus was on His way to Jairus' house to heal his daughter when He perceived that power had flowed out of Him and stopped to find out who had touched Him. As a ruler of the synagogue, Jairus had authority to have this woman stoned.

This woman had to be tenacious, stubborn, resistant to flow. She had to overcome her fear and go against religious leaders.

You know, some ministers say, "Well, you just can't be healed. God doesn't heal people anymore." When that happens, people have to override what those ministers are saying about healing in order to receive healing.

This woman had to overcome a lot—unbelief, fear, and weakness. She had to decide no matter what came against her, she would receive healing.

We must reach that same point and make that same decision: "I don't care what anyone says. I don't care what it looks like, seems like, or feels like. I stand on God's Word, and that's all there is to it!"

Confession

I won't be moved by circumstances or by what others say.
I'm moved only by what God's Word says. No sickness is
too hard for my Father to heal. I receive my healing today.

"Thou Art Loosed!"

This woman had been bowed over for eighteen years. That's a tough condition—eighteen years of looking at her shoestrings. The woman couldn't straighten her back and stand straight. She must've been in tremendous pain.

But then Jesus touched her and said, "Woman, thou art loosed from thine infirmity." Immediately, she was made straight, and she glorified God.

Jesus got her attention with His first words to her: "Woman, you are loosed." In other words, "You were set free a long time ago. Now you just need to get rid of the symptoms." She was the daughter of Abraham. She was loosed, but she didn't know it.

It's the same thing with Christians today. The Bible says those whom the Son sets free are free indeed. (John 8:36.)

We're loosed from all the works of the enemy, whether we realize it or not. But it's time to act loosed. We were re-created in Jesus to walk free of all sickness and disease, so let's do that today!

Confession

Because of Jesus, I'm loosed from any infirmity. I'm free from all circumstances and symptoms because I hear, believe, and act on the Word.

And [Jesus] was teaching in one of the synagogues on the sabbath. And, behold, there was a woman which had a spirit of infirmity eighteen years, and was bowed together, and could in no wise lift up herself.

And when Jesus saw her, he called her to him, and said unto her, Woman, thou art loosed from thine infirmity. And he laid his hands on her: and immediately she was made straight, and glorified God.

—Luke 13:10-13

Don't Miss an Opportunity To Act

And [Jesus] was teaching in one of the synagogues on the sabbath. And, behold, there was a woman which had a spirit of infirmity eighteen years, and was bowed together, and could in no wise lift up herself.

And when Jesus saw her, he called her to him, and said unto her, Woman, thou art loosed from thine infirmity. And he laid his hands on her: and immediately she was made straight, and glorified God.

—Luke 13:10-13

Jesus called the woman who was bowed over to come to Him. He didn't walk back to her in the crowd and deliver her miracle. Why did Jesus make that woman come to Him? It would've been easier for Him to walk to her than for her to hobble to Him. After all, she'd been bowed over for eighteen years, and He was young and healthy.

But Jesus was giving the woman an opportunity to *act in faith.* How do we know her faith was in operation? Because faith always acts on the Word, and the woman had been hearing the Word.

Look back at verse 10: "And he was teaching in one of the synagogues on the sabbath." Jesus was always putting something into people to believe. And when they believed and acted on it, they got results.

If the woman had told Jesus, "No, I can't come to You," it would've been evident she wasn't expecting anything. She wouldn't have struggled to come forward if she hadn't expected to walk back healthy. But this woman was in faith. And when Jesus called her to come forward, she acted on her faith and received her miracle.

Confession

Jesus has also loosed me from bondage.
As I act in faith I'm set free from sin and sickness.

Loosed From the Devil's Bondage

When Jesus healed this woman, the religious people got angry. Isn't it amazing how religious people never change? They still get angry today when people are healed. Often people are angry when someone else is healed and they're not.

This story proves something else to me. The Bible says over and over that the majority of Jesus' healings took place on the Sabbath, the Jews' sacred day. I believe Jesus was making the point that healing is sacred to God. However, the ruler of the synagogue didn't agree at all. Jesus rebuked him, saying, "You'd water your animals on the Sabbath, but you wouldn't let this little woman get healed!"

Also, notice the minute this woman got healed she glorified God. Some say, "Yes, but God gets glory through sickness." Actually, the Bible says God got glory when she got healed. The woman didn't glorify God much hobbling around with nothing to stare at but her shoes for eighteen long years. But she glorified God with all her heart when she stood straight up and was delivered from the devil's bondage.

Confession

My Father has set me free from all bondage, and I give Him all the glory.

And he laid his hands on her: and immediately she was made straight, and glorified God. And the ruler of the synagogue answered with indignation, because that Jesus had healed on the sabbath day....

The Lord then answered him, and said, Thou hypocrite, doth not each one of you on the sabbath loose his ox or his ass from the stall, and lead him away to watering? And ought not this woman, being a daughter of Abraham, whom Satan hath bound, lo, these eighteen years, be loosed from this bond on the sabbath day?

—Luke 13:13-16

Sickness–Bondage or Blessing?

And ought not this woman, being a daughter of Abraham, whom Satan hath bound, lo, these eighteen years, be loosed from this bond on the sabbath day?

—Luke 13:16

Let's see what we can learn from this verse. First of all, Jesus called sickness *bondage*. We don't know the specific disease this woman had; it could have been crippling arthritis. But we do know the Bible called it a spirit of infirmity.

Whatever it was, Jesus for sure never called her sickness a blessing. He also did *not* say, "Ought not this woman whom *God hath blessed* these eighteen years...." No, God's blessing was in sending Jesus to *loose* the woman from her infirmity.

The truth is, God never had anything good to say about sickness. In fact, He detested it so much He sent His own Son Jesus to bear all the sickness of the world upon Himself. Sickness was never called a blessing in the Bible, and anyone who calls it a blessing today doesn't know what the Bible says.

If sickness and disease are from God, then Jesus was fighting against God when He healed people. If sickness and disease are from God, then Jesus robbed God of His glory when He called sickness a bondage of Satan.

Thank God, the Bible sets us free from wrong thinking and wrong believing so we can enjoy the blessings of healing and health.

Confession

I'm not confused about where sickness comes from. Sickness is a bondage from Satan clear and simple. God wants me to live free of sickness and pain, so I choose to walk in health today.

Satan Is the Author of Sickness

Two important points are revealed in this Scripture: Sickness is a bondage, and Satan is the author of sickness.

For years I've heard people say, "God chose to have me sick." Yet Jesus said Satan *bound* the woman—not God.

The truth is that God detests sickness as much as He detests sin because sickness is a result of the original sin. Sickness didn't come into the world until sin did. When God ruled and reigned on the earth through Adam, there was no sickness on the earth. But Adam gave Satan his authority and a long-term lease on creation, and Satan brought sickness with him.

And ought not this woman, being a daughter of Abraham, whom Satan hath bound, lo, these eighteen years, be loosed from this bond on the sabbath day?

—Luke 13:16

Yet people still blame God for sickness. God had nothing to do with it! It just doesn't make any sense to call God the author of sickness.

For instance, 1 John 3:8 says, "...For this purpose the Son of God was manifested, that he might destroy the works of the devil." But if God made anyone sick under Jesus' ministry, then Jesus was destroying the works of God when He healed people. Now if Jesus destroyed God's works, then we're in trouble because the Bible says a kingdom divided against itself cannot stand. (Matt. 12:25.)

No, Jesus never destroyed one work of God. He only "went about doing good, and healing all that were oppressed of the devil" (Acts 10:38).

Confession

Any sickness that attacks my body is a bondage of Satan. No sickness is from God. Jesus came to set me free from every sickness and disease, so I accept my healing now.

Be Loosed

And ought not this woman, being a daughter of Abraham, whom Satan hath bound, lo, these eighteen years, be loosed from this bond on the sabbath day?

—Luke 13:16

We've learned from this Scripture that sickness is bondage. Then, we saw that sickness came from Satan. Now let's look at Jesus' question: "Ought not this woman...be loosed?"

Satan had kept this woman in bondage for eighteen years. But, thank God, Jesus said she ought to be loosed.

Jesus was also saying that *any* person whom Satan has bound with sickness and disease ought to be loosed. And Jesus is in the business of loosing people!

What qualified this woman to be loosed from this satanic bondage? Was she a real saint? Had she done something special? No, Jesus said she ought to be loosed because she was "a daughter of Abraham."

"Where does that leave me?" you may ask. In a good position because Galatians 3:7 says, "Know ye therefore that they which are of faith, the same are the children of Abraham." According to this Scripture, we are sons and daughters of Abraham. We've been grafted into his family through the blood of Jesus Christ.

Galatians 3:29 says, "If ye be Christ's, then are ye Abraham's seed, and heirs according to the promise." What is that promise? Well, one of the promises is that we can be loosed from every bondage of the enemy!

Confession

Because I'm a child of Abraham, I'm loosed from every satanic bondage. I not only enjoy the same rights and privileges as Abraham did, but I also live under a new and better covenant, established on better promises—including the promise that by Jesus' stripes I am healed.

"The Lord That Healeth Thee"

...If thou wilt diligently hearken to the voice of the Lord thy God, and wilt do that which is right in his sight, and wilt give ear to his commandments, and keep all his statutes, I will put none of these diseases upon thee, which I have brought upon the Egyptians: for I am the Lord that healeth thee.

—Exodus 15:26

This was God's first healing covenant with His people. Some Hebrew scholars say this verse should be translated in the permissive tense—meaning "I will *allow*" instead of "I will *put*." In that case it would read, "I will allow none of these diseases upon thee, which I have allowed upon the Egyptians."

God finishes by saying, "For I am the Lord that healeth thee." The Hebrew says, "I am Jehovah Rapha."[1]

Three million children of Israel left Egypt trusting God. They went out with silver and gold, and the Bible says there was not one feeble person among them. (Ps. 105:37.)

But God put a few conditions on this new covenant: "If thou wilt diligently hearken to the voice of the Lord thy God, and wilt do that which is right in his sight, and wilt give ear to his commandments...." You see, even in the first healing covenant, there was a correlation between hearing and being healed.

Also, notice God didn't say, "*I will be* or *I was* the Lord that healeth thee." No, He said, "*I am* the Lord that healeth thee."

That's good news because James 1:17 says God never changes. If He was the Lord who healed His people back then, He's the Lord who still heals His people today.

Confession

I'm in covenant with Jehovah Rapha, the God who heals me, and I live in in divine health.

The Arm of the Lord Revealed

Who hath believed our report? and to whom is the arm of the Lord revealed?

—Isaiah 53:1

Did you ever wonder, *to whom does God reveal His arm?* In other words, to whom does God show His strength? And for whom does He work miracles?

People say, "Oh, you never know for whom God will use His power. God works in mysterious ways." No, that isn't the way it works.

If someone starts to reveal his arm—to roll up his sleeves—he's getting ready to use some strength. If a big guy begins rolling up his sleeves, you figure he's either getting ready to work or getting ready to fight. And God reveals His arm when He's ready to go to work—and show some power—for His children.

Does God have favorite children? Does He look at some and say, "I don't know what it is, but something about you bothers me. I just don't like you, and I think I'll take all My blessings somewhere else"?

No, God is no respecter of persons. God doesn't have favorite children. What He does for one, He does for *anyone*. He loves the whole world equally. God loved us while we were yet sinners to the extent that He sent His own Son to die for us.

And yet, God doesn't reveal His arm for everyone. He reveals His arm and demonstrates His power for those who believe His report—His Word.

So really, the choice isn't God's—*it's yours*. If you want God's power revealed to you, then you must believe His report.

Confession

God's report says by Jesus' stripes I'm healed. I choose to believe and receive that report. Therefore, God reveals His healing power to me.

He Carried the Curse Away

Hundreds of years before Jesus Christ ever took on flesh and dwelt among us, God gave the prophet Isaiah a vision. Looking into the future, he saw that Jesus would go to the Cross and die for all mankind. The prophet told us not only what the Crucifixion looked like, but he also told us what Jesus would purchase and why. The book of Isaiah is called "the Gospel of the Old Testament."

Surely he hath borne our griefs, and carried our sorrows: yet we did esteem him stricken, smitten of God, and afflicted.

—Isaiah 53:4

Let's look carefully at this verse: "Surely he hath borne our griefs, and carried our sorrows." A lot of people think that means Jesus just helped us carry our burdens. But *borne* means *to lift up, bear away, convey or remove to a distance.*[1] When Jesus bore our sins, sicknesses, and pains, He did just help tote them along—He bore them and removed them. Both these words, *borne* and *carried* imply substitution, or bearing another's load.[2]

Now look at this: "Surely he hath borne *our* griefs, and carried *our* sorrows." Jesus didn't have any griefs or sorrows of His own. He didn't have any sickness, pain, or sin—*we do.*

We live in this world, and we were under the curse of the Law. But Jesus bore it all for us. He came in as our substitute and took the curse away from us. He didn't *have to* do that; He *chose to* do it.

We deserved the curse, but Jesus carried it away for us.

Confession

Jesus took upon Himself my pain and sickness because He loves me. By faith I receive the divine healing and health His sacrifice provides for me.

Jesus Purchased Our Physical Healing

Surely he hath borne our griefs, and carried our sorrows: yet we did esteem him stricken, smitten of God, and afflicted.

—Isaiah 53:4

Let's examine this Scripture closely—particularly the words, "he hath *borne our griefs, and carried our sorrows.*" Isaac Leeser's respected translation of the Old Testament—the only English translation of the Bible accepted by the Jewish council—translates the words *griefs* and *sorrows* as "sicknesses" and "pains."[1] So in the Hebrew, it actually says, "Surely He has borne our sicknesses [or our diseases], and carried our pains." That puts a little different light on this Scripture.

Of course, griefs and sorrows are very similar to sickness and disease. In fact, sickness and disease *cause* grief and sorrow. Anyone who says sickness and pain are blessings from God for sure doesn't understand God's nature.

For further understanding of this Scripture, we can go to where it was fulfilled in the New Testament. Referring to Jesus' healing the multitudes, Matthew 8:17 says, "That it might be fulfilled which was spoken by Esaias the prophet, saying, Himself took our infirmities, and bare our sicknesses."

So Isaiah 53:4 was fulfilled during Jesus' earthly ministry as He healed people physically. Isaiah's prophecy, therefore, looked ahead to the time when Jesus would purchase healing for our physical bodies.

Confession

Jesus took my sickness and carried my pain.
He paid the price so I could be well. I believe
what the Word says. I am healed.

Redeemed–Spirit, Soul, and Body

When man fell from grace in the Garden of Eden, his spirit, soul, and body fell too. God responded with a plan to redeem mankind with the blood of Jesus. God wasn't interested in doing just half a job. He wanted to redeem *all* of man.

Actually, man had a threefold problem, and Jesus gave us a threefold answer. He went to the Cross as our substitute, bearing our sins, the chastisement of our peace, and our sicknesses. He paid the same price for all three dimensions of our being, so apparently all three are equally important.

But he was wounded for our transgressions, he was bruised for our iniquities: the chastisement of our peace was upon him; and with his stripes we are healed.

—Isaiah 53:5

You may say, "Well, I thought spiritual things were more important." In the realm of eternity, that's true. But God never required us to choose whether we wanted our spirits, souls, or bodies taken care of. He said, "I paid the price for all three dimensions so receive all three benefits!"

The first benefit mentioned in Isaiah 53:5 takes care of the sin problem: "He was wounded for our transgressions, he was bruised for our iniquities." Jesus died on the Cross to pay for our sins. He shed His blood for us because without the shedding of blood, there is no remission of sins. (Heb. 9:22.) And He was raised from the dead so we could be born again. Once we receive Jesus Christ as Savior, God's report is that we're forgiven of sins.

Confession

Jesus purchased freedom for me spirit, soul, and body.
Therefore, I believe I'm saved, healed, and full of His peace.

Chastised for Our Peace

But he was wounded for our transgressions, he was bruised for our iniquities: the chastisement of our peace was upon him; and with his stripes we are healed.

—Isaiah 53:5

Consider the phrase, *"the chastisement of our peace was upon him."* Why was Jesus chastised so much? Think about it: He was beaten. He was whipped until His back was laid open. His beard was plucked out, and a crown of thorns was placed on His head. Then, finally, He was nailed to the Cross.

But none of Jesus' suffering was without purpose. Everything that happened to Him was substitutionary. Jesus wore a crown of thorns so we could be crowned with glory and honor. Because He bore our chastisement, we can now live in peace, free from depression and mental anguish.

When you go to any church in this nation and ask, "How many would like more peace?" most of the people raise their hands. Why? Because most Christians don't know that peace already belongs to them.

Jesus didn't have to put up with all that His tormenters did to Him. He said, "No man can take My life; only I can lay it down. No man has any authority or power over Me unless it comes from above." (John 10:18.) No, Jesus paid that price willingly, bearing our chastisement and shedding His blood to give us peace of mind.

Confession

Jesus was chastised for my peace; therefore,
I'm forever free from depression and mental anguish.
I live in the peace of God.

Settling the Question of Healing

Jesus was raised from the dead with a perfect, glorified body. So where did He leave our sickness and disease? He left them in hell. Jesus was then called the firstborn of all creation. (Col. 1:15.)

Jesus died on the Cross and then descended to the depths of hell, carrying our sickness and disease. But when He—the firstborn among many brethren—was raised from the dead, He came forth free of sickness that was laid on Him. Therefore, when we're born again, healing is ours to claim.

But he was wounded for our transgressions, he was bruised for our iniquities: the chastisement of our peace was upon him; and with his stripes we are healed.

—Isaiah 53:5

Here's another question: If God didn't want us healed, why in the world did Jesus bear those stripes before He went to the Cross? That was one misery Jesus could have bypassed. Yet He did it by choice.

You see, healing is no longer a promise—it's a firmly established fact. Now you and I just need to get the revelation in our own spirits that healing is God's will for us. When we do, we'll start walking in the divine health Jesus purchased for us with the stripes on His back.

Confession

Jesus willingly paid the price for me. He took my sickness;
He gave me His health. I appropriate what the
Lord did for me and receive my healing now.

Do You Believe God's Report?

But he was wounded for our transgressions, he was bruised for our iniquities: the chastisement of our peace was upon him; and with his stripes we are healed.

—Isaiah 53:5

Isaiah 53:1 says, "Who hath believed our report?" Believing the right report isn't mind over matter or the power of positive thinking. It's believing God's Word over our problems, symptoms, or circumstances. This means we have to choose whom we will believe. Will we believe God or the world? Will we believe the voice of the Holy Spirit or the voice of the devil?

Once we know what God says, we can choose to believe His report. In Isaiah 53:5, God gives us this report to believe: Jesus was wounded for our transgressions and bruised for our iniquities so we can be free from sin. He took the chastisement of our peace upon Himself so we can have peace. And He bore stripes upon His back so we can be healed.

A note in the margin of my *King James* Bible states the Hebrew word for *stripes* literally means "bruise." Now look at Isaiah 53:10: "Yet it pleased the Lord to bruise him...." Can you imagine our heavenly Father being pleased to bruise His Son?

God was pleased because He understood the end result. Jesus was bruised for our sickness, then died on the Cross for us. But in three days Jesus would be raised from the dead in a glorified, healthy body. And because of the bruises He bore, the entire body of Christ could go free from sickness. That's the report God wants us to believe.

Confession

Jesus shed His blood so I'd be free from sin, and He was bruised for my physical healing. I choose to believe the report of the Lord.

Jesus' Ministry–Then and Now

In Acts 10:38, Peter preached about the earthly ministry of Jesus to Cornelius' household: "How God anointed Jesus of Nazareth with the Holy Ghost and with power: who went about doing good, and healing all that were oppressed of the devil; for God was with him." Was Peter confused? Jesus was already gone. Why preach about His earthly ministry? It was finished, wasn't it?

The former treatise have I made, O Theophilus, of all that Jesus began both to do and teach.

—Acts 1:1

No, Jesus' earthly ministry was just getting started. He just ascended to the Father's right hand to become the Head over all things to the body. (Col. 1:18.)

Jesus is still working in and through us today. His earthly ministry didn't stop or diminish—it multiplied. Jesus told His disciples, "It's better for you if I go. I'll pray to the Father, and He'll send another Comforter to abide with you forever." (John 14:16.)

He also said, "He that believeth on me, the works that I do shall he do also; and greater works than these shall he do; because I go unto my Father" (John 14:12).

The last verse of the book of John says, "There are also many other things which Jesus did...even the world itself could not contain the books that should be written" (John 21:25). Then in Acts 1:1, the next verse in the Bible, Luke talks about "all that Jesus *began both to do and teach.*"

The body of Christ will pick up where Jesus left off. Jesus ministry of healing and deliverance will continue—*in and through us.*

Confession

While Jesus walked the earth, He healed the sick.
As I hear God's Word, I receive my healing because
Jesus' ministry is still alive today in me.

Act in Faith as God Leads You

[Jesus]...spat on the ground, and made clay of the spittle, and he anointed the eyes of the blind man with the clay, and said unto him, Go, wash in the pool of Siloam...he went his way therefore, and washed, and came seeing.

—John 9:6,7

You may wonder, *What should I do to act on my faith?*

Don't do something because it worked for someone else. God will instruct *you.*

Jesus told the blind man to wash in the pool of Siloam, but He didn't tell anyone else that. Jesus gave people a variety of different instructions to act on their faith.

I had a friend who was waiting for God to heal him from severe sugar diabetes. He heard of someone who had thrown away his insulin, so he thought, *I'm going to try that too! If I throw away this insulin, God will have to do something.* But he almost died! He tried to make something work instead of acting in faith.

Another time, I traveled with a group that included two diabetics. Throughout the summer I watched them check the amount of insulin they needed daily. Each time they said, "Thank You, Father. I believe I'm healed by Jesus' stripes. Glory to God!" Then they took whatever insulin they needed.

The insulin wasn't healing these two people, but it was keeping them alive while they believed God. Soon they needed less insulin. Again, they took whatever medicine they needed and always said, "Thank God, I believe I'm healed." By the end of the summer, both were healed—neither one needed any insulin at all.

Let God show you how to act on your faith!

Confession

God shows me how to act in faith.
I follow His instructions and see results.

Sickness Is a Work of the Devil

Why did Jesus become flesh and dwell among us on this earth? Why was He manifested? The main reason He came into this realm was to destroy the works of the devil.

Did Jesus fulfill what God called Him to do, or did He fail? Of course Jesus accomplished what God sent Him to do. He destroyed the works of the devil. So if we want to find out what the works of the devil are, we need to find out what Jesus destroyed.

Acts 10:38 tells us that Jesus "went about doing good, and healing all that were oppressed of the devil; for God was with him." What good did Jesus do? He healed people.

He that committeth sin is of the devil; for the devil sinneth from the beginning. For this purpose the Son of God was manifested, that he might destroy the works of the devil.

—1 John 3:8

Every time Jesus healed someone, He destroyed the works of the devil—sickness and disease. Every time He forgave someone, He destroyed the works of the devil—sin and separation from God. Every time He set someone free, He destroyed the works of the devil—spiritual, mental, and physical bondage.

Healing multitudes of people was a major part of Jesus' ministry. In fact, there were times when as many as touched Jesus were made whole. Jesus accomplished the purpose for which He was sent. Whenever He went about healing people, He was destroying the works of the devil.

Confession

The devil wanted to kill me, but Jesus set me free and gave me eternal life. The devil wanted to make me sick, but Jesus destroyed his efforts. I am the healed of the Lord.

Satan, a Defeated Foe

*For this purpose
the Son of God
was manifested,
that he might
destroy the works
of the devil.*

—1 John 3:8

Sickness is not a blessing from God—it's a curse from the enemy from whom we've been redeemed. If sickness is from the enemy, we don't have a thing to be concerned about. Jesus was manifested to destroy the works of the devil—and He did what He was sent to do.

And having spoiled principalities and powers, he made a shew of them openly, triumphing over them in it.

Colossians 2:15

We see in this Scripture that Jesus spoiled principalities and powers. He spoiled Satan's army—the beings that back up what little authority Satan had.

Forasmuch then as the children are partakers of flesh and blood, he also himself likewise took part of the same; that through death he might destroy him that had the power of death, that is, the devil.

Hebrews 2:14

So if sickness and disease are from the devil (and they are!), then we're in a good position because Jesus destroyed his works and ruined his army. The Rotherham translation says Jesus defeated Satan so "He might paralyse him that held the dominion of death."[1] Jesus did all of that for us!

Satan has no legal, moral, or spiritual authority to put anything on you and make it stick. He can only make you sick if you let him. His works have been destroyed, his army has been beaten, and he's been paralyzed by the blood of Jesus that covers you.

Confession

Jesus has given me authority over all the devil's
works in my life. The devil has no legal authority
to put anything on me. I am redeemed from the curse.

Choose Life

A number of years ago I heard a certain minister say, "The person who shuts his spirit away cripples himself in life and becomes an easy prey to selfish and designing people. But the individual who learns to be led by the Spirit of God will rise to the top in life."

Something rose up on the inside of me when I heard that, and I thought, *Well, now I know it's my choice!*

You see, God doesn't choose who will be successful in life. He's no respecter of persons. He isn't in a good mood on some days and in a bad mood on other days. He doesn't look at one person and say, "I like you. You get everything I've got," and then look at someone else and say, "I don't know what it is about you. You just bug me. You just rub my fur backwards. You don't get anything." *No!* God has no favorites. He loves everyone equally.

It's up to us whether or not we rise to the top in life. We are free moral agents. We can live mediocre lives, scraping the bottom of the barrel, or we can rise to the top.

Through His death, burial, and resurrection, Jesus purchased for us "all things that pertain unto life and godliness" (2 Peter 1:3). The work is already done and already paid for.

Will you walk in the blessings of God? *The choice is yours.*

> *I call heaven and earth to record this day against you, that I have set before you life and death, blessing and cursing: therefore choose life, that both thou and thy seed may live.*
>
> *—Deuteronomy 30:19*

Confession

I choose life, blessing, and health.
I choose to believe God's Word and rise to the top in life.

Whom Will You Serve?

Choose you this day whom ye will serve....

—Joshua 24:15

Man has always had a choice. God has shown us that from the beginning. He formed man and gave him authority over all the works of His hands. God told him to dress the Garden of Eden, keep it, and take care of it.

But God warned Adam, "Don't eat of the Tree of the Knowledge of Good and Evil, for in the day you do, you will surely die." (Gen. 2:16,17.)

God was talking about spiritual death, or separation from Him. So what happened? Well, Adam ate of that tree. And from then on, mankind was separated from God, except when animal sacrifices were made. Thank God, Jesus Christ came to earth and brought us back into relationship with the Father.

I used to read the account of Adam and Eve and think, *God, why did You do that? Instead of putting the Tree of the Knowledge of Good and Evil in the midst of the Garden, why didn't You put it on the southern tip of South America, where it would take 5000 years to find? By then, Adam wouldn't have wanted it.*

Some folks say, "God was testing mankind." No, this wasn't a test. God was allowing man the privilege of being a free moral agent, which meant man was free to make choices.

God doesn't want us to serve Him because we *have to,* but because we *want to.* He will allow us to go to hell and spend eternity there if we so choose. Or we can choose life and spend eternity in His presence—starting here and now.

Confession

I choose to obey God because I want to.
I choose life that I and my seed shall live.

God Heals Because He Loves

And Jesus went forth, and saw a great multitude, and was moved with compassion toward them, and he healed their sick.

—Matthew 14:14

Why did Jesus heal the multitudes? Because He was moved with compassion.

God often demonstrates His power for people who've never had the opportunity to hear His Word. Through these demonstrations, God puts His "seal of approval" on the Word and manifests His love to the people.

Janet and I were in a church service recently where God demonstrated His love to some visitors. The Holy Ghost quickened a word of knowledge to me, so I spoke it out. A woman on the front row came forward and was healed.

The woman gave her testimony and explained, "All these years, I didn't think God loved me. But I found out differently last night. God called me out of a whole church full of people and healed me. This is the first time in my life I've truly known the love of God."

I thought to myself, *God sure knows His business!*

Healing is the dinner bell for the Gospel, and we need to ring that bell. Many people are tired of religious doctrines; they're looking for something real. God demonstrates that He is real: *Healing shows God's compassion, and miracles show His power.*

Many have the idea God is a big bully with a baseball bat, sitting on a cloud, waiting to belt them every time they do something wrong. But God is love, and He proves it to the world by healing people.

Confession

God loves me. He loved me so much He sent Jesus to die for me.
Because of His love, I'm healed.

Keep the Law of Love

And hope maketh not ashamed; because the love of God is shed abroad in our hearts by the Holy Ghost which is given unto us.

—Romans 5:5

One way for us to stay healthy is to walk in love. Under the old covenant, God told His people if they served Him, He'd take sickness away from the midst of them. (Ex. 23:25.) Then He gave them a list of commandments and ordinances to obey, knowing that the Israelites had no power to fulfill them.

In essence, He was saying to them, "Here are all these rules and regulations to follow in order to live holy before Me. However, there's no way you can keep them. So when you break My laws, the blood of an animal sacrifice will cover your sins and iniquities. It will push your sins ahead for a year so you can receive My blessings."

God gave His laws and commandments to His people to prove to them that they needed a Savior. Galatians 3:24 says the law served as a schoolmaster to bring God's people to Jesus. God's people couldn't be perfected through the Law. They needed a Redeemer.

What about us? Are we able to obey Jesus' commandment to "Love one another" (John 13:34) any better than the Old Testament saints kept the Law?

Yes! When we're born again, the Holy Ghost comes to live in us and imparts God's love in our spirits. We then have the power to walk in love. As we walk in love, we keep all God's commandments. And therefore, God takes sickness from the midst of us.

Confession

God heals me and keeps me in divine health
as I walk in love and obey His Word and His Spirit.

Judge Your Love Walk

To open our hearts to God and allow Him to work in our lives, we need to judge our love walk.

That means we must know what God's love acts like, and then make sure we're doing the same thing. Sure, it's going to be an effort. Sure, we'll miss it now and then. But if we don't start endeavoring to walk in love, then we never will.

The Amplified Bible says, "Love endures long and is patient and kind; love never is envious nor boils over with jealousy, is not boastful or vainglorious, does not display itself haughtily."

> *Charity suffereth long, and is kind; charity envieth not; charity vaunteth not itself, is not puffed up.*
>
> —1 Corinthians 13:4

Love endures long. Do we endure long with people? *The Phillips* translation says, "This love of which I speak is slow to lose patience." Are we that way?

"Love envies not, love flaunteth not itself."[1] The Williams translation says, "Love never boils over with jealousy." Have we ever been jealous? That's not love. Love doesn't react that way.

The Phillips translation says, God's love "is neither anxious to impress, nor does it cherish inflated ideas of its own importance." Love never tries to impress anyone.

When we know what love acts like, we have a goal to reach toward. As we trust the greater One in us and tap into His love, which is poured out in our hearts, God will enable us to walk in love.

Confession

By the power of the Holy Ghost indwelling me, I walk in love toward people. I endure long and am patient and kind. I don't boil over with jealousy. I'm not boastful or anxious to impress. In every circumstance, I obey the law of love.

Love Always Forgives

[Love] doth not behave itself unseemly, seeketh not her own, is not easily provoked, thinketh no evil.

—1 Corinthians 13:5

Love always forgives. Forgiveness is one of the offsprings of love. *The Amplified Bible* says it this way:

[Love] is not conceited (arrogant and inflated with pride); it is not rude (unmannerly) and does not act unbecomingly. Love (God's love in us) does not insist on its own rights or its own way, for it is not self-seeking; it is not touchy or fretful or resentful; it takes no account of the evil done to it [it pays no attention to a suffered wrong].

Galatians 5:6 talks about "faith which worketh by love." Love forgives, so we could say faith works by forgiveness. Isn't that what Jesus was telling us in Mark 11:25? "And when ye stand praying, forgive...." Faith works by love, and love always forgives.

First Corinthians 13:5 goes on to say that love "seeketh not her own." *The Revised Standard Version* says, "Love does not insist on its own way." *Goodspeed* says, "It does not insist on its own rights."[1] How often have we said, "I've got my rights!" No, love doesn't insist on its own rights.

Love "is not easily provoked, thinketh no evil." *The New English Bible* says love is "not quick to take offence." Love keeps no score of wrongs. Now, our flesh will say, "I remember what that old bat did to me." But love doesn't take any account of the evil done to it, because love always forgives.

Confession

I walk in love because my Father is Love. I'm not arrogant, prideful, or rude. I don't insist on my own rights or keep a score of wrongs. I'm not quick to take offense, but I'm quick to forgive.

Walking in the God-Kind of Love

The *Amplified Bible* helps us see what it really means to walk in the God-kind of love:

> [Love] does not rejoice at injustice and unrighteousness, but rejoices when right and truth prevail. Love bears up under anything and everything that comes, is ever ready to believe the best of every person, its hopes are fadeless under all circumstances, and it endures everything [without weakening]. Love never fails [never fades out or becomes obsolete or comes to an end].

First, this Scripture says that love "rejoiceth not in iniquity." Love is never glad when others go the wrong way in life. On the other hand, your flesh is glad when someone else stumbles because that elevates you in your own mind.

[Love] rejoiceth not in iniquity, but rejoiceth in the truth; beareth all things, believeth all things, hopeth all things, endureth all things. Charity never faileth....

—1 Corinthians 13:6-8

Love is always glad when truth prevails. It overlooks faults. It's always slow to expose faults or sins and is always eager to believe the best. Love will go a long way to believe the best. It doesn't look for something wrong, but always looks for the good in every person.

So how do you measure up to this definition of love? If you find areas where you're lacking in your love walk, ask the Holy Spirit to help you make the necessary adjustments. Remember, your faith only works when love is operating in your life.

Confession

I walk in love because I'm a child of a loving God.
I don't rejoice at injustice or iniquity, but I rejoice in the truth.
I believe the best about people and endure everything
without weakening. God's love in me never fails.

Keep Your Confidence Toward God

Beloved, if our heart condemn us not, then have we confidence toward God. And whatsoever we ask, we receive of him, because we keep his commandments, and do those things that are pleasing in his sight. And this is his commandment, That we should believe on the name of his Son Jesus Christ, and love one another, as he gave us commandment.

—1 John 3:21-23

God said if our hearts don't condemn us, we have confidence toward Him and we receive what we ask for. So if we've been asking for something and haven't received our answer, we need to examine our love walk with others.

We receive what we ask for because we obey His commandments and do that which is pleasing in His sight. And these are His commandments: that we believe on the Lord Jesus, and that we love one another.

Walking in love keeps us out of trouble and in the blessings of God. Sure, it's work. It's not easy to put the body under. Most of us have been accustomed to letting the flesh dominate us in certain areas. For instance, the flesh thinks it's fun to criticize and talk about people because it makes the talker feel bigger.

But if we walk the love walk, we put ourselves in a position to walk in God's blessings. And I guarantee you, nothing the flesh offers comes close to the blessings of God.

Confession

I walk in love; therefore, I'm confident
God hears and answers my prayers.

The Command of Love

What are God's statutes and commandments for us to live by under the new covenant? In this Scripture, Jesus gives us one new commandment—that we love one another.

Under the old covenant, God said if we would keep His ordinances, statutes, and commandments, He would take sickness from our midst. (Ex. 23:25.) Similarly, 1 John 3:22 says that because we keep God's commandments, we receive what we ask of Him. So we see that the same restrictions that applied under the old covenant apply now. Under both covenants, God says, "I'll take care of you and bless you and cause you to walk in health, if you will keep My commandments."

A new commandment I give unto you, That ye love one another; as I have loved you, that ye also love one another. By this shall all men know that ye are my disciples, if ye have love one to another.

—John 13:34,35

In the Old Testament, God's people had many statutes, commandments, and ordinances to obey. In the New Testament, God condenses all His laws into one important commandment and calls it *love.*

Romans 13:10 says, "...Therefore love is the fulfilling of the law." As we walk in love, we fulfill all of God's other commandments.

Confession

I will walk in love toward others in every situation.
As I obey the commandment of love, my Father takes
sickness away from me. And I live in divine health.

What Can You Believe?

...but if thou canst do any thing, have compassion on us, and help us.

Jesus said unto him, If thou canst believe, all things are possible to him that believeth.

—Mark 9:22,23

A man brought his demon-possessed son to Jesus and said, "If You can do anything, have compassion on us and help us."

Jesus said in essence, "It's not a question of what I can do; the question is, What can you believe? If you can believe, all things become possible for you. It's not up to Me; it's up to you. I don't decide if your son gets healed—you do. I have the ability, but it's up to you whether or not My ability is released."

Over and over again in the Scriptures God "puts the ball back in our court." We've been crying out to God, saying, "Oh, God, move. Oh, God, do something!" Meanwhile, He's been saying, "You believe; then I'll move."

God gave us His Word and His faith. After we use the faith He gave us to believe the Word He gave us, it's His turn to move again.

God really gave us the easy part of the covenant. But a lot of times, we've avoided our responsibility. It's easier to just lean back and wait for God to do everything.

But that never worked for the people under Jesus' ministry. Jesus taught the Word to give people something to believe; then they had to act on their faith in that Word.

According to Jesus' own words, approximately 70 percent of the people healed under His ministry did so as a result of their own faith. As a result of your faith, all things are possible to *you!*

Confession

I believe and act on the Word and receive my miracle today.

"Help Thou Mine Unbelief"

When the man in this passage pleaded with Jesus to help his son, Jesus said to him in essence, "It's not just up to Me. It's whether you can believe that really matters." Instead of getting discouraged, the man caught what Jesus said. He said, "All right, Lord, I believe. Help my unbelief." In other words, he said, "I believe it in my heart, but my head is giving me trouble."

A lot of times people say, "I believe I'm healed, but what about the symptoms and circumstances?" or "I believe I'm healed, but when is this pain going to stop?"

Have you ever been in a spot like that? That's where this father of a demon-possessed son found himself. "I believe my son is free, Lord; I extend my faith. But please help my unbelief." In other words, doubts were trying to crowd into his head.

The minute people say, "I believe, *but...*" you just know they're looking in the wrong direction. In 2 Corinthians 4:18, Paul said, "While we look not at the things which are seen, but at the things which are not seen...." Too many times we've thought about and watched the problem. Then we've wondered why our faith hasn't worked.

We need to say, "I know the problem is there, but who cares? I'm looking at God's unseen Word, which produces victory every time."

...but if thou canst do any thing, have compassion on us, and help us.

Jesus said unto him, If thou canst believe, all things are possible to him that believeth.

And straightway the father of the child cried out, and said with tears, Lord, I believe; help thou mine unbelief.

—Mark 9:22-24

Confession

I believe God's Word that says I'm healed, so I am healed.

All Things Are Possible When You Believe

Jesus said unto him, If thou canst believe, all things are possible to him that believeth.

—Mark 9:23

Jesus made a powerful statement to the man who brought his son to Him for deliverance. He said, "All things are possible to him that believeth."

The reason Jesus could say that is shown in Hebrews 1:1-2: "God... hath in these last days spoken unto us by his Son, whom he hath appointed heir of all things...." How many is *all? All is all!* Jesus has been made heir of *all* things.

Then Romans 8:16-17 says, "The Spirit itself beareth witness with our spirit, that we are the children of God: and if children, then heirs; heirs of God, and joint-heirs with Christ...."

If you're a joint heir with someone, then whatever he inherits also belongs to you. Well, what did Jesus inherit since God appointed Him heir of all things?

Jesus said in Mark 10:27, "For with God all things are possible." That's great for God, but what about us? Jesus cleared up that question as well when He said, "All things are possible *to him that believeth.*" Why are all things possible to the person who believes? Because we're joint heirs with Jesus, the heir of all things.

Whatever God has, is, and can do is available to us as we tap our faith into His grace and His ability. If we get ahold of that, it will absolutely change our lives.

Confession

With God, all things are possible. He's greater than
any sickness, difficulty, or lack. He's greater than all, and
He lives in me—so all things are possible to me because I believe.

Let God Be True in Your Life

Paul was saying to the Romans, "You have to choose what you're going to believe." Every person in this world has to decide what is going to be true in his life.

God forbid: yea, let God be true, but every man a liar....

—Romans 3:4

Notice, Paul didn't say, "God is true." He said, "*Let* God be true." *You* is the understood subject of the sentence. That means *you are to let God be true in your life.* Are you going to let God be true or let the problem be true?

The Bible says, "By Jesus' stripes you were healed." (Isa. 53:5; 1 Peter 2:24.) A lot of people say, "I know that's what the Bible says, but I don't feel very good." Well, they've chosen to let their symptoms be truth and God a liar. They've chosen to let the problems be truth and God a liar. They're living on the negative side of life, always focusing on their problems instead of God's Word.

You can't focus on the problem and go over in victory, and you can't focus on the answer and go under in defeat. So what are you focusing your attention on?

We have to let God be true, switch over to the realm of faith, and declare, "Who cares what it looks or feels like? The Bible says I'm healed!"

You may know God's Word is true, but Paul says in this Scripture that you have to *choose* what is truth in your life. Are you going to believe symptoms and circumstances, or are you going to believe God?

Confession

I choose to let God's Word be truth in my life.
I steadfastly focus on His Word and receive what God says is mine.

Step out of the Boat by Faith

And in the fourth watch of the night Jesus went unto them, walking on the sea.

And Peter answered him and said, Lord, if it be thou, bid me come unto thee on the water.

And he said, Come. And when Peter was come down out of the ship, he walked on the water, to go to Jesus.

—Matthew 14:25,28,29

The disciples were out on the Sea of Galilee, fighting to keep afloat in a storm. Suddenly, Jesus came walking across the sea toward their boat. He'd been spending time with the Father and gotten so caught up in the glory He didn't even need a boat.

Peter called out, "Lord, if that's You, I want to come out there!" Jesus called back, "Come on out!"

I like Peter; he was a pioneer. He didn't want to walk the same road everyone else traveled. He wanted to plow a new one.

Peter stepped out of the boat and began to walk on the water toward Jesus. But it wasn't the water that held Peter up. Try it sometime, and see if water holds you up! No, it wasn't the water—it was Jesus' word that kept Peter on top of the water.

Jesus had said to him, "Come." And every time Peter put his foot down to take another step on the water, he landed on that word. Peter heard and believed what Jesus said. Then Peter acted on what Jesus said, keeping his eyes on Jesus all the while.

Like Peter, take a step of faith out on the Word and believe God for the miracle you need.

Confession

When the One who made my body tells me it's healed, it's healed.
The Word of God is the unsinkable foundation I walk on.

Keep Your Eyes on Jesus

Peter stepped out of the boat and walked on the water. But then Peter made a mistake. He was hearing, believing, and acting right, but then "he *saw* the wind boisterous." He took his eyes off Jesus and started watching the strong wind blowing on the stormy sea.

At that moment, fear entered in, faith stopped, and Peter started to sink. It was as though he was thinking, *I can't walk on water when the wind is blowing, especially when the waves are big!* He must have forgotten who had made it possible for him to walk on the water when it had been smooth.

When we're believing God, we need to hear God's Word, believe God's Word, say God's Word, and act on God's Word. But we also need to keep our eyes *off* the problem and *on* Jesus, who *is* God's Word. No matter what stormy circumstances we face, Jesus is the answer to our every need.

Confession

I keep my eyes on Jesus, not looking at the circumstances or impossibilities that surround me. I choose to believe His Word, and my faith holds me up.

And in the fourth watch of the night Jesus went unto them, walking on the sea.

And Peter answered him and said, Lord if it be thou, bid me come unto thee on the water.

And he said, Come. And when Peter was come down out of the ship, he walked on the water, to go to Jesus.

But when he saw the wind boisterous, he was afraid; and beginning to sink, he cried, saying, Lord, save me.

—Matthew 14:25,28-30

"Fear Not"

And when Peter was come down out of the ship, he walked on the water, to go to Jesus.

But when he saw the wind boisterous, he was afraid....

—Matthew 14:29,30

Does this scenario sounds familiar: You're in a trial, but you're believing right, talking right, and acting right. Then circumstances pull your eyes off Jesus and onto the problem. Suddenly, your faith is replaced with fear, and you begin to lose ground.

That's what happened to Peter. When he stepped out of the boat and began walking on the water, he was believing and acting right. But the minute Peter took his eyes off Jesus and looked back on the problem, his faith stopped working. His eyes started looking in the wrong direction, and fear entered in.

I used to be afraid of everything, but then I got a revelation of Psalm 91. If I didn't know Psalm 91 worked today, I'd never get on a plane. But Janet and I travel all the time, flying across the ocean several times a year. We never have a problem and never will because He's given His angels charge over us to keep us in all our ways. (Ps. 91:11.)

Sometimes Christians make the mistake of rebuking the fear without replacing it with anything. Jesus said, "Fear not; *only believe.*" (Mark 5:36.) In other words, He was saying, "If you want to believe God, you have to let your faith drive out fear."

How do you get rid of fear? Get in the Word! Faith comes by hearing God's Word, and faith drives out fear and enables you to keep your eyes where they belong—*on Jesus.*

Confession

God saves, heals, guides, and protects me. So I boldly say,
"The Lord is my helper, and I will not fear!" (Heb. 13:5,6.)

Don't Get Under Condemnation

Peter was actually walking on the water. But when he got his eyes off the answer and onto the problem, he began to sink. However, notice that Jesus didn't just walk over, slap him, and say, "Swim back to the boat!"

That's the impression a lot of people have of God. They think, *I missed it; God is going to get me now.* They come under condemnation because they've had a faith failure.

But God doesn't want you to feel condemned when you miss it and get out of faith. He's not condemning you. His hand is always reaching out to pull you back up on top of the situation,

Jesus didn't put Peter under condemnation. He just asked him, "Why did you doubt?" Then Jesus caught hold of Peter's hand and helped him stand up on top of the water again. And I don't believe Jesus just pulled Peter along back to the boat. I think they walked back together and had a good discussion about faith on the way.

And immediately Jesus stretched forth his hand, and caught him, and said unto him, O thou of little faith, wherefore didst thou doubt? And when they were come into the ship, the wind ceased.

—Matthew 14:31,32

Confession

Even when I miss God's best, He doesn't condemn me.
He picks me up and helps me on my way.
There is no condemnation for me because
I'm in Christ Jesus, and I walk after the Spirit of God.

Great Faith–Little Faith

And when Peter was come down out of the ship, he walked on the water, to go to Jesus.

But when he saw the wind boisterous, he was afraid; and beginning to sink, he cried, saying, Lord, save me.

And immediately Jesus stretched forth his hand, and caught him, and said unto him, O thou of little faith, wherefore didst thou doubt?

—Matthew 14:29-31

Peter was walking on the water. He had a miracle going. He'd stepped out in faith on the strength of Jesus' word, but got his eyes off the answer and onto the problem and began to sink. Jesus caught him and said, "O thou of little faith."

Do you know what *"little faith"* is? It's keeping your eye on the problem instead of the answer. Weak faith says, "I know what God says, but, man, look at the problem!" Great faith says, "I don't care what it looks like! I know what God says." The difference between great faith and weak faith is found in *what you dwell on—the problem or the answer.*

One example of great faith can be found in Romans 4:19: "And being not weak in faith, [Abraham] considered not his own body now dead, when he was about an hundred years old, neither yet the deadness of Sarah's womb."

Now, take the two *nots* out of that Scripture, and you'll see an example of weak faith: "Being weak in faith, he considered his own body now dead." *Weak faith considers the body or the problem; strong faith considers what God says or the answer.*

Abraham was *fully persuaded* God would perform what He promised. That's the mark of great faith.

Confession

I won't focus on symptoms or circumstances.
I'll look at God's Word and walk in victory every time.

Don't Observe "Lying Vanities"

They that observe lying vanities forsake their own mercy.

—Jonah 2:8

Jonah had a whale of a problem. God told him to go to Nineveh and preach, but Jonah refused. He got in to a boat to run away, but a storm arose threatening to sink it. Jonah knew he was the cause of the storm, so he told the crew to throw him overboard. As soon as he hit the water, a great fish swallowed him. (Jonah 1:1-17.)

By then, Jonah realized he'd missed it, but he also realized it wasn't too late to set things straight. So Jonah repented before God. Then he made this powerful statement: *"They that observe lying vanities forsake their own mercy."*

Every one of us needs God's mercy. So "Let us therefore come boldly unto the throne of grace, that we may obtain mercy, and find grace to help in time of need" (Heb. 4:16). Whatever we need is available by God's mercy.

But Jonah said, "If you observe lying vanities, you'll forsake your own mercy." You see, anything contrary to God's Word is a *lying vanity.* Jonah was saying, "I can sit here in this whale and dwell on my predicament, or I can dwell on mercy. I can either observe the problem or the answer. But if I observe the problem, I forsake my own mercy."

Don't forsake your mercy and watch symptoms or bad reports. Make the right choice and observe the answer.

Jonah made the right choice to trust God instead of his problem. So it wasn't long before he was out of the fish and safe on dry land.

Confession

I won't keep my eyes on symptoms or bad reports and forsake my mercy. I observe God's Word and receive His benefit of healing.

Abraham, the Father of Our Faith

God talked with [Abraham], saying, As for me, behold, my covenant is with thee, and thou shalt be a father of many nations. Neither shall thy name any more be called Abram, but thy name shall be Abraham; for a father of many nations have I made thee.

—Genesis 17:3-5

Romans 4:16 calls Abraham our father of faith. God made a covenant with Abraham, saying, "I have made you the father of many nations." He didn't say, "I *will* make you." He said, "I *have* made you."

You see, God always calls those things that be not as though they were. (Rom. 4:17.) He talks about what doesn't exist as though it already existed. That's why it's all right for us to do the same. We're not lying; we're following God's example.

But remember, God was talking to a 100-year-old man and his 90-year-old wife who were past child-bearing age. Medically speaking, it was impossible.

Abraham could've said, "Now, God, I appreciate Your enthusiasm, but we're a little old to have a baby. Why don't You talk to the nice young couple down the street who already have four kids?"

Yet Abraham had a deep awe and respect for Almighty God. He believed what God said, despite the situation looking hopeless in the natural. That's the key. *Abraham had to believe what God said before he could become what God said.* "[Abraham] against hope believed in hope, that he might become the father of many nations, according to that which was spoken..." (v. 18).

You're no different than the father of faith, so follow his lead.

Confession

God says by Jesus' stripes I'm healed. So when symptoms come against me, I call those things that be not as though they were, saying, "I am healed."

Don't Deny the Problem

Did you notice that Abraham never denied the problem? *He just didn't consider it.* He never said, "No, I'm not 100 years old. I'm more like 20 or 25."

God doesn't want us to deny problems exists. He doesn't advocate lying or "mind over matter." He's just saying, "Don't consider problems; switch over and consider the Word. Don't deny that the problem is there; just observe the Word and keep your eyes on the answer."

I once overheard someone say to another person, "Oh, you look sick, and you sound like you have a cold."

And being not weak in faith, [Abraham] considered not his own body now dead, when he was about an hundred years old, neither yet the deadness of Sarah's womb.

—Romans 4:19

The other person replied, "No, I don't. I'm not sick."

The first person said, "Well, your nose is running."

"No, it isn't."

"But you sound sick."

"No, I'm not sick," the second person insisted. But everyone around him could see he was. This person thought he was in faith, but he was really just denying the problem.

God doesn't want us to do that. He simply wants us to say, "It doesn't matter what I look like, feel like, or sound like. The only thing that matters is what God says. God tells me that by Jesus' stripes I was healed, and I believe Him!"

So don't deny the problem or try to think it away. Just look at it and say, "Who cares? The answer is mine—I have God's Word on it!"

Confession

I don't deny the problems that arise. I just believe God's Word, which is greater than problems, symptoms, or circumstances. I'm fully persuaded that what God has promised, He's able to do. (Rom. 4:21.)

Fix Your Eyes on God's Word

Wherefore let him that thinketh he standeth take heed lest he fall.

—1 Corinthians 10:12

The enemy will do anything in the world to get a believer's eyes off the answer and back on the problem.

For instance, I've heard people say, "I believe I'm healed! I believe I'm healed!" But when their bodies started to feel a little better, they've gotten their eyes off the Word and back over on their bodies. Then they say, "Oh, I know I'm getting better now because I *feel* better."

That sounds good, but if believers get their eyes off the Word for *any reason,* it could get them in trouble. If they say, "I know I'm healed because my body feels better," what will they do if their bodies feel worse the next day? More than likely, they'll fall back into doubt and unbelief.

We don't need any other reason to believe we're well except 1 Peter 2:24: "By Jesus' stripes, we were healed." If the enemy can keep us watching our symptoms—whether those symptoms are getting better or worse— he has control over us.

But as we keep our eyes on the Word, it doesn't matter what our bodies feel like. Ultimately, they will have to respond to that anointed Word.

Confession

I'm not moved by what I see or feel. I'm moved only by
the Word of God. I know I'm healed simply because
the Bible says by Jesus' stripes, I was healed.

Turn Your Face to the Wall

King Hezekiah was sick unto death. In other words, he suffered from a terminal illness. A lot of people are shaken when doctors tell them they're not going to live. Imagine what it was like for Hezekiah when God gave him that message.

The prophet Isaiah came to the king and said, "Thus saith the Lord, Set thine house in order: for thou shalt die, and not live." It's important to understand that God wasn't judging the man. God was simply giving Hezekiah a natural diagnosis: He was going to die. Therefore, Hezekiah was supposed to set his house in order.

But the king decided he would rather live. The next verse says, "Then Hezekiah turned his face toward the wall, and prayed unto the Lord." Hezekiah not only prayed, but he also *turned his face to the wall.* What does that mean? Well, the prophet Isaiah had just laid out King Hezekiah's situation before him. The king was keenly aware of his symptoms, pain, and dismal future. But in response, he turned his face to the wall—away from all natural circumstances—and talked to God.

He turned his back on everything but Almighty God. What happened? King Hezekiah *lived!*

In those days was Hezekiah sick unto death. And Isaiah the prophet...said unto him, Thus saith the Lord, Set thine house in order: for thou shalt die, and not live.

Then Hezekiah turned his face toward the wall, and prayed unto the Lord.

—Isaiah 38:1,2

Confession

When symptoms attack my body, I turn my face to the wall and say, "Father, thank You that Your Word is true." I don't deny symptoms, but I don't dwell on them either. I look to Almighty God and receive the healing He's provided for me.

Believing God Is Easy

Have faith in God. For verily I say unto you, That whosoever shall say unto this mountain, Be thou removed, and be thou cast into the sea; and shall not doubt in his heart, but shall believe that those things which he saith shall come to pass; he shall have whatsoever he saith.

Therefore I say unto you, What things soever ye desire, when ye pray, believe that ye receive them, and ye shall have them.

—Mark 11:22-24

Jesus gives His disciples some good instruction on the subject of faith here. He starts out by saying, "Have faith in God." Then in verse 23, Jesus explains the two foundational principles: *Believe in your heart and say with your mouth.*

Verse 24 starts with the word *therefore,* which connects verse 24 with the previous verses. That tells us Jesus is still teaching on the subject of faith.

"When ye pray, *believe,*" Jesus said. But why? It all seemed so hard.

I wondered, *Lord, why did You make it so hard? Why do we have to believe? Why can't we just throw a prayer out and see if You take it or leave it?* But I tried that method for years, and it didn't work.

Then one day I realized, *Lord, believing isn't hard! It's the easiest thing in the world!*

You see, you've never prayed a prayer in your life without believing something. Believing is the easiest, most natural thing in the world. The question is, *what do you believe?*

And what does God want you to believe? "When ye pray, *believe that ye receive.*" Believe that your request is granted—and you *shall* have it.

Confession

God says He's the God who heals me. I ask Him
now to heal me and believe I receive my request.

Believe That You Receive

I remember when I first got saved, I'd pray, "Oh Lord, I ask You to heal me in Jesus' name. I ask You for healing now. Amen." Then when someone would ask, "Did you get anything?" I'd check my body and say, "Well, no, I don't think so." And according to my faith it would be done unto me. I'd pray and then I'd believe I wouldn't get anything, so I wouldn't get anything. My faith worked all the time.

Therefore I say unto you, What things soever ye desire, when ye pray, believe that ye receive them, and ye shall have them.

—Mark 11:24

But Jesus did *not* say, "When you pray, believe you *don't receive anything,* and you'll have it." It sounds funny, but a lot of us prayed that way for years. A lot of people still do. They pray and then check to see whether their bodies feel any better or whether the symptoms are gone. And if nothing is different, they don't believe they received anything.

That's not what Jesus said to do. If we want His results, we have to follow His instructions. He didn't say, "When you pray, believe you didn't receive." He said, "When you pray, *believe you receive.*"

Confession

When I pray for healing, I don't check to see if symptoms are gone or if anything in my body has changed. I believe I receive when I pray, and God sees to it that my healing manifests.

The Present Tense of Faith

Therefore I say unto you, What things soever ye desire, when ye pray, believe that ye receive them, and ye shall have them."

—Mark 11:24

Here's another way to pray that sounds really spiritual but is *wrong:* "Oh Father, I ask You to heal me in Jesus' name. I ask You for results. Amen." Now, so far this person is doing fine.

But when someone asks the person, "Well, did you get anything?" the person checks to see and says, "Well, I tell you one thing. I believe God *is going* to heal me."

That sounds really good because the person is saying, *"I believe."*

I've heard people do this. They're sincerely believing in their hearts, but they're sincerely wrong in the way they're believing.

I was talking with a friend who mentioned a person we both knew. He said, "Man, he didn't get his healing, and I know he was in faith."

"Really?" I asked.

"Yes, I heard him. He kept saying, 'You watch—I believe God *is going* to heal me.'"

But Jesus didn't say, "When you pray, believe you're *going to* get something, and you'll have it." No, *faith always speaks in the present tense.*

If we analyze that person's words, it becomes obvious what he's saying: "I prayed, but I don't feel any better. Therefore, I don't believe I'm better. But although I haven't received a thing yet, you can bet I'll believe it when I feel better!"

But Jesus told us exactly how to pray in faith: "When you pray, believe that you receive"—right now, present tense.

Confession

Healing belongs to me as a child of God. I'm not going to be healed— I'm already healed because I believe I receive my answer when I pray.

Two Points in Time

We're still talking about the prayer of faith—the kind of prayer that receives from God.

I always thought the prayer of faith involved just one point in time. I thought, *Well, you're supposed to pray and then check to see if anything happened. If it didn't, too bad—try again later. See if you can catch God in a better mood.*

But this Scripture shows us that the prayer of faith includes *two points in time.* Jesus said, (1) "When you pray, believe you receive your answer"—*present tense.* Then He said, (2) "And you shall have it"—*future tense.*

> *Therefore I say unto you, What things soever ye desire, when ye pray, believe that ye receive them, and ye shall have them.*
>
> *—Mark 11:24*

When will you have it? *After* you believe you receive it. When do you believe you receive it? *Before* you have it.

"Well, I can't believe because I don't have it." But you have to believe *before* you have it. "How can I believe I have it when I don't?" You believe you receive when you pray, and *then you shall have* your answer. "Yes, but I don't have it." But you have to *believe you receive first.*

Some people get hung up on this key point and put the cart before the horse. They want to receive their answer before they believe they received.

The first step is to pray and believe we receive the answer, "walking by faith and not by sight." (2 Cor. 5:7.) The second step is to actually see our answer in full manifestation.

Confession

When I need healing in my body, I ask God for it and believe I receive what He said is mine. Then I stand in faith until my healing manifests.

First the Believing, Then the Having

Therefore I say unto you, What things soever ye desire, when ye pray, believe that ye receive them, and ye shall have them.

—Mark 11:24

We are to pray, believing we receive, and then the answer comes. But well-meaning Christians say, "You know, I have trouble believing I have something until I feel it." Or, "I'm not going to believe I'm healed until I feel better. I just can't believe I've received anything I can't see."

In case that thought has ever come to you, let me ask you this: Do you believe you have a brain? Have you ever seen your brain? That may seem like a strange question, but it proves a point. You have no proof that you have a brain. The anatomy book says it's there; a doctor may say it's there. But otherwise, you have no proof.

When you stop to think about it, about 80 percent of the things we believe are accepted as truth without feeling or seeing them. In school, I believed what I read in the history books. For instance, I wasn't around when George Washington was alive, but I believed the history book when it said he was our first president.

Well, we need to attribute more credibility to God's Word than we do history books. Sometimes we're willing to believe anything we read except the Bible; then we say, "Lord, give me a sign."

We have to believe we receive; *then* we will have. First comes the believing; then comes the having. When we operate in that kind of faith, we get so excited believing we forget to check when the answer manifests.

Confession

I believe I receive the healing God has provided for me,
and I shall see it manifested in my body.

Believe Without Seeing First

Therefore I say unto you, What things soever ye desire, when ye pray, believe that ye receive them, and ye shall have them.

—Mark 11:24

Some ask, "Is it scriptural to believe you receive before you see or feel anything?" Let's look at a Bible illustration to find the answer.

Remember, Jesus told the disciples over and over again, "I'm going, but I'll be back." But when He went to the Cross, the disciples thought He was dead and gone for good.

But then Jesus was resurrected and appeared to His disciples, though Thomas wasn't present at the time. When Thomas showed up later, the others told him, "We've seen the Lord!" Thomas replied, "Except I shall see in his hands the print of the nails, and put my finger into the print of the nails, and thrust my hand into his side, I will not believe" (John 20:25).

Thomas, who probably thought he was being spiritual, was saying, "I won't believe anything until I can see and touch Him."

A few days later the disciples were all together, and Jesus walked in. The first thing He did was say to Thomas, "Reach hither thy finger, and behold my hands; and reach hither thy hand, and thrust it into my side: and be not faithless, but believing" (John 20:27). In other words, Jesus told him, "Quit being faithless; just believe."

Jesus set doubting Thomas straight: "Because thou hast seen me, thou hast believed: blessed are they that have not seen, and yet have believed" (John 20:29).

Jesus said the blessed ones are those who believe without seeing first. I want to be on the blessed side of life, don't you?

Confession

I'm blessed because I believe I receive the promises of God's Word—now—before I see them.

Move Up to the Next Faith Level

And there was a certain nobleman, whose son was sick at Capernaum. When he heard that Jesus was come out of Judea into Galilee, he went unto him, and besought him that he would come down, and heal his son: for he was at the point of death.

Then said Jesus unto him, Except ye see signs and wonders, ye will not believe.

—John 4:46-48

Understand this situation. This man was a nobleman; he was a ruler, and he was important. When he said, "Come to my house," people didn't question him; they just asked, "What time?" I'm sure no one refused.

The nobleman had heard of Jesus and came to see the Miracle Worker. He said to Jesus, "Come down to my house; my son is at the point of death. Come and heal him."

Jesus turned to him and said, "If you don't see signs and wonders, you won't believe." Jesus had instantly located this man's faith level.

Think back to Jairus, the ruler of the synagogue in Mark 5, who came to Jesus and said, "Come to my house. My little daughter is at the point of death. But if You lay hands on her, she will live." Jesus went with him, and the child was healed.

Why did Jesus go with one father and not the other? I don't know why, but I do know Jesus was always led by the Holy Ghost. And He got results in both cases.

I believe Jesus wanted to grab the nobleman by his faith and yank him up to a higher level so his life would be changed forever.

Confession

I step out this day on God's Word of healing and expect it
to effect a healing and a cure in my physical body.

Faith Comes Before the Physical Evidence

The nobleman said, "Jesus, if You come, my son will live; if You don't, he'll die."

Jesus replied, "Go your way, and believe what I say: Your son lives."

That put the nobleman in a difficult spot. He'd traveled more than twenty miles to see Jesus, which was a long trip even if he had the fastest chariot around. He didn't see or feel anything—no burning bush, no goose bumps, no gifts of the Spirit in manifestation. All he had to hold on to were the bare words of Jesus.

So the nobleman had to make the choice: Should I stand here and argue with Jesus or take Him at His Word?

The nobleman decided to turn around and head home, believing the word that was spoken. As he traveled back to his home, the devil probably talked to his mind, saying, *How can you just accept Jesus' words? Your son is in bad shape, and Jesus isn't coming back with you.*

The nobleman saith unto him, Sir, come down ere my child die.

Jesus saith unto him, Go thy way; thy son liveth. And the man believed the word that Jesus had spoken unto him, and he went his way.

—John 4:49,50

Yet the nobleman demonstrated true faith. He traveled home, believing his son was well, with nothing but God's Word to stand on. He probably traveled at least ten miles before he met his servants who gave him the good news: "Thy son liveth" (v. 51).

This is a picture of faith toward God. The minute the nobleman took Jesus at His word and headed for home, his son began to amend.

Confession

I count my healing done—no matter what I see or feel.
My body amends from this very hour.

Amending "From That Hour"

And as he was now going down, his servants met him, and told him, saying, Thy son liveth.

Then inquired he of them the hour when he began to amend. And they said unto him, Yesterday at the seventh hour the fever left him. So the father knew that it was at the same hour...Jesus said unto him, Thy son liveth: and himself believed, and his whole house.

—John 4:51-53

Jesus told the nobleman, "Thy son liveth" (v. 50). The next day, the servants who met the nobleman on the road home said the same thing word for word. When the man believed the word Jesus spoke, his son was healed, and it changed his entire household.

God's Word is just as powerful as His physical presence. If we'll take Him at His Word, it will do anything He could do if He stood right here in the flesh. That's what God is trying to teach His Church.

Take God at His Word. Believe what He says no matter what the situation looks like, sounds like, or feels like.

Now, notice that the nobleman inquired the hour his son *began* to amend. He understood that his son's healing had been *gradual.*

This is where a lot of people have trouble receiving. Many people stand in healing lines then return to their seats thinking, *I don't feel better; guess I didn't get anything.* These people think all healings have to be instant.

Instant healings are available, but it's just as scriptural to amend "from that hour." The truth is, more people are healed gradually than instantly. All we should care about is that God heals us—whether it takes minutes, hours, or longer.

Confession

The minute I take God at His Word, my body begins to amend.

Healed as They Went

The ten lepers cried out, "Jesus, Master, have mercy on us." Apparently, they'd heard of Jesus the Healer because they called Him "Master." And since faith comes by hearing, they came in faith.

However, under the Levitical Law, lepers were to be stoned if they came within 100 paces of a healthy human. So these ten lepers stood afar off and cried out to Jesus for help. Jesus instructed them to go show themselves to the priests. Verse 14 says, "And it came to pass, that, as they went, they were cleansed."

Did you notice that the lepers weren't cleansed until *after they went?* Many people don't get healed because they don't "went"! They sit around hoping they will somehow receive a miracle. Meanwhile, God wants them to believe they receive and go their way in faith.

That "went" part was the lepers' act of faith. When Jesus told them to show themselves to the priests, they immediately turned around and started on their way. In the natural, their condition wasn't any better. But when they obeyed Jesus' words, they were healed.

And as he entered into a certain village, there met him ten men that were lepers, which stood afar off: and they lifted up their voices, and said, Jesus, Master, have mercy on us.

And when he saw them, he said unto them, Go shew yourselves unto the priests. And it came to pass, that, as they went, they were cleansed.

—Luke 17:12-14

Likewise, we have to take God at His Word, regardless of what we see or feel, and go our way.

Confession

Symptoms may seem to keep me "afar off" from victory, but as I go my way—believing—God's healing power works wholeness in me.

Healing Is the Work of God

*...Jesus...saw a man
which was blind
from his birth. And
his disciples asked
him, saying, Master,
who did sin, this
man, or his parents,
that he was born
blind?*

*Jesus answered,
Neither hath this
man sinned, nor his
parents: but that the
works of God should
be made manifest in
him. I must work the
works of him that
sent me.*

—John 9:1-4

In Jesus' day, religious people thought if someone were born sick, either the parents sinned before the child was born or the child sinned in the womb. So the disciples asked Jesus, "Who sinned—the man or his parents?"

Now, Jesus' response in the *King James Version* is unclear. It sounds as though God made this man blind just so Jesus could heal him and give God the glory.

But, remember, the New Testament was originally written in Greek with no punctuation—no periods, no commas. All punctuation was later inserted by Bible translators. Therefore, you could change a period or question mark without changing anything in the original manuscripts.

So let's look at this verse another way. "Neither hath this man sinned, nor his parents [*period*]." Jesus answered their question. "But that the works of God should be made manifest in him [*comma*], I must work the works of him that sent me."

Changing two punctuation marks, not in the original manuscripts, changes the whole meaning and takes the blame off God. Suddenly the verse lines up with the rest of Scripture.

Jesus did work the works of the One who sent Him all right—and healed the blind man.

Confession

Jesus never made anyone sick, but healed all who came
to Him in faith. I come to Him now in faith and
receive God's work of healing in my body.

Jesus Bore Our Sickness

Jesus took our infirmities and bore our sicknesses. Some people have said to me, "Now, Brother, you must realize this verse is talking about a spiritual healing." But that erroneous thinking has put people in early graves. The infirmities and sicknesses God is talking about here aren't spiritual in nature. Just back up about four verses, and you'll see what Jesus did to fulfill that Old Testament Scripture.

A centurion had come to Jesus and said, "My servant is home sick of the palsy. Just speak the Word and my servant will be healed." (Matt. 8:8.) "And Jesus said unto the centurion, Go thy way; and as thou hast believed, so be it done unto thee. And his servant was healed in the selfsame hour" (v. 13). *That's physical healing.*

Then Jesus went to Peter's house, where Peter's mother-in-law lay sick with a fever. "And he touched her hand, and the fever left her: and she arose, and ministered unto them" (v. 15). *That's physical healing.*

Finally, verse 16 says, "When the even was come, they brought unto him many that were possessed with devils: and he cast out the spirits with his word, and healed all that were sick." *That's physical healing.*

Then, after all those physical healings, Matthew comes back to verse 17 where we began reading and said Jesus fulfilled Isaiah's prophecy by physically healing people. That means Jesus bore our physical infirmities on the Cross so we could live healthy and whole all the days of our lives.

That it might be fulfilled which was spoken by Esaias the prophet, saying, Himself took our infirmities, and bare our sicknesses.

—Matthew 8:17

Confession

Jesus paid for my sins and sicknesses.
I'm free because He already bore them for me.

Let God Use You To Heal the Sick

And he said unto them, Go ye into all the world, and preach the gospel to every creature.

And these signs shall follow them that believe; In my name...they shall lay hands on the sick, and they shall recover.

—Mark 16:15,17,18

Jesus listed several signs that are to follow those who believe in Him. One important sign is that "they shall lay hands on the sick, and they shall recover." This sign is not just for preachers. It's for *all* believers.

Some say, "Well, I don't know why God never uses me that way." I made the mistake of thinking that one time. I read that Scripture and thought, *Boy, I don't know why God never uses me to heal anyone. He never works through me to lay hands on the sick.*

But then I got quiet for a minute. (You know, if you'll get quiet, you'll receive some answers.) All of a sudden, I heard down on the inside: "How many people have you laid hands on recently?"

Well, that woke me up. I started laying hands on people, and guess what? They got healed!

If we'll just be obedient to the Word, it will work. We don't have to wonder why God never uses us. As we start laying hands on the sick, He will. It's up to us. It's our job. Healing the sick is part of the Gospel, and we're to take the Gospel into all the world.

Confession

I'm a believer, so I expect signs to follow me according to the Word.
When I lay hands on the sick, they are healed.
God's Word works in me, for me, and through me.

Tell the World, "God Wants You Well!"

Jesus Christ was the Word that became flesh and dwelt among us. During His earthly ministry, Jesus healed all who came to Him in faith. Now we have the written Word, and it's full of healing from one end to the other.

No wonder God said, "He sent his word, and healed them, and delivered them from their destructions" (Ps. 107:20). No wonder He said, "Attend to my words; incline thine ear unto my sayings. Let them not depart from thine eyes; keep them in the midst of thine heart. For they are life unto those that find them, and health to all their flesh" (Prov. 4:20-22).

In the beginning was the Word, and the Word was with God, and the Word was God.

And the Word was made flesh, and dwelt among us....

—John 1:1,14

If we take time to read and study the Word, the revelation knowledge that God wants us healthy will become a part of us. We'll be able to step into a life of divine health. You see, we can only receive healing by faith when we know it's God's will to heal us because faith is believing God's known will and acting like it's true. We have to know the Word says healing is ours.

Jesus, the Word made flesh, was sent to heal us. When we received Him as Savior, Jesus also became our Healer. Now, by inspiration of the Holy Ghost, we've been given the Word in written form. And no matter how we look at it, we'll find healing from every angle. Jesus is the Word, and Jesus is the Healer.

Confession

God's Word was sent to heal me. I keep it before my eyes, and it becomes life and medicine to all my flesh.

Under the Shadow of His Wings

But unto you that fear my name shall the Sun of righteousness arise with healing in his wings....

—Malachi 4:2

One day I was meditating on the Word, when suddenly this Scripture rose up in me. I got to thinking, *Who is the "Sun of righteousness"? Jesus!* Then I thought, *Glory to God! He arose with healing in His wings.*

I asked the Lord, "Why is healing in His wings, and how do I get under those wings?"

I remembered Psalm 91:1-4 AMP:

> He who dwells in the secret place of the Most High shall remain stable and fixed under the shadow of the Almighty [Whose power no foe can withstand]. I will say of the Lord, He is my Refuge and my Fortress, my God; on Him I lean and rely, and in Him I [confidently] trust.

> For [then] He will deliver you from the snare of the fowler and from the deadly pestilence. [Then] *He will cover you with His pinions, and under His wings shall you trust and find refuge.*

You find refuge under God's wings when you say, "Thank God for Jesus! He's my refuge, my fortress, my healer, and my Savior." Once you've confessed Jesus as Lord, you're under His wings full of healing. So just reach out and grab hold!

Confession

Jesus, my God, my healer, my refuge, my fortress.
He arose with healing in His wings, and I take refuge
under those wings. I put my trust in the Sun of
righteousness and His healing power.

Present Your Body a Living Sacrifice

Paul tells us here to present our bodies as a living sacrifice to God. It's interesting to note what God says about sacrifices in Malachi 1:7-8,13.

Ye offer polluted bread upon mine altar; and ye say, Wherein have we polluted thee? In that ye say, The table of the Lord is contemptible. And if ye offer the blind for sacrifice, is it not evil? and if ye offer the lame and sick, is it not evil?...

...And ye brought that which was torn, and the lame, and the sick; thus ye brought an offering: should I accept this of your hand? saith the Lord.

I beseech you therefore, brethren, by the mercies of God, that ye present your bodies a living sacrifice, holy, acceptable unto God, which is your reasonable service.

—Romans 12:1

God isn't saying He gets angry with us when we present our sick, broken, lame bodies as a sacrifice to Him. He's saying we need to line our bodies up with His Word and believe that Jesus took our infirmities and bore our sicknesses. Then we can present our bodies as a living sacrifice to Him, and He'll make them whole.

He said in His Word that by Jesus' stripes, you were healed. So just begin to believe that in your heart, say it with your mouth, and act like it's true. Then you can present your body as a living sacrifice, no matter what it looks like or feels like, and the power of God will make it whole.

Confession

I present my body to the Lord as a living sacrifice, believing I'm healed because Jesus took my sicknesses and carried my pains.

In Remembrance

...Jesus...took bread: and when he had given thanks, he brake it, and said, Take, eat: this is my body, which is broken for you: this do in remembrance of me. After the same manner also he took the cup, when he had supped, saying, This cup is the new testament in my blood: this do ye, as oft as ye drink it, in remembrance of me. For as often as ye eat this bread, and drink this cup, ye do shew the Lord's death till he come.

—1 Corinthians 11:23-26

In Exodus 12, God told His people living in Egypt in bondage, "Slay a spotless lamb and put its blood on the doorposts; then roast it and eat it. But before you do, pack your bags, put your marching shoes on, and get ready to travel because you're coming out of bondage."

As the Israelites ate the Passover lamb, they looked ahead to the redemptive work Jesus would accomplish on the Cross. Under the new covenant, we take Communion to remember what Jesus already accomplished for us.

We also were once trapped in bondage, but the perfect Lamb shed His blood to redeem us. Therefore, God's message to us is similar to what He told the Israelites. He says to us, "When you partake of Communion, put your marching shoes on, and get ready to come out of bondage!"

Communion services should be some of the biggest healing rallies around because we should partake of the emblems, saying, "Thank You, Jesus, by Your shed blood my sins are washed away. By Your broken body, I'm healed. And by Your chastisement, I have peace of mind." (Isa. 53:5.)

Confession

On the Cross, Jesus freed me from every yoke of bondage.
In remembrance, I thank You, Jesus, for the price You've paid.

Seated in Heavenly Places

We're seated in heavenly places in Christ Jesus. Ephesians 1:3 says, "Blessed be the God...who hath blessed us with all spiritual blessings in heavenly places in Christ." We're blessed to be a part of the body of Christ because all things have been put under His feet. We may just be the skin on the bottom of the left foot; but sickness is still beneath us, and we walk on top of it!

Sickness cannot exist in heavenly places, and that's where we are. That's the way God looks at us. When we beg or plead for healing, He doesn't know what we're talking about. He sees every satanic bondage beneath our feet.

Sickness keeps trying to crawl up on the body of Christ, but it's up to us to resist it. James 4:7 says, "Resist the devil, and he will flee from you." And Paul exhorts us never to give place to the devil. (Eph. 4:27.)

Even when we were dead in sins, hath quickened us together with Christ, (by grace ye are saved;) and hath raised us up together, and made us sit together in heavenly places in Christ Jesus.

—Ephesians 2:5,6

Jesus gave us all authority over the devil. He told His disciples, "All power is given unto me in heaven and in earth. Go ye therefore" (Matt. 28:18,19). He also said, "Behold, I give unto you power to tread on serpents and scorpions, and over all the power of the enemy: and nothing shall by any means hurt you" (Luke 10:19).

Jesus has overcome the enemy, so keep sickness under your feet where it belongs. Refuse to let the devil rob you.

Confession

I'm part of the body of Christ, seated with Jesus in heavenly places. Sickness is under my feet.

Draw Strength From Jesus

I can do all things through Christ which strengtheneth me.

—Philippians 4:13

Jesus Christ is our strength. Yet, when sickness has tried to attach itself to me, it hasn't given me strength; it's drawn strength out of me. But then I turn to the promises in God's Word. As I continually keep my eyes on Jesus and draw strength from Him, sickness has to go.

In the Old Testament, when the children of Israel were bitten by serpents, they had to look steadfastly at the brass serpent on the pole in order to be healed. (Num. 21:8,9.) That brass serpent was a type of Jesus who became sin for us when He hung on the Cross. (2 Cor. 5:21.) If we fix our gaze upon Jesus and His redemptive work, we also can receive healing.

Yet that means we must look at Him—not at symptoms. The reason some have trouble getting rid of symptoms is because they spend too much time looking at them. Second Corinthians 4:18 says, "We look not at the things which are seen, but at the things which are not seen: for the things which are seen are temporal; but the things which are not seen are eternal."

That which is seen is temporal, or subject to change. That which is not seen is eternal, or not subject to change. In other words, we could say, "For we look not at the symptoms but at the promises of God's Word because symptoms are subject to change according to the promises of God's Word."

Confession

As I keep my eyes on Jesus, circumstances and symptoms
must change. God's Word will never change. I attend to
God's Word, and it's life and medicine to my flesh.

Don't Accept the Devil's Package

If the devil is trying to put symptoms on you, you have the authority to make him go away.

The reason Christians have so much trouble getting rid of sickness and disease is because they accept the symptoms to begin with. The devil rings the front doorbell delivering the package. Then some folks say, "Oh, let's see—watery eyes, runny nose, sore throat, headache. Yes, I do believe I'm getting the flu!" They sign for the package and then suddenly say, "Hey, wait a minute! I don't want this!" But once received, the package is difficult to give back.

Submit yourselves therefore to God. Resist the devil, and he will flee from you.

—James 4:7

So when sickness comes knocking on your door, remember not to accept the package. Say, "Let's see—watery eyes, runny nose, headache, sore throat. No, no, no! I won't take it. Devil, I resist you in the name of Jesus! You won't give that to me! I've been redeemed from poverty, sickness, and death. In the name of Jesus, you take your symptoms and get out of here!"

You have the authority to do that. So take your stand against the enemy. Refuse every package of symptoms he tries to deliver to your doorstep.

Confession

I rebuke sickness when it tries to come on me.
I exercise my faith when I first notice symptoms,
and those symptoms have to go, in Jesus' name.

Fear Not—Only Believe

For God hath not given us the spirit of fear; but of power, and of love, and of a sound mind.

—2 Timothy 1:7

Do you know what happens when you fear something? Job tells you in Job 3:25: "For the thing which I greatly feared is come upon me...." Fear opens the door for the very things you fear to enter your life.

Fear often opens the door to sickness by producing worry. In fact, about 80 percent of hospital patients got there because of worry. They say, "I'm afraid I'll catch the flu," or "I'm afraid I'll get cancer," or "I'm afraid I'll have an accident." They continually confess, "I'm afraid of this; I'm afraid of that."

The Bible says, "Fear not; only believe." (Luke 8:50.) You see, you can't fear and believe at the same time. Fear opens the door to the devil and gives him room to move. In fact, fear is faith in the devil. Fear receives the worst the enemy comes up with. Faith in God receives the best God has for you.

But fear can't just latch onto you. It has to present itself to you; then it's up to you whether you receive it or resist it.

So when fear hits you, realize you have the ability to get rid of it. You can say, "Fear, I resist you in the name of Jesus! You'll have no part of me, and I'll have no part of you!"

It's your choice. If you're experiencing all kinds of fear in your life, don't focus on the fear. Just get full of God's Word, and the fears will disappear.

Confession

Jesus said, "Fear not; only believe."
I do not fear sickness, for God sent His Word to heal me.

Know God's Will

It's important to know God's will regarding the healing you need because faith only operates on God's known will.

For example, if I told you I had $1000 in my pocket, you wouldn't come running over to me to get it because I never promised I'd give it to you. You'd realize I had the money, but that wouldn't necessarily mean it was for you.

Now faith is the substance of things hoped for, the evidence of things not seen.

—Hebrews 11:1

But suppose I said to you, "I have $1000 in my pocket, and I want to give it to you. Just come and get it." At that point, you'd have my promise as a foundation for your faith. And undoubtedly you'd quickly take hold of my promise and come receive your money. Once you knew my will on the matter, you would be confident to receive or operate in faith.

It's the same way with God. You can't operate in faith until you know what His will is in a matter. But as you go through His Word, you can find His will concerning anything you need, including healing. You can find out Jesus took your infirmities and bore your sicknesses. You can discover by Jesus' stripes, you are healed. You can know beyond a shadow of a doubt God wants you well.

Confession

I know absolutely and without a doubt God's will for me regarding healing. Jesus took my infirmities and bore my sicknesses because my Father wants me well.

Faith Turns God Loose

And, behold, there cometh one of the rulers of the synagogue, Jairus by name; and when he saw him, he fell at his feet, and besought him greatly, saying, My little daughter lieth at the point of death: I pray thee, come and lay thy hands on her, that she may be healed; and she shall live.

And Jesus went with him....

—Mark 5:22-24

Jesus started walking with Jairus toward his house. About that time, the woman with the issue of blood came up behind Him and touched the hem of His garment. Jesus turned and asked, "Who touched Me?" The woman fell down and told Jesus how she'd been healed. (Mark 5:25-33.)

All this was going on while Jairus' daughter was at home near death. When Jesus finished with the woman, they all started again toward Jairus' house. But just then someone came running from Jairus' home, saying, "It's too late. Your daughter has died."

Jesus immediately turned to Jairus and made a profound statement: *"Fear not; only believe."* Jesus laid out a choice for Jairus, telling him, "If you keep operating in faith, your child will be healed. But if you step over into fear, you shut off My power."

You see, our words open the door for the devil to attack us. Proverbs 6:2 says, "Thou art snared with the words of thy mouth, thou art taken with the words of thy mouth."

But Jairus made the right choice. He didn't speak one word of doubt or fear, and his little girl was raised from the dead. His faith turned God loose to work in his daughter's life.

Confession

I refuse to allow fear in my life. I speak words of life
and truth that turn God loose to work in my behalf.

Paul's "Thorn"–Persecution

The subject of Paul's thorn is a common argument against healing. Many have taught Paul's thorn was a disease in his body. But in context, you can see that Paul was talking about *persecutions:*

> Of the Jews five times received I forty stripes save one. Thrice was I beaten with rods, once was I stoned, thrice I suffered shipwreck, a night and a day I have been in the deep.
>
> In weariness and painfulness, in watchings often, in hunger and thirst, in fastings often, in cold and nakedness.
>
> 2 Corinthians 11:24-25,27

Unquestionably, there were many persecutions in one form or another. Every place Paul went, there was a spirit stirring people up to persecute him. But Paul never said anything to indicate his thorn in the flesh was even remotely connected to disease.

However, Paul did say the thorn was a messenger of Satan, *not* a messenger of God: "There was given to me a thorn in the flesh, the messenger of Satan to buffet me." So we see that Paul's thorn wasn't disease and it wasn't from God.

Confession

Paul's thorn wasn't from God and neither are diseases that attack me. I overcome the devil in every situation, and I'm the healed of the Lord.

And lest I should be exalted above measure through the abundance of the revelations, there was given to me a thorn in the flesh, the messenger of Satan to buffet me, lest I should be exalted above measure.

For this thing I besought the Lord thrice, that it might depart from me. And he said unto me, My grace is sufficient for thee: for my strength is made perfect in weakness.

Most gladly therefore will I rather glory in my infirmities, that the power of Christ may rest upon me.

—2 Corinthians 12:7-9

Paul's "Thorn in the Flesh"

And lest I should be exalted above measure through the abundance of the revelations, there was given to me a thorn in the flesh, the messenger of Satan to buffet me, lest I should be exalted above measure.

—2 Corinthians 12:7

People have been telling me for years that Paul's "thorn in the flesh" was sickness. Some say it was an eye disease God gave him to keep him humble. But that explanation contradicts the Scriptures.

How was Paul exalted? He received visions and revelations from the Lord. God revealed to him great mysteries, which those who walked and talked with Jesus for three years didn't yet understand. Paul was also in the process of writing two-thirds of the New Testament, which we live by today.

Paul said, "There was given to me a thorn in the flesh, a messenger of Satan, to buffet me." Well, God wouldn't have sent a messenger of Satan to Paul. And God certainly wasn't going to exalt Paul by giving him visions and revelations just to make him sick and to keep him from being exalted.

The word *messenger* in the original Greek is the word "angelos." It refers to an angel or "one sent."[1] In this case, it refers to a demon spirit Satan sent to harass Paul. Satan wanted to hinder Paul any way he could because he knew those who read Paul's letters would follow his Holy Spirit-inspired instructions and walk in victory. So let's defeat Satan's purpose and start walking in God's victory today.

Confession

God didn't send sickness to humble Paul, and He doesn't send sickness to humble me. I rebuke disease in Jesus' name, for it has no part in God's will for me. I receive healing that belongs to me.

His Grace Is Sufficient

Some people interpret this Scripture by saying, "After Paul prayed three times, God replied, 'No, I want you to keep that thorn. You need it to keep you humble and pious.'"

But that isn't what God meant. God said, "My grace is sufficient for thee."

What is God's grace? It's God's *unmerited favor* given to us in the form of His Word, name, Spirit, healing, power, and authority. God's grace is the source of the unmerited blessings He sent us through Jesus Christ. We didn't deserve any of those blessings, but Jesus made us righteous so we *could* deserve them. That's the measure of God's grace, and He told Paul, "My grace is sufficient for thee."

One aspect of God's grace is the name of Jesus. Jesus delegated His authority, might, and dominion to us through His name. Then He said in Mark 16:17, "In my name shall [believers] cast out devils."

Jesus was telling Paul, "Look, I've given you everything you need to get rid of that evil messenger. Take authority over it. My grace is sufficient for you. But don't go after that messenger of Satan in your own strength—go in Mine. Use My strength to resist the devil in Jesus' name, and he'll flee from you!"

For this thing I besought the Lord thrice, that it might depart from me. And he said unto me, My grace is sufficient for thee: for my strength is made perfect in weakness.

Most gladly therefore will I rather glory in my infirmities, that the power of Christ may rest upon me.

—2 Corinthians 12:8,9

Confession

God's grace is also sufficient for me. He's given me the name of Jesus, which is greater than any power that comes against me.
I'm healed and strong in Jesus' name.

The End Result

Now a certain man was sick, named Lazarus, of Bethany, the town of Mary and her sister Martha.

Therefore his sisters sent unto him, saying, Lord, behold, he whom thou lovest is sick.

When Jesus heard that, he said, This sickness is not unto death, but for the glory of God, that the Son of God might be glorified thereby.

—John 11:1,3,4

Don't misunderstand Jesus' comment about Lazarus' sickness. Jesus was *not* saying, "Lazarus' sickness isn't unto death; nevertheless, he's suffering with this sickness to bring God glory."

If we're not careful, we can get confused because we don't study the Word enough to rightly divide it. Jesus wasn't talking about the problem; He was talking about the *end result.* Jesus always talked about the end result. He was saying here, "The end result of this sickness will not be death but the glory of God."

Again in John 11:40, Jesus told Martha, "I told you if you'd believe, you'd see the glory of God." The sickness took Lazarus' life for a while, but his life was given back to him when Jesus raised him from the dead. Thus, Lazarus' sickness wasn't for God's glory; it was his resurrection from the dead that brought God glory. That was the end result.

Confession

God is glorified when I'm healed and walking in health. The end result of my life will be to God's glory. I walk in health and run my race, and I will finish my course with joy.

Speak the Word and Go Your Way

Jesus came to a fig tree looking for fruit, but there was no fruit. So He cursed the fig tree and just walked away.

We can learn a faith lesson here. Although the tree didn't change immediately, Jesus didn't wonder whether His words had worked. He just walked away in faith knowing His words were working.

When they returned from Jerusalem the next day, His disciples said, "Master, the fig tree you cursed is withered away! It died from the roots!" (v. 21.) *Of course!*

Second Corinthians 5:7 says, "For we walk by faith, not by sight." You see, it didn't matter what Jesus *saw*. It was what He *believed* that made the difference.

That's the very basis of faith. Faith is walking by what God says instead of what you see—*because what God says will change what you see!*

Faith is placing your confidence in the truth. Romans 3:4 says, "Yea, let God be true, but every man a liar...." In John 17:17 Jesus says, "Thy word is truth." The only real truth we find in this world is the Word of God, and it takes precedence above experiences, opinions, or doctrines.

Speak words of faith, and your words will surely come to pass.

And on the morrow, when they were come from Bethany, he was hungry: and seeing a fig tree afar off having leaves, he came, if haply he might find any thing thereon: and when he came to it, he found nothing but leaves; for the time of figs was not yet. And Jesus answered and said unto it, No man eat fruit of thee hereafter for ever.

—Mark 11:12-14

Confession

I speak in faith over my body and call myself healed, whole, well, strong, and victorious.

Have the Faith of God

And in the morning, as they passed by, they saw the fig tree dried up from the roots. And Peter calling to remembrance saith unto him, Master, behold, the fig tree which thou cursedst is withered away.

And Jesus answering saith unto them, Have faith in God.

—Mark 11:20-22

Jesus was about to teach His disciples about faith. I can't think of a better Bible subject to get ahold of than faith. It touches every other area of life. Everything we do should be in faith, "for whatsoever is not of faith is sin" (Rom. 14:23).

Faith is the easiest thing in the world to understand. When faith is taught, little children usually understand it first; then they teach the adults. Faith is so simple most adults spend their time trying to figure it out. They think, *It can't be that simple.*

But Jesus made things simple for us. He taught about everyday things, such as fishing and farming. He explained spiritual principles so everyone could understand them.

Jesus started the faith lesson to the disciples by saying, "Have faith in God." That's easy. After all, God is the One who works miracles. He's the One who heals bodies. He's the One who purchased all things that pertain to life and godliness. Therefore, our faith is to be placed in Him.

Margin notes for Mark 11:22 in some Bibles say, "Have the faith *of* God." In other words, Jesus is telling us, "God gave you the same kind of faith He has, and it will operate for you the same way it operates for Him." After all, you're the child of a faith God.

Confession

As God's child, I have the God-kind of faith,
and I use that faith to call my body well.

You Have the Faith To Receive

Here Jesus gives us the two basic foundational principles of operating in faith: *believing in the heart* and *saying with the mouth.*

Have you ever thought the believing part sounded hard? People say all the time, "Oh, it's so hard to believe. I wish I could believe God."

One fellow replied to that comment, "Well, if you can't believe, you ought to get saved." Let me explain what he meant by that.

Ephesians 2:8 tells us how we get saved: "For by grace are ye saved *through faith;* and that not of yourselves: it is the gift of God." Then Romans 10:10 says, "With the *heart man believeth* unto righteousness; and with the mouth confession is made unto salvation."

So the simple fact that you're saved proves you have faith. *You've already used your faith to believe God for the biggest miracle in existence— the new birth.* When you were born again, God took out that heart of stone and put in a heart of flesh, giving you a brand-new spirit.

And Jesus answering saith unto them, Have faith in God. For verily I say unto you, That whosoever shall say unto this mountain, Be thou removed, and be thou cast into the sea; and shall not doubt in his heart, but shall believe that those things which he saith shall come to pass; he shall have whatsoever he saith.

—Mark 11:22,23

You used your faith to receive the gift of salvation. That proves you have the ability to believe God. Now it's just a matter of learning how to point your faith in another direction to receive God's other benefits and blessings.

Confession

I've already believed and received salvation. Now, I believe and receive healing just as easily as I received eternal life.

Faith Is of the Heart

For verily I say unto you, That whosoever shall say unto this mountain, Be thou removed, and be thou cast into the sea; and shall not doubt in his heart, but shall believe that those things which he saith shall come to pass; he shall have whatsoever he saith.

—Mark 11:23

Let's consider the two major principles of faith in this verse: *believing in the heart* and *saying with the mouth.*

People often make mistakes in the believing side of faith. You see, real faith is of the *heart, not the head.* Romans 10:10 confirms this, saying, "For with the heart man believeth unto righteousness...."

Now, it's important to understand that you can have faith in your heart with doubts in your head. For instance, I find Scriptures that cover my need, then I believe I receive what God has promised. On the inside, I have peace and rest, knowing I'm in faith. But at the same time, doubts hit my mind like machine gun bullets: *What if it doesn't work? It's not working.*

When doubts start coming to your mind, it's easy to think, *Well, I thought I believed, but I guess I didn't.* But just realize those doubts aren't yours. Cast them down and get rid of them in the name of Jesus. Don't try to believe with your head, or your faith will be up and down like a yo-yo.

Remember, it's with the heart—or spirit—that man believes. So if your mind gives you fits when you stand in faith, just shut your mind off and follow what's in your spirit.

Confession

I believe with my heart and refuse to allow doubts to hinder me.
I pray for healing—and despite what I feel or see—I believe I'm healed.

The Power of Words

Years ago I heard a minister teaching on faith, and he said something that got my attention. Once as he was meditating on Mark 11:23, the Spirit of God spoke to his spirit and asked, *Did you notice that in Mark 11:23, Jesus talked about saying three times as much as believing?*

The minister said, "Apparently, we need to hear about *saying* three times more than we need to hear about *believing*. And if we're having trouble in our faith walk, it's three times more likely to be in the saying part than in the believing part."

Why? Because we're a direct result of our words. Our lives today are a direct result of what we've been saying up until now. And what we say today is what we will be or have tomorrow. So as someone once said, "If you don't like what you are, quit saying what you're saying."

This is not "mind over matter" or "mind science"; these are Bible truths. Hebrews 11:3 says, "Through faith we understand that the worlds were framed by the word of God...." How did God create the earth? *By His words.* "God said, Let there be light: and there was light" and so on. (Gen. 1:3.) How did God bring this to pass? *By speaking.*

How do we operate in faith? We also believe and *say*—which ultimately determines our lives.

...Whosoever shall say unto this mountain, Be thou removed, and be thou cast into the sea; and shall not doubt in his heart, but shall believe that those things which he saith shall come to pass; he shall have whatsoever he saith.

—Mark 11:23

Confession

The words I speak today create who I'll be and what I'll have tomorrow. I speak healing and abundance in my life.

Change From the Inside Out

Man shall not live by bread alone, but by every word of God.

—Luke 4:4

Man is a three-part being: He is a spirit, he has a soul, and he lives in a body. The Bible also describes man as having an inward man and an outward man. (2 Cor. 4:16.)

The outward man is your flesh or "earth suit," and it's the vessel you live in that keeps you here on this earth. The outward man, which includes the soul and the body, is the part of you everyone sees.

The Bible says, "Therefore if any man be in Christ, he is a new creature: old things are passed away; behold, all things are become new" (2 Cor. 5:17). Where are old things passed away? In your spirit. You have the same body and mind you had before you were saved. Your body has to be healed, and your mind has to be renewed through God's Word. However, your inner man is a brand-new creation.

The inward man is the spirit man. The outward man is simply a reflection of the inward man. So if I have problems in my flesh, I better make adjustments in the inward man because those inside changes reflect on the outside.

For instance, suppose you have health problems. What should you do? Meditate on healing scriptures until they're planted deep in your spirit. Jesus said, "Let these sayings sink down into your ears" (Luke 9:44).

When you get full of the Word on the inside, it will show up on the outside, bringing health to your body.

Confession

God's Word works mightily in my spirit, bringing health to my body.

Locate Your Faith

You can locate your faith by your own words. Your words are your faith speaking.

Now, it's good practice to consciously speak good words over your circumstances. But if you want to find out where you really are in your faith walk—or why some things aren't going right in your life—then listen to yourself talk when the pressure is on. See what comes out of your mouth when you're not making a conscious effort to speak something good. In other words, see what comes out of the abundance of your heart. Then you'll know if you need to make some adjustments.

It's like a bank account. The bank sends you a statement each month. If you want them to add more to the final balance, what do you do? Put more money in the bank, and the next statement will show the difference.

A good man out of the good treasure of his heart bringeth forth that which is good; and an evil man out of the evil treasure of his heart bringeth forth that which is evil: for of the abundance of the heart his mouth speaketh.

—Luke 6:45

It's the same way spiritually. When you want something to show up outside, deposit the treasures of God's Word inside. Feed on the Word continually. Treat your inner man like a bank vault and just keep depositing God's Word in there. Once the Word is deposited in your inner man, you'll believe it; once you believe it, you'll say it. And then your entire being will reflect the treasure of God's Word.

Confession

I deposit healing Scriptures in my heart. I don't talk about symptoms, even when the pressure is on. I open my mouth and say, "Thank You, Father. Your healing power is working in me."

What Are You Believing?

..,for of the abundance of the heart his mouth speaketh.

—Luke 6:45

Usually you can find out why a person is struggling in faith just by listening to him for a few minutes. For instance, people have come up to me after being prayed for in a healing line and said, "Well, I still have such-and-such in my body. I don't know why I can't get rid of it."

I want to say, "You just told me why you haven't gotten rid of your condition!" You see, they're *believing they can't* get rid of it.

I've had other folks say, "I never get healed. When someone prays for me, I never receive anything." These people receive nothing because *nothing is exactly what they're believing* for.

When people come to receive prayer, they ought to be saying, "I've come to get rid of these symptoms."

"What do you have?"

"Well, I don't 'have' anything, but the devil is trying to put symptoms of sickness on me. I've come to get rid of them. You lay hands on me in the name of Jesus, and I'll receive my healing!"

Not only can we locate other people's faith by their words, but we can also discover what we really believe as we listen to our own words. When things aren't working right, we must listen to what we say.

Our words are important. If we can get our thinking, believing, and speaking straightened out, our lives will get straightened out. It may not happen instantly, but it will come to pass.

Confession

I believe and speak that by Jesus' stripes I am healed.
These faith-filled words are working in my body even now.

Choose Words of Life

Sometimes Christians take God's sovereignty too far. They think they're supposed to walk through life "rolling with the punches," taking whatever comes. I did that for years. But I got punched most of the time and spent the rest of my time rolling.

No, we choose in life whether we walk in blessing or cursing. We're not puppets. God doesn't arbitrarily decide who gets His blessings and who doesn't. We aren't supposed to walk around wondering what God has for us on this earth. God has already told us what He has for us. It's all written in the pages of the Bible.

Death and life are in the power of the tongue: and they that love it shall eat the fruit thereof.

—Proverbs 18:21

God gives us a choice to either accept or reject His blessings. Deuteronomy 30:19 says, "I call heaven and earth to record this day against you, that I have set before you life and death, blessing and cursing: therefore choose life, that both thou and thy seed may live." The choice is ours.

But how do we choose between death or life, blessing or cursing? Proverbs 18:21 tells us: "Death and life are in the power of the tongue...." We make the choice between death or life by what we say.

Now, I didn't say that—*God did.* Our tongues point us in one direction or the other. They're like the rudders on ships. The direction we turn them is the direction our bodies and lives will go. That's why it's so important that we choose words of life.

Confession

My future is affected by the words I speak today. Therefore,
I choose to speak God's Word over my life, circumstances,
and body. And I say I'm blessed, healthy, and victorious.

Control Your Mouth—Control Your Life

...If anyone does not offend in speech [never says the wrong things], he is a fully developed character and a perfect man, able to control his whole body and to curb his entire nature.

—James 3:2 AMP

In the last part of this verse, James says, "If you can control your mouth, you can control your body and your entire nature." That's a strong statement.

In verse 3 AMP, we learn more about the tongue: "If we set bits in the horses' mouths to make them obey us, we can turn their whole bodies about." Now, I'm not a horseman, but I know horses are too big to grab around the neck and pull around wherever you want. However, if you put a bit in a horse's mouth, you can control the direction it goes.

James continues: "Likewise, look at the ships: though they are so great and are driven by rough winds, they are steered by a very small rudder wherever the impulse of the helmsman determines" (v. 4 AMP). Ships are big, and winds are strong. But when you control the rudder, you control where the ship goes.

Think about it this way: A horse wants to go a particular direction by its own inner will. A ship has no will, but outside forces, such as wind and waves, try to drive it. So, putting a bit in a horse's mouth and directing a ship by its rudder are examples of controlling inside desires and outside forces.

Apply this to your life. No matter whether you face problems from *within* or forces from *without*, control your tongue and you'll control your life.

Confession

My words control my life. So I say I'm headed straight toward victory.

Control Your Tongue With God's Word

James is saying a spark can set a forest ablaze to destroy it or set a fire ablaze to keep us warm. In other words, we can use our tongues to destroy ourselves or make ourselves victorious.

Our words will make us or break us. If we allow our tongues to speak words of doubt and complaint, they will defeat us every time. But when we line up our words with God's Word, our tongues will put us over every time—no matter what comes against us.

Even so the tongue is a little member, and it can boast of great things. See how much wood or how great a forest a tiny spark can set ablaze.

—James 3:5 AMP

Sometimes Christians are the most negative people in the world. Many say things like, "I'm just an unworthy worm," or "Here I wander like a beggar through the heat and the cold."

We used to think we were being humble and spiritual when we talked like that. But what we thought was humility was really spiritual pride.

To be spiritual is to line up with God's Word. True humility is admitting God knows more than we do. True humility says, "I don't feel worthy or righteous. But, Lord, if You said I'm the righteousness of God in Christ, then I must be. I'm going to humble myself to Your Word and believe what You said, no matter what I feel." (Rom. 3:22.)

So make a decision to line your words up with the Word of God in every area of your life!

Confession

God's Word says I have abundant life, health, strength, and victory.
And God's Word is working mightily in me right now!

Break out of Captivity With Your Words

Thou art snared with the words of thy mouth, thou art taken with the words of thy mouth.

—Proverbs 6:2

The words of your mouth can snare you. Or, to paraphrase this verse, "Thou art taken captive with the words of thy mouth." Have you ever been in captivity? If so, more than likely your words put you there.

Job 42:10 bears this out when it explains why Job's ordeal ended: "And the Lord turned the captivity of Job, when he prayed for his friends."

Job first got himself into trouble through fear: "For the thing which I greatly feared is come upon me, and that which I was afraid of is come unto me" (Job 3:25). Job was saying, "That which I greatly feared has come upon me. I didn't have any peace; I didn't have any rest. I thought my good fortune was too good to be true."

Many folks say that today. Everything is going well in their lives, but they still speak negative words: "Man, this can't last. This is too good to be true." Sometimes they talk themselves right out of the good things that are happening.

Don't make that mistake. When something good comes into your life, say, "Glory to God! I'm walking in abundant life. Thank God, I'll just keep right on going from glory to glory!"

Confession

My life just keeps getting better and better. Blessings are overtaking me more and more. My needs are met; my body is healed. And the best is yet to come.

Be Satisfied With Good

A man shall be satisfied with good by the fruit of his mouth: and the recompence of a man's hands shall be rendered unto him.

—Proverbs 12:14

You could actually say the first phrase of this verse another way: "A man shall be satisfied with all kinds of good." But notice this verse does *not* say, "A man shall be satisfied with good if it's God's will or if God decides to smile upon him."

I don't know about you, but I like the promise in this Scripture because I want to be satisfied with good.

You have a choice between good and evil in life, and that choice is determined by the fruit of your mouth. In other Scriptures, God associates "good" with healing. (Acts 10:38; Luke 6:9.) So you could say, "A man shall be satisfied with healing by the fruit of his mouth."

I'm telling you, there is power in your words. Your mouth can get you over your circumstances and into the blessings of God. Proverbs 18:20 says, "A man's belly shall be satisfied with the fruit of his mouth; and with the increase of his lips shall he be filled." (I suggest that you read through Proverbs and see everything God says just in this one book about your words. After all, Proverbs is called the Book of Wisdom.)

Now look at Proverbs 15:4: "A wholesome tongue is a tree of life...." Adam had access to eat from the Tree of Life, and so do we—by making our tongues line up with God's Word.

Confession

I'm satisfied with good by the fruit of my mouth. I speak God's Word concerning healing, and those words produce life, strength, and wholeness in my body. Healing is mine now.

Our Words Preserve Us

...God, who quickeneth the dead, and calleth those things which be not as though they were.

—*Romans 4:17*

Words are important to God. This Scripture says God uses words to call those things that are not as though they were. Some people say, "Well, that's fine for God, but we shouldn't be doing that." But the Bible says our words are important as well.

First, look at Proverbs 14:3: "In the mouth of the foolish is a rod of pride: but the lips of the wise shall preserve them." Notice it doesn't say the lips of the wise will pickle them; it says their lips will preserve them.

Then in 1 Thessalonians 5:23, Paul told the Thessalonian church how he prayed for them: "I pray God your whole spirit and soul and body be preserved blameless unto the coming of our Lord Jesus Christ."

Paul prayed that we'd be preserved blameless while we walk on this earth. But what preserves us from the enemy who wants to steal from, kill, and destroy us? Proverbs 14:3 gives us the answer: "the lips of the wise."

As our own mouths speak forth God's wisdom, our faith-filled words will preserve us from the enemy's strategies arrayed against us. That's why it's wise to follow God's example and call those things that be not as though they were.

Confession

I call those things that be not as though they were.
In Jesus' name, I speak healing to my body and
health and wholeness to all my flesh.

Refrain Your Lips From Evil

What does it mean to "think evil"? You are thinking evil when you dwell on any kind of thoughts that are contrary to God's Word.

What are you supposed to do if you are guilty of thinking evil? "Lay thine hand upon thy mouth." God is telling you, "If you've thought evil, that's one thing. But don't verbalize it, or you might get it. If you've spoken foolishly or thought evil, lay your hand on your mouth."

If thou hast done foolishly in lifting up thyself, or if thou hast thought evil, lay thine hand upon thy mouth.

—Proverbs 30:32

Proverbs 10:19 says, "In the multitude of words there wanteth not sin: but he that refraineth his lips is wise." Sometimes the smartest thing we can do is to keep our mouths shut. James 1:19 says, "Wherefore, my beloved brethren, let every man be swift to hear, slow to speak, slow to wrath."

So refuse to dwell on evil thoughts of doubt, unbelief, complaint, or worry. Don't let them come out of your mouth. Be slow to speak. Refrain your lips from doubtful and evil speaking. Put your hand on your mouth if you have to. In fact, do whatever you have to do to make sure your words line up with the Word of God.

Confession

I speak victory and health to my life and body.
The words of my mouth and the meditation of my
heart are acceptable in Your sight, Father,
my strength and my redeemer. (Ps. 19:14.)

The Tongue of the Wise

There is that speaketh like the piercings of a sword: but the tongue of the wise is health.

—Proverbs 12:18

Our words have a lot to do with our physical healing and health. We have the ability to talk ourselves into all kinds of problems or to speak words of faith, which cause miracles to manifest. Many times people get sick or don't receive healing because they believe and speak according to natural symptoms. These people may receive temporary relief when they're prayed for. But if they don't straighten out what their saying, they'll eventually find themselves back in the same unhealthy conditions.

These very same people who've talked themselves into sickness often say, "I don't know why God put this on me. I don't know why He allowed this to happen."

But God didn't have anything to do with it. You see, faith is a law, and we operate it with our words—either to our benefit or destruction. Proverbs 12:18 says, "The tongue of the wise is health." We could turn that around and say, "The tongue of the unwise is sickness."

It's your choice. You can operate the law of faith by hooking up your mouth with your symptoms and what the devil tells you. Or you can operate the same law of faith by hooking up your mouth with God's Word full of blessings. Faith in God works by believing and saying what God says. So speak His words of healing, and receive the healing God has reserved just for you.

Confession

I speak words of health to my body because the tongue of the wise is health. Disease cannot attach itself to me because Jesus bore my sicknesses and pains so I don't have to. I walk in excellent health.

Keep Your Soul From Trouble

Many people have trouble in their soul, which includes the mind, will, and emotions. But God gives the answer right here.

We've all dealt with doubts and fears at one time or another. Fear often starts as a *single thought*. As we dwell on that thought, it produces fear. And if we continue to dwell on fearful thoughts, fear escalates into panic.

Whoso keepeth his mouth and his tongue keepeth his soul from troubles.

—Proverbs 21:23

The devil likes to attack your mind with fearful thoughts. He may say, *I'm going to kill you. You won't live out your full life. You'll get cancer and die.* Most of the time there's no basis at all for what the enemy is saying to your mind. He doesn't care. He just wants you to dwell on his evil suggestions long enough for fear to take over.

I finally realized demonic thoughts come to our minds because the devil isn't big enough to pull off his schemes on his own. He's trying to convince us to agree with him so he can operate in our lives.

Cast down the enemy's thoughts the second they come. How do you stop his thoughts? Well, you can't think one thing while you're saying something else. So open your mouth and start confessing, "Glory to God! God sent His Word and healed me and satisfies me with long life. It's so good to be well!"

When you start speaking God's Word, thoughts stop and fear leaves. That will keep your soul from trouble.

Confession

I refuse to allow fear and doubt to control me.
I keep my soul from trouble by speaking God's Word. I live
a long, healthy life, and God will fulfill the number of my days.

Speaking the Word Works

*The tongue of the
wise is health.*

—Proverbs 12:18

When I was a youth minister in Colorado, we scheduled a youth camp in the mountains a couple of times a year. One morning I led a group of teenagers on a hike to the top of a small, nearby mountain. We ate lunch and had a Bible study before we started back.

On the way down, one of the girls stepped on a rock and injured her ankle and foot. When I reached her, her ankle was already swollen. I didn't know whether she'd broken her foot or sprained it, but she couldn't stand on it.

We prayed and some of her pain was relieved. Then another man and I took turns piggybacking the girl down the mountain.

As I carried her, I started talking to her about the power of the tongue. I told her, "The Bible says, 'The tongue of the wise is health.'" I also explained the principles of Mark 11:23—we can have what we say if we believe.

So she started confessing, "Thank God, it's so good to be healed!" We praised and worshipped God together down the mountain.

About a third of the way down, the girl said, "Put me down!" We supported her as she hobbled for a few minutes. The whole time she kept saying, "Thank God, it's so good to be healed." Pretty soon, she took off walking on her own.

The more she walked, the better it got. By the time she got to the bottom, she said, "See you later!" and ran all the way to the bus.

The Word works!

Confession

In times of pressure, I speak God's Word and circumstances change.
Thank You, Father, for the power in Your Word that's healing my body.

Pray the Answer, Not the Problem

And all things, whatsoever ye shall ask in prayer, believing, ye shall receive.

—Matthew 21:22

I was born again right in the middle of the Charismatic move. I visited a small full gospel church and was filled with the Holy Ghost. I had a lot of enthusiasm, but I didn't know much about the Bible.

I prayed constantly at the church so the pastor finally gave me my own key. The problem was, I didn't how to pray. Over and over, I prayed, "Dear God, You see how bad my problems are." But if anything changed, it was always for the worse.

I had a plaque hanging at home that said "Prayer Changes Things," but I was saved, filled, and defeated. Everything went wrong. After a year of this, I couldn't decide whether to throw that plaque away or burn it.

Finally I thought, *The answer has to be in the Bible someplace.* So I started searching the Scriptures. Matthew 21:22 is the verse that got my attention. Jesus said, "And all things, whatsoever ye shall ask in prayer, believing, ye shall receive."

This verse was a key that unlocked my understanding of the prayer of faith. Suddenly I realized I'd been talking to God about the *problem* instead of the *answer.*

Another key is found in Isaiah 43:26: "Put me in remembrance: let us plead together...." I realized God wants to be reminded of what He's already said about our needs.

So pray God's answer, then believe you receive it by faith. That's the true prayer of faith.

Confession

Father, I put You in remembrance of Your Word.
I thank You because You said by Jesus' stripes, I was healed.

Choose To Believe God's Word

How then shall they call on him in whom they have not believed? and how shall they believe in him of whom they have not heard?

So then faith cometh by hearing, and hearing by the word of God.

—*Romans 10:14,17*

Believing is a result of hearing. Once you hear the Word, you have the ability and the capacity to believe it, but you still have to choose what you will believe. I've seen people hear and hear the Word. But then when the pressure was on, they believed their symptoms instead of what God says.

In John 20, the resurrected Jesus had already appeared to His disciples when Thomas wasn't present. Before His death, Jesus had told His disciples over and over again that He would be raised from the dead. After He appeared to the other disciples, they all told Thomas, "We've seen the Lord!"

So Thomas had the capacity to believe in Jesus' resurrection because he'd already heard about it from Jesus and the other disciples. But Thomas made his choice. He said, "Except I shall see in his hand the print of the nails, and put my finger in the print of the nails, and thrust my hand into His side, *I will not believe*" (John 20:25).

Thomas wasn't alone in his unbelief. That's where a lot of folks get in trouble. We hear the Word but then choose to believe the natural circumstances. As a result, we don't receive the blessings God wants to give us.

Don't make that mistake. Hear the Word and make a quality decision to believe what you hear. That's how you'll keep God's blessings flowing in your life.

Confession

I choose to believe God's Word over adverse circumstances or symptoms. Victory and healing belong to me.

Be a Doer of the Word

If you want to walk in the divine health God desires for you, you'll have to be a doer of the Word. For one thing, that means meditating on God's healing promises. As you do, you'll find His Word getting so big on the inside of you that you'll start acting like a healthy person.

God told Joshua the results he could expect for being diligent in His Word: "For then thou shalt make thy way prosperous, and then thou shalt have good success." Did you notice that it doesn't say, "For then *God* will make your way prosperous"? No, it says, "For *you* will make your way prosperous." I've also heard it put this way: "Then you will deal wisely in all the affairs of life."

God has made health and success available in every area of your life. Now He says, "I give you the wisdom and ability to deal wisely in all the affairs of life. But it's your choice whether or not you become a doer of My Word and actually receive what I've given you."

This book of the law shall not depart out of thy mouth; but thou shalt meditate therein day and night, that thou mayest observe to do according to all that is written therein: for then thou shalt make thy way prosperous, and then thou shalt have good success.

—Joshua 1:8

Confession

I have planted God's Word in my heart, and that Word is life to me and health to all my flesh. Because I meditate on God's Word, I deal wisely in all the affairs of life.

"Mutter" the Word

This book of the law shall not depart out of thy mouth; but thou shalt meditate therein day and night, that thou mayest observe to do according to all that is written therein: for then thou shalt make thy way prosperous, and then thou shalt have good success.

—Joshua 1:8

The word *meditate* means "to read, to study, to think about, *to mutter.*"[1] Notice the final word in that list of definitions is to *mutter*—or in other words, to keep God's Word coming out of our mouths.

It's ironic when you stop to think about it. The enemy has propagated a theory in this world that people who talk to themselves are going crazy. But we Christians ought to be speaking the Word to ourselves all the time. We ought to be meditating on the Word of God continually—reading it, studying it, thinking about it, "chewing on it," and saying it to ourselves.

For instance, you can use the time when you're driving in your car to speak the Word aloud to yourself. You can say: "Thank God, He sent His Word and healed me. Jesus had compassion on the multitudes, and He healed them all. Jesus went about all the cities and villages, teaching and preaching and healing every sickness and every disease among the people. And by His stripes I am healed!"

The world might think you're a little strange when they see you muttering to yourself. But that's okay. You know something they don't know—you're on the edge of a miracle!

Confession

I keep God's Word before me and meditate on it day and night.

His Word is seed planted in my heart, and I speak it continually.

God's Word is working mightily in me to produce a harvest of healing.

The Same Measure of Faith

We having the same spirit of faith, according as it is written, I believed, and therefore have I spoken; we also believe, and therefore speak.

—2 Corinthians 4:13

Paul starts out in this Scripture saying, "We having...." I like that. The great apostle Paul was talking to the entire body of Christ, not just to apostles, prophets, evangelists, pastors, and teachers.

Then Paul said, "We having the same spirit of faith...." We have the same spirit of faith that the apostle Paul had. He had a measure of the God-kind of faith, and we have the same measure and the same faith.

God didn't give Paul a greater dose of faith than He gave us. If He did, He'd be a respecter of persons because the Bible says, "This is the victory that overcometh the world, even our faith" (1 John 5:4). If God gave Paul a greater dose, Paul would've had a greater ability to overcome the devil's attacks.

But no, God gave each and every one of us the same exact dose, or measure, of the God-kind of faith. (Rom. 12:3.) But it's up to us what we do with it.

Think about how muscles work. Think back on a time when you physically exerted yourself exercising or doing yard work and discovered a muscle you hadn't used for a while. Maybe it hurt for a few days, having become weak from lack of use. Yet if you exercise that muscle every day, it will grow in size and strength.

Faith is also like a muscle. So keep your faith working all the time, and it will grow to overcome any and every obstacle.

Confession

I exercise my faith by believing God's promises.
I'm free from all disease. Praise God, it's good to be well.

Exercise Your Faith

We having the same spirit of faith, according as it is written, I believed, and therefore have I spoken; we also believe, and therefore speak.

—2 Corinthians 4:13

Our capacity to operate in faith comes from hearing God's Word. However, our faith doesn't grow because we hear. We can feed and feed a muscle, but it only grows in strength as we *exercise* it.

Faith is the same way. All over the world believers sit back in their church pews week after week, just hearing and hearing the Word. Then they can't figure out why their faith doesn't work for them. I could tell them why: *They're not using their faith.*

Our faith needs to be working on something all the time. When one answer comes in, our faith should still be out working in four or five other areas. We have to keep our faith muscles flexed.

Then when a new problem arises, we won't flinch and say, "Oh, Lord, what am I going to do?" We'll look it square in the face and say, "Thank God, another opportunity to exercise my faith."

We don't like problems, and God doesn't send them. But we can take anything the devil throws against us and turn it around for our good. We can use our faith to push problems away from us like a weight lifter uses weights. Every time he pushes the weights away, he gets stronger.

So the next time a problem comes along, count it all joy. Consider it one more opportunity to prove God's Word works. Your faith will drive the problem away and come out stronger than ever.

Confession

When symptoms come against me, I count it all joy. The Word was sent to heal me, and it's working mightily in me right now.

The Connection Between Saying and Believing

We having the same spirit of faith, according as it is written, I believed, and therefore have I spoken; we also believe, and therefore speak.

—2 Corinthians 4:13

I heard a minister say, "Any time you see a *therefore* in the Bible, stop and see what it's *there for.*" In this verse, Paul uses the word *therefore* to combine the two parts of faith: "I *believed* and therefore have I *spoken;* we also *believe,* and therefore *speak.*"

If we're going to believe something, we also have to speak it; believing alone doesn't make it come to pass.

Jesus said, "If you believe in your heart that what you say will come to pass, you'll have whatever you say." (Mark 11:23.) The truth is, we can spend a lot of time feeding on God's Word, but what we continually say is what we'll ultimately believe.

When I was growing up, I had a friend who'd make up a whopper of a lie about some situation; then six months later, no one could convince him it hadn't happened that way. He actually believed it.

If that can be done with a lie, it can be done with God's Word. When someone starts saying, "By Jesus' stripes I was healed," it can sound hollow. It's easy to think, *I know the Bible says by His stripes I was healed, but I feel sick from head to toe.* But as we keep saying it, soon we'll believe it no matter what we feel like.

Feed on God's Word and continually speak it. Once you believe in your heart what God says, you'll declare it with faith-filled words. Then get ready—your answer is coming.

Confession

I believe God's truth, I declare God's truth, and I receive God's truth.

Faith for Salvation–Faith for Healing

But the righteousness which is of faith speaketh on this wise...

But what saith it? The word is nigh thee, even in thy mouth, and in thy heart: that is, the word of faith, which we preach; that if thou shalt confess with thy mouth the Lord Jesus, and shalt believe in thine heart that God hath raised him from the dead, thou shalt be saved.

—Romans 10:6-9

This passage of Scripture tells you not only how to be saved, but also how to be healed.

Notice what Paul says in verse 6: "But the righteousness which is of faith speaketh...." Faith always speaks. What you say is your faith speaking. I don't mean just what you say once, but what you say over a period of time.

Then in verse 8, Paul asks, "But what saith it?" What does the righteousness which is of faith say? "The word is nigh thee, even in thy mouth, and in thy heart." Faith has to be in two places: in your heart and in your mouth.

Verse 9 goes on to say, "That if thou shalt confess with thy mouth...." You may say, "I don't believe in Bible confessions." If you don't, you have to throw out the whole book of Romans.

You may argue, "But that verse is talking about salvation." Yes, I know, but the same faith that got you saved will get you healed. You just have to take your faith and point it in a different direction. Remember, Jesus said, "All things are possible to him who believes." (Mark 9:23.)

Confession

God's Word in my heart and in my mouth says
Jesus is my healer. I speak healing to my body, and
according to my faith, it will be done unto me.

Release Your Faith With Your Words

The apostle Paul is saying *with the heart you believe unto the reality of God's Word.* In other words, when you get a revelation of God's Word in your heart, it becomes more real or alive to you.

Then Paul is also saying *with the mouth confession is made unto the manifestation, or experience, of God's Word.*

In other words, when you believe the Word, it becomes real; when you say it, it manifests. If you say it without believing it, it isn't real to you. If you believe it without saying it, it isn't manifested for you. But when you believe and say the Word, it will produce for you.

For with the heart man believeth unto righteousness; and with the mouth confession is made unto salvation.

—Romans 10:10

We like it when God's Word becomes real in our spirits. But there's something about having it actually manifest in our lives that makes it more enjoyable yet. When we're actually walking in good health, it feels good to "feel good".

To experience the manifestation of God's promises, you must continually speak God's Word about your situation. That's how faith is released. You can have a heart full of faith, but it won't do you any good until you release it.

It's like having a bank account full of money. That money will sit in the vault and do no good unless it's spent. In the same way, you spend or release faith by the words you speak. That's how to put your faith to work.

Confession

As I feed on God's Word, my heart grows full of faith. Now I release my faith and say, God's power is healing me from head to toe.

Have the God-Kind of Faith

Through faith we understand that the worlds were framed by the word of God, so that things which are seen were not made of things which do appear.

—Hebrews 11:3

In Mark 11:22, Jesus said, "Have faith in God," or "Have the God-kind of faith." What is the God-kind of faith? Hebrews 11:3 gives us a clue; it says God spoke the universe into existence by faith.

Did you notice when God decided to create the worlds, He didn't say, "Hmmm, I've never tried speaking worlds into existence before. I sure hope it works!" No, God knew He could do it.

Isaiah 40:12 says God measured out the heavens in the span of His hand and measured the waters in the hollow of His hand. God thoroughly believed He could create the universe, and He knew exactly what it would look like when He was through.

In fact, God could've stepped out on the first day and said, "Universe, be!" and everything would've spun into existence. I believe one reason God created a day at a time is to show us how the God-kind of faith works.

So God said, "Let there be light," and there was light. (Gen. 1:3.) But since God already believed He could speak the worlds into existence, how come the whole universe didn't appear right then? The point is, even God didn't get what He believed; He got what He *said*. Nothing more, nothing less. God believed He could create the entire universe, but only what He actually said came into manifestation at that point.

Faith works the same for us. You might believe a lot of things, but you'll receive what you believe and *say*.

Confession

From a believing heart I release my faith, saying
healing and wholeness are mine.

Call That Which Is Not as Though It Were

We are to call those things which be not as though they were. As someone once said, "We don't want to get that mixed up. God didn't say to call those things which are as though they were not."

In other words, God didn't say to deny the symptoms, the circumstances, or the problems. We're not supposed to say, "No, I don't have any pain. No, there aren't symptoms in my body. No, my leg is not broken. No, my nose isn't running."

...even God, who quickeneth the dead, and calleth those things which be not as though they were.

—Romans 4:17

No! We are to call those things that be not as though they were. That means a person in faith should say, "Well, I don't feel healed. But thank God, the Bible says I am, so I believe I'm healed. I don't feel strong; but the Bible says I am, so I believe I'm strong."

You should talk about healing as though it already existed in your body. You should say, "It doesn't matter what my body feels like, by Jesus' stripes I was healed. (Isa. 53.) Jesus took my infirmities and bare my sicknesses and pains. (Matt. 8:17.) God sent His Word and healed me. (Ps. 107:20.) It doesn't matter what the problem is, no weapon formed against me shall prosper. (Isa. 54:17.) Since God is for me, no one can stand against me. (Rom. 8:31.) And I believe I receive my healing by faith now in Jesus' name."

Confession

I don't deny symptoms or circumstances; I just call forth God's promises to be manifested in my life. I call my mind strong and at peace. And I call my body healthy and whole.

Call Forth Your Miracle by Faith

...I have made thee a father of many nations, before him whom he believed, even God, who quickeneth the dead, and calleth those things which be not as though they were.

—Romans 4:17

Our faith has to speak if we're going to see results. God calls those things which be not as though they were. Abraham called those things which were not as though they were. Certainly, if our heavenly Father and the father of our faith operated in that kind of faith, we ought to do the same.

"*Call* those things...." To *call*, you have to say something. In other words, you'll have to speak out loud.

Which of God's blessings is not in your life? Is healing not in your life? Then call it as though it were: "Everywhere I go, healing and health overtake me causing my body to be strong, healthy, and whole!"

Is that scriptural? Well, I like what Joel said: "Let the weak say, I am strong" (Joel 3:10). He didn't say, "Let the weak say I'm weak and unworthy." No, the weak are supposed to say they're strong. So calling those things that be not as though they were is very scriptural.

And the weak aren't supposed to wait until they feel strong. If they did that, they'd never feel it. No, let the weak say, "I'm strong" while they still feel weak.

Why? Because with your mouth, confession is made unto the manifestation of God's Word in your life. (Rom. 10:10.) So continually call your body healed as though it already were. And soon you'll experience the manifestation of your miracle.

Confession

Jesus took my sin and sickness and gave me His righteousness and health. So, I call my body healed and strong.

Making a Statement of Fact

Someone may say, "If I say I believe I'm healed when I still feel sick, that's a lie."

No, it isn't. Number one, it's calling those things which be not as though they were. (Rom. 4:17.) If that's lying, then God lies all the time; and He can't lie.

Number two, it's a statement of fact. If I say, "I believe I'm healed," all I'm doing is telling you what I believe. However, if I say, "I don't have any symptoms in my body" when I do have symptoms, that's a lie. Or if I say, "I have five $100 bills in my pocket" when I don't, that's a lie. But if I say, "I believe I'm healed by the stripes on Jesus' back," I'm making a statement of truth because I believe it.

Paul, a servant of God, and an apostle of Jesus Christ, according to the faith of God's elect, and the acknowledging of the truth which is after godliness; in hope of eternal life, which God, that cannot lie, promised before the world began.

—Titus 1:1,2

You can believe anything you want to believe. If you choose to believe what God's Word says instead of what symptoms tell you, is that a lie? No, that's truth.

Jesus said, "Thy word is truth" (John 17:17). Paul says, "Yea, let God be true, but every man a liar" (Rom. 3:4). And Hebrews 6:18 states it's impossible for God to lie. So when you believe what God says, you come in line with the highest form of truth in the universe—the Word of God, exalted even above His name. (Ps. 138:2.)

Confession

I believe God's healing power is working in my body now, driving out every symptom and making my body completely whole.

Hook Up With What God Says

Let the words of my mouth, and the meditation of my heart, be acceptable in thy sight, O Lord, my strength, and my redeemer.

—Psalm 19:14

When I first learned you can have what you say, I shut up for about three weeks. I thought, *If I get what I've been saying, I'm in trouble!* For instance, when I was in high school I was a good driver. But, like everyone else in my family, I drove too fast. I remember laughingly saying, "Boy, the way I drive, I'll never live to be thirty years old."

I thought it was funny back then. But when I found out what the Bible said, I adjusted that in a hurry. I said, "The way I drive, I'll live to be 125." (Of course, I had to change a few driving habits too!)

We need to listen to ourselves. So often we speak negative phrases over and over without thinking. If we thought about it, we'd realize, dear Lord, that's not what I want in my life.

If we keep speaking the same negative things over and over, eventually we'll believe what we're saying—then we'll have it. For example, I've heard people say, "I'm afraid I'll have an accident." Then when they do, they ask, "Why did God do this to me?"

God didn't have a thing to do with it. Those people stepped into a spiritual law that works either positively or negatively: They believed it, they said it, and they received it.

Let's use this spiritual law to our advantage and hook up with what God says.

Confession

I listen to my words. When I discover I'm contrary to God's Word, I change it. I speak divine health into my body. In Jesus' name, I'm whole.

Speak the Word From Your Heart

How did this woman with the issue of blood get faith? "When she had *heard* of Jesus...." Faith comes by hearing. But did you notice how she started releasing her faith? "For she *said*...." *The Amplified Bible* says, "For she *kept saying*, If I only touch His garments, I shall be restored to health." She *kept saying* those words that released her faith.

Someone may ask, "How long do you speak the Word over a situation?"

Speak it until the answer manifests.

When she had heard of Jesus, came in the press behind, and touched his garment. For she said, If I may touch but his clothes, I shall be whole.

—Mark 5:27,28

But don't rely on simple confession alone to do the job. Feed on God's Word at the same time. Take time to read and study the Word. Meditate on it; speak it to yourself.

Matthew 9:20-22 provides another account of the same healing. Verse 21 says, "For she said within herself...." I like to say it this way: "For she said from within herself...."

Many people just mimic the way others speak the Word; they do it out of their heads instead of their hearts. They grab some Scripture and start saying it without even concentrating on it. These people need to keep on speaking God's Word until it registers in their heart and they believe it.

So plant the Word down in your heart until its truth is alive and real to you. Then you can release faith-filled words that produce results.

Confession

I abide in Jesus, and His words abide in me. I make my request according to God's Word, and He answers me. I believe and speak now that Jesus took my infirmities and bare my sicknesses. I am healed.

The Simplicity of Faith

For the Word that God speaks is alive and full of power [making it active, operative, energizing, and effective]; it is sharper than any two-edged sword.

—Hebrews 4:12 AMP

God operates in faith by believing and saying, and God gets exactly what He says. Everything God does, He does by speaking.

Did you ever notice that everything God does in the world today, He does by His Word on the lips of believers? That's how God carries out His plan on this earth.

How did you get saved? By believing in your heart and saying with your mouth. Then how are you going to get healed? By believing in your heart and saying with your mouth. How are you going to get your needs met? By believing in your heart and saying with your mouth. How does faith work? By believing in the heart and saying with the mouth.

Thank God, He made it easy for us. Faith is so simple. Faith is just taking God at His Word.

So feed on God's Word until you get it on the inside. Read it, study it, mutter it, meditate on it, and think about it until it is lodged deep down in your spirit. Then declare God's promises with your mouth and watch God bring them to pass.

James 2:20 says faith without actions is dead. So act on your faith: Open your mouth and boldly declare, "Thank God, by Jesus' stripes I am healed!" It's that simple!

Confession

I believe with my heart and say with my mouth that God's Word is true in my life. His Word says I'm healed by the stripes of Jesus. The power in that Word is working in me now, healing, strengthening, and restoring me to health.

Slay Your Giant of Sickness by Faith

Who is this uncircumcised Philistine, that he should defy the armies of the living God?

—1 Samuel 17:26

Believing and saying is a spiritual law, just as gravity is a natural law. You can find the law of faith all through the Bible.

Remember David and Goliath? David was a shepherd boy working out in the fields with a sling and a handful of stones. But in 1 Samuel 17, he fought against Goliath, a giant and a warrior from his youth. Notice what David said: "I come to you in the name of the Lord of Hosts. This day He's going to deliver you into my hands!" (vv. 45,46.)

That might seem pretty cocky for a little guy, but David wasn't cocky or arrogant. He just knew he had a covenant with God.

David spoke out of confidence in his God, asking, "Who does this ugly Philistine think he is, defying the armies of the living God?"

Notice what David's motives were. He didn't challenge Goliath for his own glory. He didn't say, "I'm going to make myself famous over this." He just didn't like people defying the armies of the living God. He was proclaiming, "We have a covenant—why don't we walk in it?"

So David boldly told Goliath, "I'm going to take your head off your shoulders today!" Goliath may have laughed, but he didn't laugh long. David sank one of those stones in his forehead; then cut off Goliath's head with the giant's own sword.

What did David get? Exactly what he believed and said. A spiritual law of faith was in operation.

Confession

Sickness and pain are my Goliath. I face the giant, saying Jesus bore my sicknesses and carried my pains. By His stripes I'm healed.

What Do Your Words Carry?

The words of a wise man's mouth are gracious; but the lips of a fool will swallow up himself.

—Ecclesiastes 10:12

Words are powerful "carriers"; they carry faith or unbelief. And whatever we fill our words with will directly affect our lives.

Sit down sometime and take a look at your life. I'm sure you'll find things you like. But if you look hard enough, you'll probably find some aspects you don't like. Then ask yourself, "What have I been saying about those parts I don't like?"

If you don't like where you are in life, change your words. Quit saying what you're saying. Proverbs 18:21 says, "Death and life are in the power of the tongue...."

For instance, have you ever said, "I never get anything from God. I tried that faith stuff, but it didn't work for me"? If so, switch over to speaking words of faith: "I've been feeding on God's Word for years, and my faith grows exceedingly. God's Word is seed planted in my heart, and it's working mightily in me."

You see, we're a direct result of what we've believed and said about ourselves in the past. So to make sure our future is better than our past or present, we need to renew our minds and straighten out our thinking.

Once you get your thinking lined up with God's Word, it's amazing how easily your believing will line up right behind it. After your believing is straightened out, your mouth will straighten out.

Then you're ready for your faith-filled words to carry you straight into a future of health and abundance.

Confession

My words are carriers of faith. They create the blessings I live in.
I walk in health and abundance all the days of my life.

The Problem Is With Your Mouth

Many years ago I attended a campmeeting when the minister in charge asked me to preach. New to the ministry I prayed, "Dear Lord, what am I going to do now?"

Back then, I taught from sermons I'd written out word for word. So I got out my notes and found a sermon I was comfortable with.

I sat reviewing my notes before the service, and all of a sudden, I heard on the inside: Your problem is not with your faith, and it's not with God; it's with your mouth. I knew it was for someone other than me.

Hear; for I will speak of excellent things; and the opening of my lips shall be right things. For my mouth shall speak truth....

—Proverbs 8:6,7

When I got up to teach I looked at my notes and went blank. "All right, Lord, You win," I said. "I'll just start off with what You said." So I repeated what the Lord had spoken to me before the service.

To this day I don't know what else I preached, but after the service a lady came up to me who'd driven a long way. She could only stay for one service but told me, "I'm in a life-and-death situation. I've battled this physical condition for quite awhile and tried to figure out why I haven't been healed.

"First I thought maybe there was some reason God wasn't healing me. Then I thought, *No, the problem is I don't have any faith.* But now I know the answer. The problem is with my mouth. Well, I'm changing what I'm saying. And you just watch—now I'll live and not die!"

Confession

I line up my words with God's words.
God satisfies me with a long and healthy life.

Understanding Biblical Confessions

In those days came John the Baptist, preaching in the wilderness of Judaea, and saying, Repent ye: for the kingdom of heaven is at hand.

Then went out to him Jerusalem, and all Judea, and all the region round about Jordan, and were baptized of him in Jordan, confessing their sins.

—Matthew 3:1,2,5,6

People have gone to extremes with the subject of Bible confession. Many misunderstand this subject because so much tradition and religious doctrine have been taught. But we shouldn't throw out the whole principle because of a few extremes. We just have to go back to the Word and find the truth.

You can find four basic types of confession in the Bible. Usually when the word *confession* is mentioned, people automatically think of confessing sin. This is the first type of confession, and it's discussed in Matthew 3:1-6.

This passage addresses John's baptism—the baptism of repentance and the confession of sins. However, we need to understand this was before the death, burial, and resurrection of Jesus. Under the old covenant, people couldn't be born again because Jesus hadn't been to the Cross yet. So to be in right relationship with God, they had to confess their sins.

This type of confession is biblical under the old covenant. However, confessing each and every sin to get in right relationship with God—or to be born again—doesn't apply to us today because we've changed covenants. Hebrews 8:6 explains that today we live under a new and better covenant established on better promises.

Confession

I confess Jesus is my Lord and Savior and my healer. He redeemed me from sin and sickness so I could have life and health.

Confessing Jesus as Lord

This Scripture shows us the second type of Bible confession. Paul talks about confessing with our mouths, so he's talking about a verbal, audible confession. What do we confess? We confess Jesus as Lord and Savior in a confession or prayer of salvation.

Just after I got saved, I went with a college group to share Jesus with people on Daytona Beach. I used to tell people, "If you'll confess your sins, God will save you." But technically, that's not true. The new birth does not come as a result of confessing all your sins. You couldn't remember them all anyway.

Paul did *not* say, "If you will confess with your mouth every mistake you ever made...." No, he said, "If thou shalt confess with thy mouth that Jesus is Lord...."

You see, the Bible says, "Go ye into all the world, and preach the gospel to every creature" (Mark 16:15). Is the Gospel bad news? No, it's good news! Too often we've given people bad news: "You old rotten sinner, if you don't get saved, you're going straight to hell." But here's the Good News: God was in Christ, reconciling the world unto himself, not imputing their trespasses unto them..." (2 Cor. 5:19). Your sins have been paid for!

So, the confession of salvation is not a negative confession—it's a positive confession of Jesus as Lord.

If thou shalt confess with thy mouth the Lord Jesus, and shalt believe in thine heart that God hath raised him from the dead, thou shalt be saved. For with the heart man believeth unto righteousness; and with the mouth confession is made unto salvation.

—Romans 10:9,10

Confession

Jesus, I believe in my heart God raised You from the dead, and I confess You as my Savior and Healer.

Confession and Cleansing for the Believer

If we confess our sins, he is faithful and just to forgive us our sins, and to cleanse us from all unrighteousness.

My little children, these things write I unto you, that ye sin not. And if any man sin, we have an advocate with the Father, Jesus Christ the righteous.

—1 John 1:9; 2:1

This Scripture reveals the third type of Bible confession—the believer's confession of sin. We know that John is talking to the Church because he began by saying, "My little children."

When we're born again, God looks at us through the blood of Jesus as though we *never* sinned. Old things are passed away; all things have become new. (2 Cor. 5:17.)

But what happens if we make a mistake after we're born again? God tells us not to sin, but He's made provision in case we do. He knows as long as we're on this earth, we'll have difficulty. The devil pushes us toward sin on one side, and our flesh drags us toward sin on the other side.

If we sin, we go right straight to our Advocate, a legal representative, in heaven who goes to the Father on our behalf. How do we make use of that Advocate? "If we confess our sins, he is faithful and just to forgive us our sins, and to cleanse us from all unrighteousness." If we do our part, God does His.

So this third type of confession is how the Church stays in fellowship with the Father.

Confession

I seek to please God, but when I miss it,
I simply ask God to forgive me and He does.

Hold Fast to Your Confession of Faith

Let us hold fast the profession of our faith without wavering; (for he is faithful that promised).

—Hebrews 10:23

The fourth type of confession is the confession of faith, or the confession of what we believe. This is an important type of Bible confession that many in the body of Christ have missed.

Let's examine the phrase, "hold fast the profession of our faith." In the *King James Version,* the word *profession* is used. But the same Greek word *homologeo* is translated as "confession" elsewhere in the New Testament and means "to speak the same thing as; to agree with."[1] So the writer of Hebrews is actually saying, "Let us hold fast the confession of our faith without wavering, for He who promised is faithful."

God *is* faithful and will keep His promises, but He also requires something of us. God is faithful to perform His Word—*if* we believe and act on it. We have a part to play. If we want His faithfulness to operate in our lives, we must hold fast the confession of our faith without wavering.

What does *confession of faith* mean? *Faith* is what you believe or put your trust in. For instance, you put your trust in the Word that says by Jesus' stripes you were healed. Then even if your body feels and looks sick, you'll hold fast to the unchangeable truth of God's Word. You'll hold fast to what you believe, and you won't waver or doubt.

Line up your mouth with what you believe, and say, "Thank God, I believe I'm healed!"

Confession

I hold fast to my confession that Jesus took my sicknesses
and bore my pains no matter what I feel or see.

Unwavering Faith

Let us hold fast the profession of our faith without wavering; (for he is faithful that promised).

—Hebrews 10:23

What does Paul mean when he tells us not to waver? Let's look at another Scripture that addresses this issue. James talks about not wavering as well:

If any of you lack wisdom, let him ask of God, that giveth to all men liberally, and upbraideth not; and it shall be given him. But let him *ask in faith, nothing wavering.* For he that wavereth is like a wave of the sea driven with the wind and tossed. For let not that man think that he shall receive any thing of the Lord.

James 1:5-7

James was talking about asking for wisdom, but he also gave us a Bible truth that applies to every area of our lives. He said, "Ask, and it shall be given—*but....*" Then he gave a condition to the promise. We have to "ask in faith, *nothing wavering.*"

How do people waver? Most wavering comes in what you say. Nothing wavering means you're not wavering in what you believe or in what you say.

You get to that place of unwavering faith by getting your heart full of the Word. You see, you talk about what is closest to your heart. So when your heart is full of the Word, you can't talk about anything else. Every time you open your mouth, God's Word comes out. That's how you hold fast to your confession of what God says.

Confession

God sent His Word to heal me, so I won't waver by speaking
doubt and unbelief. Symptoms don't move me because
I believe in my heart that I've already received my healing.

Seek Healing, Not Sympathy

Notice that this verse talks about holding fast to your profession of faith. Think about that. If you have to *hold fast* to something, it usually means it's trying to get away from you. You'll find in life that it will take some work at times to hold fast to the confession of your faith.

Folks will say to you, "You look terrible. How do you feel? I know what you believe, but how do you feel?" It's so tempting to switch over into the natural realm and just spew it all out, telling people how bad you really feel, how bad it looks, and how bad the doctor's report says it's going to get. Flesh just likes to get down and wallow in that mire of doubt and self-pity, looking for sympathy.

Let us hold fast the profession of our faith without wavering; (for he is faithful that promised).

—Hebrews 10:23

But I'd rather have healing than sympathy. Sympathy feels good for a few seconds, but healing feels good for a long time. I can hold fast to my symptoms and get sympathy. But I'd rather hold fast to my confession of faith and get results.

Confession

Jesus was faithful to heal those who came to Him in faith, and He's still the same today. I hold fast to my confession that I am healed because God is faithful to keep His promises.

Return God's Word Unto Him

For my thoughts are not your thoughts, neither are your ways my ways, saith the Lord. For as the heavens are higher than the earth, so are my ways higher than your ways, and my thoughts than your thoughts.

For as the rain cometh down, and the snow from heaven, and returneth not thither, but watereth the earth, and maketh it bring forth and bud, that it may give seed to the sower, and bread to the eater: So shall my word be that goeth forth out of my mouth: it shall not return unto me void....

—Isaiah 55:8-11

God's ways and thoughts are so much higher than ours. But, thank God, He had His ways and thoughts written down in sixty-six books called the Bible and handed them to us so we can walk in victory.

But some folks say, "I tried the Word, and it didn't work for me." The truth is, the Word *always* works *if you work it*. So if the Word doesn't seem to be working in your life, perhaps you aren't returning it to Him. God said "[My Word] shall not return unto me void," (v. 11).

How do you *return* God's Word to Him? With your mouth. You say, "Father, thank You no weapon formed against me shall prosper. Thank You by Jesus' stripes I'm healed. Thank You I walk in abundant life."

Fill your heart with God's promises pertaining to your need, then return the Word to Him by holding fast your confession of faith. As you do, God will make sure His Word returns with the answer!

Confession

Father, I return Your Word to You. I say, by Jesus' stripes I'm healed. Jesus took my infirmities and bare my sicknesses. And You satisfy me with long life.

Go Forth With Joy

God's talking here about an abundant, blessed life. God plans for His people to "go out with joy, and be led forth with peace." This is a provision under the old covenant, and today we live under a new and even better covenant established on better promises.

Folks say, "Well, that's just a blessing for the Jews." But the Bible says we are grafted in through the blood of Jesus.

...they which are of faith, the same are the children of Abraham.

Galatians 3:7

If ye be Christ's, then are ye Abraham's seed, and heirs according to the promise.

Galatians 3:29

Some folks say, "Well, we're redeemed from the Old Testament." No, we're just redeemed from the curse of the law. (Gal. 3:13.) We still have a right to all the old covenant blessings. And on top of that, we have the new birth, the infilling of the Holy Ghost, and the life, nature, and ability of God living on the inside of us.

So shall my word be that goeth forth out of my mouth: it shall not return unto me void, but it shall accomplish that which I please, and it shall prosper in the thing whereto I sent it. For ye shall go out with joy, and be led forth with peace....

—Isaiah 55:11,12

How do these blessings operate in our lives? They operate as you believe and speak God's Word, which *cannot* return to Him void. Think about that. When you speak God's Word, it must come to pass and accomplish what it's sent to do because God's words wouldn't dare return to Him empty and void!.

Confession

God's Word doesn't return to Him void so I speak joy, peace, health, blessings, and abundance in my life, knowing God's Word will accomplish it.

God's Insurance Policy

He that dwelleth in the secret place of the most High shall abide under the shadow of the Almighty. I will say of the Lord, He is my refuge and my fortress: my God; in him will I trust.

There shall no evil befall thee, neither shall any plague come nigh thy dwelling.

—Psalm 91:1,2,10

I thank God for insurance policies protecting houses and cars and so on, but I thank God even more for the divine insurance policy He gave us in Psalm 91. I have more confidence in that policy than in any earthly one.

Janet and I have seen the 91st Psalm work many times in our lives. For instance, we frequently travel overseas, and all you have to do is ride in traffic to witness firsthand how angels protect you. In some countries, whichever car bumper sticks out the farthest is the car with the right of way. I love it, but Janet closes her eyes and prays while I drive.

Now, verse 1 of our divine policy says, "He that dwelleth in the secret place of the most High shall abide under the shadow of the Almighty." If we want to stay within the boundaries of God's protection, we must walk closely with Him.

How do we appropriate our Psalm 91 insurance policy? Verse 2 tells us: "I will *say* of the Lord, He is my refuge, and my fortress: my God; in him will I trust."

As you speak God's promises of protection and deliverance, His Word will not return unto Him void. No evil will befall you, and no plague shall come near you.

Confession

Psalm 91 works for me. My God is my refuge and my fortress. No plague comes near my dwelling place because I put my trust in Him.

Walk in Agreement With God

Adam walked and talked with God in the cool of the day. That's the fellowship the first Adam had with God, but he lost it through the Fall.

Can two walk together, except they be agreed?

—Amos 3:3

The Bible calls Jesus the last Adam, the One who came to restore to us what the first Adam lost. So under the new covenant, we have the ability to walk and talk with God again. In fact, He said, "I will dwell in them, and walk in them; and I will be their God, and they shall be my people" (2 Cor. 6:16).

But when we're in disagreement with someone, it's hard to walk with that person in comfortable fellowship. It's the same way in our relationship with God.

Sometimes we unconsciously disagree with God and then wonder why He won't help us. We ask, "Why isn't God helping me? Why isn't He working for me? He knows how bad things are!"

Yes, God knows the situation. Nothing catches Him by surprise. He doesn't look down in surprise and say, "Wow! When did that happen?"

It isn't that God refuses to help us if we disagree with Him. There's just very little He can do. That's why Amos 3:3 says, "Can two walk together, except they be agreed?"

One particular meaning of the word *confess* is "to agree with."[1] In order to hold fast to the confession of your faith, you have to agree with God. The best way to develop agreement is to get in His Word. Then make a choice to agree with it, believing in your heart and saying with your mouth.

Confession

God says I'm healed. God says I'm more than a conqueror.
God says He satisfies me with long life. And I agree.

Guard Your Words

But the angel said unto him, Fear not, Zacharias: for thy prayer is heard; and thy wife Elisabeth shall bear thee a son, and thou shalt call his name John.

And Zacharias said unto the angel, Whereby shall I know this? for I am an old man, and my wife well stricken in years.

—Luke 1:13,18

Zacharias, a priest under the old covenant, was in the temple fullfilling his duties when the angel Gabriel appeared. The angel told Zacharias that he and his wife would bear a child named John. This was big news because they were old and had no children.

"How can this be? We're too old," Zacharias said. In other words, he doubted the word of the Lord.

A person who doubts at some point will speak doubt. So Gabriel said, "And, behold, thou shalt be dumb, and not able to speak, until the day that these things shall be performed, because thou believest not my words, which shall be fulfilled in their season" (v. 20).

The son born to Zacharias would become John the Baptist, who was a crucial part of God's plan; he came to prepare the way for the first coming of Jesus. If Zacharias had spoken doubt against that divine plan, he could've messed up the whole thing. So Zacharias was made dumb until the plan was fulfilled. God wasn't punishing Zacharias; He was protecting His divine plan.

God may not strike you dumb, but He does tell you to guard your mouth. Your words can put you on a path to victory or defeat. Protect God's plan for your life by guarding your words.

Confession

My words keep me in the midst of God's plan for my life.
I will finish my course with joy and live a long and healthy life.

"Be It Unto Me According to Thy Word"

When the angel appeared to Mary and told her she, a virgin, would have a son, she didn't say, "I don't believe this." She didn't say, "Give me a sign that this is really true." She simply questioned how it could happen, saying, "How shall this be, seeing I know not a man?" (Luke 1:34).

She was saying, "I don't know how it's going to happen; but you said it so I believe it." Verse 38 says, "And Mary said...be it unto me according to thy word."

The angel Gabriel appeared to Zacharias and Mary, bringing the promise of a child to both. To Zacharias it was difficult to believe because he and his wife were old. To Mary it was impossible to believe because she was a virgin.

Zacharias doubted and said, "I don't know whether I can believe that." He had to have his mouth closed for months so he wouldn't disagree with God's plan.

And the angel came in unto her, and said, Hail, thou that art highly favoured, the Lord is with thee: blessed art thou among women.

And, behold, thou shalt conceive in thy womb, and bring forth a son, and shalt call his name Jesus.

—Luke 1:28,31

But Mary simply said, "I believe it!" Verse 45 tells us the result of Mary's faith: "Blessed is she that believed: for *there shall be a performance of those things which were told her from the Lord.*"

Words make a difference! So, pick yours carefully so there will also be a performance of those things which have been told you from the Lord.

Confession

My words cause me to walk in God's plan of abundance and health.
Be it unto me according to Your Word, Lord.

Tell Yourself How You Are

...Whosoever shall say unto this mountain, Be thou removed, and be thou cast into the sea; and shall not doubt in his heart, but shall believe that those things which he saith shall come to pass; he shall have whatsoever he saith.

Therefore I say unto you, What things soever ye desire, when ye pray, believe that ye receive them, and ye shall have them.

—Mark 11:23, 24

In this passage, Jesus gives us the most complete, condensed instruction of faith found in the Bible. In verse 23, He gives the two basic principles of faith—believing in the heart and saying with the mouth. Then in verse 24, He shows us how to apply our faith in prayer.

Now, I remember hearing that Smith Wigglesworth once said, "I never get up in the morning and ask Smith how he is. I get up in the morning and tell him how he is."

You can do the same. Take yourself to God's Word every morning and say, "This is how you are. You're more than a conqueror. This is the victory that overcomes the world—even your faith. (1 John 5:4.) By Jesus' stripes you were healed. (1 Peter 2:24.) You've been delivered. (Col. 1:13.)"

We have to feed on the Word until we not only know what God says, but we also believe it in our hearts. Then when a situation arises, we can just lean back, look the problem square in the face and say, "I don't care what you look like, seem like, sound like, or feel like. I believe God!"

Confession

Every day I tell myself how I am according to God's Word. I'm healed. I'm blessed. And I believe it shall be even as He told me in His Word.

Taking Our Promised Land

The things that happened to Israel happened as examples for us. Many are types and shadows, or pictures, we can learn from because they point to our new covenant in Christ.

God delivered Israel from the bondage of Egypt. He supernaturally parted the Red Sea and then closed up the Red Sea on the Egyptian army. God "brought them forth also with silver and gold: and there was not one feeble person among their tribes" (Ps. 105:37).

When the Israelites came out of Egypt and walked across that Red Sea, they were free, happy, healthy, prosperous, and delivered from their enemies.

Now all these things happened unto them for ensamples: and they are written for our admonition, upon whom the ends of the world are come.

—1 Corinthians 10:11

That's what the new birth looks like. And the minute we're born again, that's the way God sees us. If we trust Him, we can walk in that kind of life. Challenges will come along, but the Bible says, "This is the victory that overcometh the world, even our faith" (1 John 5:4).

God led the Israelites into the Promised Land, which isn't a type of heaven; it's a type of our abundant Christian life on earth.

God told them, "Giants live there, but don't be concerned about them. I'll drive them out. You just go possess what I've given you!"

We're in a similar position. Victory already belongs to us. The devil has already been defeated. Sickness and disease have already been conquered. Now we just have to exercise our rights and privileges to take what already belongs to us.

Confession

God wants me free, healthy, and delivered from my enemies.
That's my promised land! I take health that is mine in Jesus' name.

Enter Your Promised Land Through Faith

And Moses sent them to spy out the land of Canaan, and said unto them, Get you up this way southward, and go up into the mountain: and see the land, what it is....

—Numbers 13:17,18

God told the Israelites about a land flowing with milk and honey, so the twelve spies went in to check it out. When they returned, they brought back a cluster of grapes so large it took two men to carry it.

That looked mighty good to these children of Israel who'd been living in the desert getting water from a rock and living on manna from heaven. They were ready to move in and possess this Promised Land. However, Israel didn't go in; they stayed back in the desert.

You'll find that in the church world today. Some folks are satisfied to stay out in the "desert," getting a little water out of a rock and a bit of manna from heaven each morning. They could move over into the promised land and enjoy an abundance of blessings, but they're satisfied where they are. "Don't push healing on me," they say. "I'm not interested. I'm happy as I am."

You see, the choice is ours. God doesn't force anything on anyone. I don't know about you, but I have a burning desire to move over into my promised land—the best God has for me.

The Bible says the Israelites "could not enter in because of unbelief" (Heb. 3:19). What will you do? Whether you move into abundance or just barely get along is the extent to which you believe God. No wonder God says, "Without faith, you can't please Me."

Confession

Healing is part of the abundant life Jesus provided for me.
I'm strong, healed, and able to possess my inheritance.

Nevertheless–Believe God

Faith is a law that operates by believing and saying. Just like the natural law of gravity, this spiritual law works for everyone. If we jump off a platform, the law of gravity says we will hit the floor. And according to the law of faith, what we believe and say is what we will get.

The ten spies returned to report that the land overflowed with milk and honey, and offered huge clusters of grapes.

If the spies had stopped there, they would've been in good shape. But they said, "*Nevertheless....*" Then verse 32 says, "They brought up an evil report of the land...."

That word *nevertheless* gets a lot of people in trouble because it's a sign of their unbelief. "Lord, we know what Your Word says; *nevertheless....*"

But I like the way Peter used the word. One morning after a bad night of fishing, Jesus told him, "Launch out into the deep, and let down your nets for a draught" (Luke 5:4).

...We came unto the land whither thou sentest us, and surely it floweth with milk and honey; and this is the fruit of it. Nevertheless the people be strong that dwell in the land, and the cities are walled, and very great: and moreover we saw the children of Anak there.

—Numbers 13:27,28

Peter replied, "Master, we have toiled all the night, and have taken nothing: *nevertheless* at thy word I will let down the net" (v. 5). As Peter obeyed Jesus, he and the other fishermen caught so many fish their boats almost sank.

Let's use the word *nevertheless* the way Peter did—to believe God.

Confession

Symptoms and circumstances may try to come against me;
yet nevertheless, I overcome through the
power in God's Word and Jesus' name.

The Spirit of Faith

Surely they shall not see the land which I sware unto their fathers, neither shall any of them that provoked me see it: but my servant Caleb, because he had another spirit with him, and hath followed me fully, him will I bring into the land whereinto he went; and his seed shall possess it.

—Numbers 14:23,24

When the twelve spies went to check out the Promised Land, they discovered it was flowing with milk and honey, exactly as God had said.

But when the spies came back out, three million and ten of the people said, "We can't possess that land." Only Joshua and Caleb stood up and said, "Yes, we can. If God said it, we can do it!"

The other unbelieving children of Israel wandered in the wilderness for forty years and eventually died there. Forty years later, Joshua and Caleb led the next generation of Israelites into the Promised Land.

But notice, they all got what they believed and said. And if that spiritual law worked under the old covenant, it works under the new.

God said, "But my servant Caleb because he had another spirit with him, and hath followed me fully...." What did God mean by "another spirit"? Caleb had the same spirit of faith Paul talked about in 2 Corinthians 4:13: "We having the same spirit of faith, according as it is written, I believed, and therefore have I spoken; we also believe, and therefore speak."

We're a direct result of what we've believed and said up to this point in time. So, don't believe evil reports. Hook up with God, agree with His Word, and walk in His blessings.

Confession

I believe, and therefore, I say that You sent Your Word and healed me. You've delivered me from destruction.

What Kind of Witness Will You Be?

There are two different witnesses talking to us in every situation.

On one side, there's the witness of the problem. Problems speak loud and clear, whether it's pain, symptoms, bad reports, depression, or fear. It says, "Man, you're sick! You won't make it. You're defeated."

In the mouth of two or three witnesses shall every word be established.

—2 Corinthians 13:1

On the other side is the witness of God's Word. It says, "By Jesus' stripes, you were healed. (Isa. 53:5; 1 Peter 2:24.) Thanks be unto God who always gives you the victory through the Lord Jesus Christ. (2 Cor. 2:14.) This is the victory that overcomes the world, even your faith. (1 John 5:4.)"

But notice, it takes two witnesses for any of those words to stand. The word *establish* means "to cause to stand."[1] So God said, "In the mouth of two or three witnesses, let every word be established, or be made to stand."

The devil is on one side. God is on the other. And *you're* in the middle. The side *you* line up with becomes the side with the majority vote. If you line up with the problem, it's established in your life, and there's little God can do about it. However, if you choose to line up with God's Word, you're on your way to victory.

How do you line up? The witness you *believe* and *verbally agree with* is the one that becomes established in your life.

Confession

With my mouth, I establish the Word in my life. God sent His Word and healed me. I believe I'm healed according to His Word.

Choose To Receive by the Hand of Faith

I call heaven and earth to record this day against you, that I have set before you life and death, blessing and cursing: therefore choose life, that both thou and thy seed may live.

—Deuteronomy 30:19

Some folks agree with every problem that comes along: "Oh, I'm sick. I'm broke. I'm defeated. I'm discouraged. I'm depressed. Nothing ever goes right for me." Some people constantly talk the blues, believe the blues, and get the blues. Then they wonder why God doesn't—and cannot—help them.

The truth is, if it were up to God we'd never have a problem. The Bible says He *has already given* us all things that pertain to life and godliness. (2 Peter 1:3.) He *has already redeemed* us from sickness, disease, poverty, lack, failure, and fear.

Yet, God left the matter of whether or not we walk in these redemptive blessings in our hands.

In Deuteronomy 30:19, He said, "I have set before you life and death, blessing and cursing: therefore choose life." It's our choice. God doesn't force anything on us. God already provided His best for us when He purchased everything we'd ever need that pertains to life and godliness. He made it available and then said, "If you want it, you can have it—just come and take it by faith."

Faith is the hand that receives from God. When we choose to reach out and take hold of God's blessings by faith, we become overcomers in this world, walking in the fullness of His blessings.

Confession

I choose to take hold of God's blessings by faith. I'm not moved by what I see or feel. I'm only moved by what I believe. God says I am healed; therefore, I agree and say, "I am healed."

Boldly Proclaim God's Truth

...For he [God] hath said, I will never leave thee, nor forsake thee. So that we may boldly say, The Lord is my helper; and I will not fear what man shall do unto me.

—Hebrews 13:5,6

Notice those two phrases "he hath said" and "that we may boldly say." As Christians, we ought to boldly say whatever God says about us. If He said, "By Jesus' stripes, you were healed," then we ought to boldly say the same. If He said, "I've delivered you from your fears," then we ought to boldly say the same.

We need to search the Scriptures to find out what God has said about us and our situation, then boldly proclaim that truth. Not timidly—*boldly!*

Now, we don't have to speak out in front of everyone; some won't believe or understand. But we can get before God and boldly agree with His Word.

So when the devil tries to remind you of mistakes you've made, you can boldly say, "Therefore if any man is in Christ, he's a new creature. Glory to God, I'm a new creature in Christ. Old things have passed away. All things have become new." (2 Cor. 5:17.)

Or when the devil says, "You're just an old, unworthy thing, a miserable creature," you can say, "He who knew no sin was made to be sin for me so I could be made the righteousness of God in Him. (2 Cor. 5:21.) I've been given the free gift of righteousness. I reign as a king in life. Glory to God!" "God hath said," so that you may boldly say the truth, then watch the enemy flee.

Confession

I boldly say the Lord is my strength and helper. No plague comes near my dwelling. No weapon formed against me prospers.

Jesus, Our Advocate

Wherefore, holy brethren, partakers of the heavenly calling, consider the Apostle and High Priest of our profession, Christ Jesus.

—Hebrews 3:1

The Greek word for *profession* is also translated *confession*, meaning Jesus is the apostle and High Priest of our confession. First John 2:1 tells us even more about Jesus' role and says, "If any man sin, we have an *advocate* with the Father, Jesus Christ the righteous." In other words, Jesus is our Mediator—our attorney.

Consider a big court case where God is the judge. In the far corner is the prosecutor—or the devil and accuser of the brethren. (Rev. 12:10.) Thank God, our attorney—Jesus—is in our corner.

Now, think about this scenario. The devil whispers to your mind, *I'm going to make you sick.* Then your attorney Jesus leans toward you saying, "All right, give Me something to work with."

But you agree with your accuser: "Oh, I'm so sick and getting sicker. Everything goes wrong for me. I hurt from head to toe."

Jesus looks at the Father and says, "I haven't got a thing to work with here."

Now, consider this instead. When the devil whispers in your mind, *I'm going to make you sick,* suppose your attorney Jesus finds you boldly saying: "Thank God, by Jesus' stripes I was healed. (Isa. 53.5; 1 Peter 2:24.) This is the victory that overcomes the world, even my faith. (1 John 5:4.)"

That's the kind of confession Jesus has been waiting to hear. He turns to the Judge and says, "Father, be it unto Your child according to his faith!"

Confession

God is the strength of my life. He heals me from
the top of my head to the soles of my feet.

Redeemed From Every Curse of Sickness

Sometimes people get sick and think, *There must be some deep, dark, hidden sin in my life I don't even know about that's caused this curse to come on me.* Yet, some problems in our lives are without cause; they're simply attacks from the enemy. So if you don't know about a hidden sin in your life, it's probably not there.

Even if you have sinned—repent, receive forgiveness, and walk in the provision of healing Jesus purchased for you.

I talked to a fellow in Europe who was upset because a physical ailment had come on his relative. He told me, "We've gone all through her childhood to see if she had any bitterness in her past that caused this condition. We found out she got angry at her mother one time when she was a little girl."

This man was trying to view his relative's sickness from a psychological perspective. Now, sometimes bitterness can cause illnesses. But we need to be careful about getting into the realm of psychology. Although psychology can sometimes help locate problems, it can seldom free us from them.

We don't need to go digging past the time we were born again. At that moment, we became new creatures, and our old man died. Any problems we had before that are gone.

Thank God, we've been redeemed from every curse of the enemy.

> *Christ hath redeemed us from the curse of the law, being made a curse for us: for it is written, Cursed is every one that hangeth on a tree.*
>
> *—Galatians 3:13*

Confession

I'm a new creature in Christ Jesus. My past was wiped away.
Therefore, I come boldly to the throne of grace to obtain
mercy and find grace to help in time of need.

"God's Word Works for Me!"

The secret things belong unto the Lord our God: but those things which are revealed belong unto us and to our children for ever....

—Deuteronomy 29:29

Sometimes God won't tell us why a particular individual didn't get his or her healing.

For instance, one time Janet and I were asked to pray for a very ill man in the hospital. When we visited, he was lying in bed saying everything right: "By Jesus' stripes I'm healed. (Isa. 53:5; 1 Peter 2:24.) Himself took my infirmities and bore my sicknesses. (Matt. 8:17.)"

But as we left, we knew in our spirits he would go home to be with the Lord. We sensed he was talking right because he didn't want his family angry at him for wanting to go to heaven. He'd seen a glimpse of it and was tired of fighting.

In just a short time, the man did go home to be with the Lord.

Some said of his death, "I guess this faith stuff doesn't work. He was believing God and died." *Yes, but he was believing God to go home.*

You can't let someone else's experience affect you because you never know what's in that person's heart. Don't look at another person's situation and say, "Well, if it didn't work for him, it will never work for me." Get your eyes back on God's Word that assures us it's God's will to heal *every* person *every* time of *every* disease. Then say, "Well, I don't know why it didn't work for that person, but it will always work for me!"

Confession

By Jesus' stripes I'm healed, and I'm never letting go of that.
My faith isn't based on people's experience, but
on the solid foundation of God's Word.

You Can Finish Your Course

Some people think there's an appointed time to die, and when that time comes the person dies. But that's wrong thinking, and it leaves the door open to the devil.

This verse doesn't say there's an appointed time to die. It says *it is appointed unto man to die once.* I heard someone say, "It's appointed unto man once to die, but we don't have to let the devil set the appointment."

It is appointed unto men once to die, but after this the judgment.

—Hebrews 9:27

The apostle Paul said in Philippians 1:23-24, "For I am in a strait betwixt two, having a desire to depart, and to be with Christ; which is far better: nevertheless to abide in the flesh is more needful for you." In other words, Paul was saying, "I haven't decided yet whether to go or stay." He was writing from prison, and they were ready to take his head off. Yet Paul was saying he hadn't decided whether to go or stay—as though he had a choice.

Paul did have a choice. Later in his writings, he said, "For I am now ready to be offered, and the time of my departure is at hand. I have fought a good fight, I have finished my course, I have kept the faith" (2 Tim. 4:6,7). He left when he was good and ready—and that was when he'd finished his course.

You should desire to do the same. Dare to believe God for a long, satisfying life. Determine in your heart you won't leave this earth until you can say with confidence, "I've finished my course!"

Confession

I'll live out my full time on this earth. I'll fight the good fight
of faith; I'll finish my course with joy.

Faith in God's Word Prolongs Life

My son, forget not my law; but let thine heart keep my commandments: for length of days, and long life, and peace, shall they add to thee.

—Proverbs 3:1,2

Someone might say, "What is our full length of time on this earth?" Perhaps it's one age for one person and another age for another person. If God were making the appointment, we'd know that from the Bible.

But look at what Ephesians 6:1-3 says:

Children, obey your parents in the Lord: for this is right. Honour thy father and mother; (which is the first commandment with promise;) that it may be well with thee, and *thou mayest live long on the earth.*

In other words, the Bible tells children, "There's something you can do that will cause you to have a long life."

The book of Proverbs also talks about increasing the length of our lives:

The fear of the Lord is the beginning of wisdom: and the knowledge of the holy is understanding. For by me thy days shall be multiplied, and the years of thy life shall be increased.

Proverbs 9:10,11

The fear of the Lord prolongeth days: but the years of the wicked shall be shortened.

Proverbs 10:27

There are many other Scriptures that say, "If you do this, you'll live long on the earth," or "If you do that, you'll cut your life short on this earth." But the Bible doesn't say, "There's an appointed time, and when your time comes, you're going." No, God tells us how to prolong our lives.

Confession

The life I find in God's Word drives disease far from me.
My days are multiplied, and the years of my life
are increased as I fear and reverence Him.

Believe God for Length of Days

I knew a man who was only thirty-nine years old when he went home to be with Jesus. He'd been sick for a while and never received healing.

Later, this man's brother told someone, "You know, it's the strangest thing. When my brother and I were younger, we spent a lot of time together. Every now and then, he'd get really serious and say, 'I'll never live to be forty.'"

The man didn't have any particular reason for believing that, but he kept thinking and planning for an early death. Just a matter of weeks before he turned forty, he went home to be with the Lord. He could've had thirty, forty, or fifty more years on this earth and fulfilled God's will for his life.

And if thou wilt walk in my ways, to keep my statutes and my commandments, as thy father David did walk, then I will lengthen thy days.

—1 Kings 3:14

Now, I don't mean to criticize people who go home early, but we need to keep our thinking right. The Bible says believers can enjoy abundant blessings in this life. We don't have to die sick.

The good news is whether a Christian gets healed or goes home to be with the Lord, he can't be defeated. If he gets healed, he's going to go tell everyone about it. If he dies and goes to heaven, he'll be with Jesus.

We have an eternity to spend in heaven, so let's get the job done here first, and then go home to be with the Lord.

Confession

I obey God's commandments with my whole heart.
Therefore, long life and peace are added unto me.
I'll live on earth until I'm satisfied.

Live Out Your Full Life on Earth

With long life will I satisfy him, and shew him my salvation.

—Psalm 91:16

God wants you to live out your full life on the earth. Yet if you don't, He won't be mad at you.

We should never criticize anyone for going home to heaven early. For instance, Janet and I had a friend who was extremely ill and couldn't seem to get his healing. He was too young to die, but he saw a glimpse of the other side and told his family, "I'm not staying. I just can't stay anymore."

Sometimes people get a glimpse of heaven, and you can't hold them back. When we say it's not the will of God for people to go home early, we're not being critical of those who have. We're just saying to those who are still here, "Let's press on and stay as long as we can!"

Don't ever feel sorry for someone who has gone to heaven. Don't try to figure out why he didn't get his healing. Faith is a matter of the heart, and the only One who can look into the heart is God.

Someone may say, "Well, I knew so-and-so. He was believing God, and it didn't work."

No, that isn't right. It may have looked as if that person was believing God, but *God doesn't—and cannot—fail.*

Don't try to figure it all out. Rejoice with those who have made it to the other side, and keep the Word working for yourself in this life.

Confession

My God shows me His salvation. He preserves my life.
He heals my body. God's Word works mightily in me.
And I'll be satisfied with a long, fruitful life for His glory.

Believe the Word, Not the Symptoms

For we walk by faith, not by sight.

—2 Corinthians 5:7

I heard about a lady who attended a particular church and had a big, visible cancerous growth on her face. She'd prayed and believed she received her healing, but there was no change in her appearance.

Later at a testimony service, this woman stood and said, "I want to thank God for healing me." She sat down, and people started looking at her funny. The next Sunday, she stood and said, "I want to thank God for healing me." This went on for several weeks.

Some people got upset, and one person said to her, "Everyone can see you're not healed. You're causing confusion. You can't keep standing up telling people you're healed."

The woman went home and stood in front of her mirror praying, "Now, Father, in Jesus' name, I know I'm healed by the stripes of Jesus. I know what the Bible says, and I know I believe it. I'd sure appreciate it, though, if You'd get rid of these ugly symptoms."

All of a sudden, while the woman still stood at the mirror, that big cancer just fell off and hit the floor! She looked in the mirror and saw that the area where the growth had been a moment before was covered in fresh baby skin!

You see, even though we reach out by faith and believe we receive our answer, we may not look different immediately. But we don't have to look different—we just have to believe what the Bible says and say what we believe. *Then* we have what we say!

Confession

Thank God, I'm healed. No matter how I feel or what
I see or what comes at me, I believe I have the victory.

Switch Over to the Realm of Faith

We having the same spirit of faith, according as it is written, I believed, and therefore have I spoken; we also believe, and therefore speak.

—*2 Corinthians 4:13*

Perhaps you need a miracle and have been waiting for God to manifest Himself through the gifts of the Spirit. But no gift has come. What should you do now?

Do what the Bible says you're supposed to do. Switch over to the realm of faith. Believe God, and draw power out of Him.

You see, Jesus ministered to people in two different ways when He walked on this earth. At times Jesus sovereignly performed miracles that required no faith from the individual. Other times people crawled up behind Jesus in a crowd and pulled power out of Him when He didn't even know they were there. (Matt. 14:36.) Their faith released the power of God.

Jesus still ministers both ways. Sometimes He sovereignly works miracles—*at His will*. But our faith in His Word will work every time *at our will*.

So don't wait for a miracle to happen—make one happen with your faith in God's Word!

Someone once said to me, "Oh, you make God sound like a heavenly butler." No, I don't make God sound like anything. I just tell you what He's already said in His Word.

Beside that, there's a big difference between a heavenly butler and a heavenly Father. You tell a butler what to do. But with your heavenly Father, you find out what He's already said and done for you, then take hold of it by faith.

Confession

My God always makes His healing power available to me. I draw on that healing power by faith and appropriate what I need from Him.

"Ask, and It Shall Be Done Unto You"

Jesus was telling His disciples, "If you abide in Me, and My words abide in you, *My words abiding in you will produce faith.* Then you'll ask whatever you will, and it will be done unto you." I didn't say that—Jesus did!

Now, Jesus did put limits on that promise. He did not give us carte blanche. In other words, He didn't say, "Ask for anything—period." No, Jesus said, "If you abide in Me and My words abide in you...."

If ye abide in me, and my words abide in you, ye shall ask what ye will, and it shall be done unto you.

—John 15:7

You see, if His Word is abiding in you and you're walking with Him, you won't be able to ask in faith for anything that's unscriptural; you'll only ask for things that line up with the Word. That's God's checks-and-balances system.

Actually, in this verse Jesus is saying that *you can have a miracle at your own discretion.* You don't have to sit back and wait to see whether it's God's own good time to perform a sovereign miracle. God said, "If you abide in Me and My words abide in you, ask whatever you will, and it shall be done for you!" You have Jesus' word on it—you can initiate a miracle any time you want.

Confession

I abide in Jesus, and His Word abides in me. Therefore, I ask whatever I will, and it's done unto me. I ask for healing, and it's done unto me. God's healing power is released and working in me even now.

The Power in Prayer

Is any sick among you? let him call for the elders of the church; and let them pray over him, anointing him with oil in the name of the Lord: and the prayer of faith shall save the sick, and the Lord shall raise him up; and if he have committed sins, they shall be forgiven him. Confess your faults one to another, and pray one for another, that ye may be healed....

—James 5:14-16

Who is the "ye" in the phrase "that ye may be healed"? "Ye" is the body of Christ. Each of us in the body of Christ is to pray for one another so those in the Church may be healed.

We Christians will be healthier when we start praying for one another. We need to understand that we have great power in prayer. James 5:16 AMP puts it this way: "The earnest (heartfelt, continued) prayer of a righteous man makes tremendous power available [dynamic in its working]."

Praying for each other can make the difference. You see, there are people in the Church and in the world who need your help to understand and take hold of their healing. Why? Some people have never even heard about divine healing. Isaiah 5:13 says, "Therefore my people are gone into captivity, because they have no knowledge...." Others have never been taught how to receive from God. These people need someone to go to the throne of God in prayer for them, praying that the eyes of their understanding are enlightened. (Eph.1:16.)

You can be that someone! Your earnest, heartfelt, and continued prayers for another can make tremendous power available.

Confession

As I pray, tremendous power is made available to effect a healing and a cure in others and in me.

Coming to Jesus for Others

You'll find cases again and again in the Bible where people were healed because someone went to Jesus on another's behalf.

For instance, did you ever notice in Matthew 8 that the centurion's servant who needed healing stayed home? This servant had palsy, but he was healed because someone went to Jesus on his behalf. (vv. 5-13.)

In Matthew 15, the woman from Canaan came to Jesus on behalf of her daughter, who was grievously vexed with a devil. This girl was healed because of her mother's faith. (vv. 22-28.)

In John 4, the nobleman traveled approximately twenty-five miles to reach Jesus. The nobleman said, "My son is at home at the point of death. Come and heal him." Jesus said, "Go your way; your son is all right." The man went his way believing the word Jesus had spoken. And because he had gone to Jesus on his son's behalf, his boy was healed. (vv. 47-53.)

When the even was come, they brought unto him many that were possessed with devils: and he cast out the spirits with his word, and healed all that were sick.

—Matthew 8:16

Years ago, when someone in a church was sick, it was a common occurrence for the church to rally around and pray twenty-four hours a day until that person was healed. It wasn't something they organized; it was Holy Ghost inspired. We need to continue that practice today because "the earnest (heartfelt, continued) prayer of a righteous man makes tremendous power available [dynamic in its working]" (James 5:16 AMP).

Confession

It's God's will that *all* be healed. Today I can bring people before God's throne in prayer so Jesus can work His healing power in them. Healing belongs to them and to me because we serve a good God.

Persistence in Prayer

*One of [Jesus']
disciples said unto
him, Lord, teach us
to pray, as John also
taught his disciples.*

—Luke 11:1

The disciples were impressed by Jesus' prayer life, and no wonder, for He got results. So they asked Him to teach them how to pray. Jesus first taught the Lord's Prayer. Then He shared another key to prayer:

And he said unto them, Which of you shall have a friend, and shall go unto him at midnight, and say unto him, Friend, lend me three loaves; for a friend of mine in his journey is come to me, and I have nothing to set before him?

Luke 11:5,6

What is *bread?* Well, when the woman of Canaan in Matthew 15 asked for healing for her daughter, Jesus called healing the children's bread. (v. 26.) So in this parable, when the man asked for three loaves of bread, he could've been asking for healing for his friend.

And he from within shall answer and say, Trouble me not: the door is now shut, and my children are with me in bed; I cannot rise and give thee. I say unto you, Though he will not rise and give him, because he is his friend, yet *because of his importunity,* he will rise and give him as many as he needeth.

Luke 11:7,8

Jesus said the man finally gave the bread to the petitioner because of his importunity. One meaning of that word *importunity* is "persistence." *The Amplified Bible* says, "because of his shameless persistence and insistence...."

Do you know someone in need who can't seem to make contact with God for himself? Go to God on his behalf. He will hear your persistent prayers and serve your friend exactly what he needs—the children's bread of healing.

Confession

I boldly go to my Father in behalf of others. I persistently ask and faithfully believe God will serve them the children's bread of healing.

Helping Others Make Contact With God

Have you been in a situation where you knew what the Word said, you knew how to believe God, your words lined up with the Bible—but still, you got nowhere fast?

Those are the times you need to go before the Father and say, "God, You never miss it because You can't change. So, tell me where I'm missing it, and I'll make the adjustment."

Sometimes people get in situations where, for one reason or another, they just can't seem to make contact with their answer. In many of those cases, other believers can go before God's throne and help them.

Confess your faults one to another, and pray one for another, that ye may be healed. The effectual fervent prayer of a righteous man availeth much.

—James 5:16

For example, years ago the daughter of a friend of ours became very ill and continually grew worse.

Another friend of ours told his wife one day that he sensed a strong urge to pray for this sick young lady. The couple prayed about five hours before the unction to pray lifted off them. They knew they had the answer.

Later, the couple found out that the very evening they prayed for the young woman, she suddenly started getting better, until soon she was perfectly normal.

We may never know why the young woman had trouble connecting with her answer. But God supernaturally moved on another believer to pray and "make tremendous power available" for her.

Confession

I'm faithful to pray fervently for others, and God's power is made available for their healing. When I don't know how to pray as I should, the Holy Spirit helps me pray, making intercession with groanings that cannot be uttered. (Rom. 8:26.)

Do the Works of Jesus

Believest thou not that I am in the Father, and the Father in me? the words that I speak unto you I speak not of myself: but the Father that dwelleth in me, he doeth the works.

—John 14:10

Jesus said, "I'm not healing people. The Father inside Me is the One doing the works. He's healing them through Me." He also said, "The Son can do nothing of himself, but what he seeth the Father do: for what things soever he doeth, these also doeth the Son likewise" (John 5:19).

Any time a Christian gives God the opportunity, God will start doing the same works He did through Jesus. That's why in John 14:12, Jesus said, "...He that believeth on me, the works that I do shall he do also; and greater works than these shall he do; because I go unto my Father."

God's plan is to dwell inside of us: "Know ye not that ye are the temple of the living God, and that the Spirit of God dwelleth in you?" (1 Cor. 3:16). We are the temple of the Holy Spirit, and that's why the believer's ministry is so powerful.

If you're a believer, God already lives inside you. Now it's up to you to release His power through faith. As you do, He will start doing the same works through you that He did through Jesus.

Confession

I'm the temple of the living God; the Spirit of God dwells in me.
Jesus said that as I believe on Him, I'm able to do the works He did—and even greater works because my Father does the work through me.

The Holy Spirit–God's Powerhouse

I've heard people say, "Miracles don't happen anymore. God doesn't heal today." But people sure don't get that idea from the Bible. There's no Scripture that will back up that statement.

Of course, Jesus is our healer. He purchased and provided healing for us on the Cross. Yet the Holy Spirit is the powerhouse who manifests that healing in our physical bodies. The Scripture above says the Spirit who raised Jesus from the dead is the same Spirit who quickens our mortal bodies or makes them alive.

Still today, the Holy Ghost is the One doing the mighty works of God through those who yield to Him. But the Holy Ghost didn't even come into the fullness of His ministry until the Day of Pentecost, when He was poured out on all flesh.

But if the Spirit of him that raised up Jesus from the dead dwell in you, he that raised up Christ from the dead shall also quicken your mortal bodies by his Spirit that dwelleth in you.

—Romans 8:11

So I ask this question: How can some say healings and miracles have stopped at the very time the Holy Spirit who manifests them came into the fullness of His ministry? The truth is, healings and miracles have not stopped. The Holy Spirit is still moving like a mighty wind over all the earth.

Confession

When Jesus ascended to the Father, He sent the Holy Spirit. That Holy Spirit dwells in me and manifests the healing power that Jesus purchased for me. That healing power is working in me right now.

Was It Profitable That Jesus Went Away?

Nevertheless I tell you the truth; It is expedient for you that I go away: for if I go not away, the Comforter will not come unto you; but if I depart, I will send him unto you.

—John 16:7

Jesus is the healer, but the Holy Ghost is the means by which Jesus manifests healing to us.

Jesus said in John 16:7 that it was *expedient,* or *profitable,* for us that He should go away. Yet how could it be profitable if it would mean we'd have to live below what Jesus provided for us? It couldn't. That's why Jesus said, "I will pray the Father, and he shall give you another Comforter, that he may abide with you for ever" (John 14:16).

Jesus was saying, in essence, "There's only one of Me. But if I go, I'll pour out the Holy Ghost. He will come into anyone who accepts Me as Lord and Savior, and that same power will dwell in him."

Jesus was also saying, "I'm not taking away healing when I go away. When I send the Holy Ghost, My healing power in the earth will be multiplied many times over!"

Regardless of what some say, healing didn't stop when Jesus ascended to heaven. It hasn't dwindled down to nothing. On the contrary, it has been multiplied hundreds of thousands of times over. Just ask the countless people living on this earth today who have been healed by God's power.

Confession

The greater One dwells within me and infills me with His power.
Healing is mine because the Spirit who breathed life back into
Jesus' body also quickens life to my mortal body.

The Holy Spirit, Our Teacher

Does God use sickness to teach us?

This Scripture says the Comforter will teach us all things. How much is "all things"? All means *all!* Well, if the Holy Spirit teaches us all things, how much does God reserve for us to learn through sickness and disease?

Absolutely nothing! You'll never find one place in the Bible where sickness is the teacher of the Church. It's always the Holy Ghost who guides and teaches.

"Well, yes," someone might say, "but God sometimes teaches us through sickness too." No, He doesn't. How could He when He doesn't have any sickness to give?

Second Timothy 3:16-17 shows us how the Holy Spirit uses the Word of God to teach us:

> *But the Comforter, which is the Holy Ghost, whom the Father will send in my name, he shall teach you all things, and bring all things to your remembrance, whatsoever I have said unto you.*
>
> *—John 14:26*

All scripture is given by inspiration of God, and is profitable for doctrine, for reproof, for correction, for instruction in righteousness: That the man of God may be perfect, thoroughly furnished unto all good works.

The Holy Ghost is our teacher, and God's Word is our perfecter, correcter, and instructor. So draw on the ministry of the Word and the teacher within. Don't look for lessons to be learned from sickness and pain. Let the Holy Spirit take you higher in God while you enjoy divine health.

Confession

Sickness is not my teacher; it's my enemy, and I rebuke it in Jesus' name. The Holy Ghost and the Word teach me everything I need to know to walk victoriously in life.

Tap Into God's Higher Ways

...My thoughts are not your thoughts, neither are your ways my ways, saith the Lord. For as the heavens are higher than the earth, so are my ways higher than your ways, and my thoughts than your thoughts.

—Isaiah 55:8,9

If God's point ended in verse 9, we might as well throw in the towel because God's ways and thoughts are so far above ours. But don't quit! Look at what God goes on to say: "...My word...shall not return unto me void, but it shall accomplish that which I please, and it shall prosper...whereto I sent it" (v. 11).

How can it prosper if we can't reach the height of His thoughts and ways? Well, God says, "Moved on by the Holy Ghost, I had holy men of old write down my ways and thoughts and give them to you in sixty-six books called the Bible. Now you have My old ways and thoughts as well as My new ways and thoughts. The new ones are even better than the old, so live by the new."

You see, God is always the same, but He enacted two covenants. Don't try to live under the old covenant He gave to people who were lost, or spiritually dead and separated from God. Their sinful, old nature was covered, not cleansed.

Today we are new creatures in Christ, living under a new covenant. We aren't just forgiven; we're made new. We're alive, redeemed, liberated, and healed.

So let God's Word renew your mind and bring life to your body. As you do, God promises His Word will help you walk in His higher ways of freedom, abundance, and health.

Confession

God's Word heals my body and renews my mind so
I can think His thoughts and follow His ways.

Walk in God's Ways

He made known his ways unto Moses, his acts unto the children of Israel.

—Psalm 103:7

God's acts are the miraculous deeds He performs, and His ways are the road that takes you to the miraculous.

Now, you see, everything God does on the earth, He does through the Holy Ghost. Think of it in terms of electricity. A power plant has plenty of electricity, but that power has to be moved from the power plant to electrical outlets so people can access it. That takes a conductor.

Well, God has plenty of power, and He wants to manifest the benefits of salvation in our lives. I once heard salvation defined as the sum total of all the blessings bestowed on man by God in Christ, through the Holy Ghost. Jesus purchased our salvation and God sends forth the blessings, but the Holy Ghost is the conductor.

That's why it's important for us to know more about the Spirit of God. He delivers salvation to our spirits and healing to our bodies. He's the One who transmits to us what the Father has.

Psalm 103:7 says that God made His ways known to Moses. As the leader of God's holy nation, Moses in particular had to know God's ways.

But Holy Ghost-filled believers must also know His ways. We're not supposed to just sit back and watch God move. He wants us to know His ways so we can be right in the middle of what He's doing on this earth.

Confession

God is making His ways known to me. I walk in the ways of God, and the Holy Ghost delivers the healing Jesus purchased for me.

The Two Flows of Anointing

How God anointed Jesus of Nazareth with the Holy Ghost and with power: who went about doing good, and healing all that were oppressed of the devil; for God was with him.

—Acts 10:38

Two major flows of anointing operated in Jesus' ministry, and these same flows are still on the body of Christ today.

One flow is like lightning. It hits every now and then; we don't know when, where, or how. These "bolts of lightning" are manifestations or gifts of the Spirit that operate as God wills.

The other flow of anointing is like electricity, flowing freely when activated by faith.

A man named Bullinger, who wrote most of the notes in the *The Companion Bible,* said, "There are fifty-two times in the New Testament where the term 'Holy Ghost' should literally be translated *not* 'the Person of the Holy Ghost,' but 'the manifestations of the Holy Ghost.'"[1]

Acts 10:38 is one of those times. So it should say, "God anointed Jesus of Nazareth with the manifestations of the Holy Ghost and with power."

At times, Jesus operated in the manifestations of the Spirit, delivering a miracle with no faith on the recipient's part. These were manifestations of God's sovereign side, where His power flowed like lightning.

But a majority of the time, Jesus would teach and preach to develop faith in people. Then by faith, individuals would activate His power and release it to flow like electricity.

Jesus hasn't changed. If the majority received by faith back then, that's how the majority will receive today. Let the hand of faith release God's power to flow in you.

Confession

By faith I tap into God's healing power and release it to flow in me. I say healing is mine, and I receive it now.

The Spirit Without Measure

We've been talking about learning the ways of God's Spirit—how He works, how He moves. Of course, the best way to understand God's ways is to look at Jesus.

Jesus had been with the Father from the beginning, but He set aside His glory and took on flesh. He left the rightful dignity and privileges He had enjoyed with the Father and was born on this earth as a baby. Then at the age of thirty, Jesus worked His first miracle after the Holy Ghost had come upon Him.

The Bible says, "God giveth not the Spirit by measure unto him." In plain English, that means God gave Jesus the anointing *without limitations.* Jesus didn't have one strong point, because He had all strong points. But when Jesus left this earth and went to the Father's right hand, He distributed the anointing that was on His earthly body throughout His new body of believers.

For he whom God hath sent speaketh the words of God: for God giveth not the Spirit by measure unto him. The Father loveth the Son, and hath given all things into his hand.

—John 3:34,35

Individually, no other person will ever walk in the anointing without measure. But the body of Christ as a whole has the anointing without measure. So whatever manifestations of God's power we saw in Jesus' ministry, we should see operating through the Church today as believers learn more about the ways of God.

Confession

I'm a child of God, and I'm learning to follow the ways of my Father. He wants me to be healthy and whole. Healing is mine. It's bought and paid for by the blood of His Son, and I receive it by faith.

Our Family Is Cheering Us On

...One of his disciples said unto him, Lord, teach us to pray, as John also taught his disciples. And he said unto them, When ye pray, say, Our Father which art in heaven, Hallowed be thy name. Thy kingdom come. Thy will be done, as in heaven, so in earth.

—Luke 11:1,2

Jesus' disciples asked Him to teach them to pray. One part of the prayer Jesus taught them said, "Thy will be done, as in heaven, so in earth." You see, God doesn't have one will for His children in heaven and one will for His children down here on earth.

Many of us have thought the early Church and latter Church are two separate churches. No, there's just *the* Church.

Then we've thought there are two different families of God: the family already in heaven and the family still on the earth. No, it's just *one* family.

Paul wrote to the Ephesians and said, "For this cause I bow my knees unto the Father of our Lord Jesus Christ, of whom the whole family in heaven and earth is named" (Eph. 3:14,15). Our family members in heaven are just as real as we are. They're leaning over the balcony of heaven, cheering us on, saying, "Go for it! Get with it, folks!"

All those great faith men and women in Hebrews 11 are watching along with our loved ones who've gone on before us. They're all cheering us on, encouraging us to overcome every obstacle in our spiritual race. That ought to get us excited!

Confession

I want God's will done on earth, as it is in heaven. There's no sickness in heaven, so sickness must leave my body in Jesus' name. God's healing power is working in me, making me whole.

One Will on Heaven and on Earth

Is it ever God's will for His children here on earth to be sick? Well, God doesn't have one will for those in heaven and another will for His family on earth. God's will is the same for *all* His children. He's no respecter of persons; He doesn't play favorites.

You don't plan to be sick when you get to heaven, do you? No! There's no sickness in heaven. Beside, sickness wouldn't be able to touch you even if it were there. It couldn't attach itself to you because you'll have a changed, glorified body like Jesus had when He was raised from the dead and walked through walls. No, you won't be sick when you get up there.

And he said unto them, When ye pray, say, Our Father which art in heaven, Hallowed be thy name. Thy kingdom come. Thy will be done, as in heaven, so in earth.

—Luke 11:2

Now, there is sickness here in this world, and it does attack. It even has the bold audacity to attack Christians. Can you imagine that? But, thank God, we don't have to take it. We don't have to put up with it. We can rise up in the name of Jesus, and our faith in God's Word will run it off. Why? Because healing belongs to us!

Confession

God's will for me is that I walk in perfect health.
So when sickness tries to attack me, I don't wonder whether
or not it's from God. It isn't! So, I don't put up with it.
I command sickness to leave in Jesus' name. God's power
is effecting a healing and a cure throughout my body.

Take Care of the Temple

Wherefore take unto you the whole armour of God, that ye may be able to withstand in the evil day, and having done all, to stand.

—Ephesians 6:13

Let's cover reasons we sometimes fail to receive healing. We may need to make some adjustments so God is free to give us what we ask for.

On one whirlwind trip to Europe, Janet and I flew all night, arrived the next morning, and then over the course of the next three days we traveled to three countries and preached I don't know how many services in all. The anointing we operate under in a service quickens our bodies and gives us an extra dose of strength. We can go on like that for weeks.

But during the trip symptoms came on my body that concerned me. I believed I received my healing. I rebuked the symptoms, but they didn't leave. So I thought, *I'll do what Ephesians 6:13 says to do: "Having done all, to stand."*

But I had misinterpreted that verse. I was trying to stand *without having done all to stand.*

Janet and I had arranged a short time off and checked into a guest house. Over the next thirty-six hours or so, I ended up sleeping more than 25 hours off and on. When I finally woke up, I told Janet, "I know what's been wrong with me!"

I'd made the same mistake as Epaphroditus; he almost worked himself to death in the ministry, but God had mercy on him. (Phil. 2:25-30.)

I learned to treat my body right so I can walk in divine health and finish my course.

Confession

I take good care of my body and stand in faith
on God's promise of healing and health.

Take Care of Your Temple

Sometimes the reason we're experiencing difficulty getting rid of sickness in our bodies is that we've left a door open someplace. Either we're doing something wrong, or we're not doing something right. This isn't a hard-and-fast rule because the devil will still try to attack when we're doing everything right.

...that ye may be able to withstand in the evil day, and having done all, to stand.

—Ephesians 6:13

For instance, I was a youth minister in Colorado for about thirteen months. I lived in a couple's home, and the wife was an amazing cook. I gained about twenty-five pounds.

But then life got very busy. I had an opportunity to minister in two different schools, and I was on a flat run all the time. For a couple of months, I ate a lot of very unhealthy junk food. All of a sudden, my stomach started giving me trouble.

Now, I'm not a nervous, high-strung person. But when I tried to eat, I'd almost get sick to my stomach. My stomach just burned all the time. I had unknowingly opened the door for the devil to bring me stomach problems.

I prayed, "Lord, I'm sorry. My body is the temple of the Holy Ghost, and I've been misusing it. Lord, I repent." Then I believed I received my healing and got healed instantly.

So don't mistreat your body and leave a door open for the devil to bring in sickness and disease. Eat right and get adequate rest and exercise. Never forget—you are the caretaker of your body.

Confession

I'm responsible for taking care of my body. So I purpose to take good care of it by eating right, and getting plenty of exercise and rest.

Be a Person of Your Word

Wherein God, willing more abundantly to shew unto the heirs of promise the immutability of his counsel, confirmed it by an oath: That by two immutable things, in which it was impossible for God to lie, we might have a strong consolation, who have fled for refuge to lay hold upon the hope set before us.

—Hebrews 6:17,18

Hebrews 6:18 says it's impossible for God to lie. He doesn't have the capacity to be dishonest or to fail to keep His Word. God and His Word cannot be separated.

As God's children, we should also be people of our word. Now, sometimes a situation arises that makes it impossible to keep our word, even though our intentions are good. With the exception of these extreme cases, we need to be people of our word.

If we can't believe in our own word, our faith will never work because faith is believing what we say will come to pass. Our faith has nothing to stand on when our word is no good. We never know what to believe.

As humans, we often have to choose whether we're going to tell the truth or "fudge" just a little bit. The flesh wants to rise up and say whatever it takes to keep us out of trouble. But compromising the truth even in little ways will short-circuit our faith.

In 1 Corinthians 9:27, Paul said, "I keep under my body, and bring it into subjection...." Well, if Paul had to keep his body under, we certainly do too. Your mouth is part of your body, so keep it under and keep your word.

Confession

I'm a person of my word, and I'm a person of God's Word.
Truth lives and abides in me and produces health and wholeness.

Live a Long, Healthy Life

Wrong thinking can open the door to the devil. For instance, one time Janet and I were in another country talking to an older gentleman who'd been on the mission field for many years. He'd built church after church, but his denomination had recently called him back home.

This older gentleman said to me, "Young man, you believe God wants to heal people, don't you?"

"Yes, sir, I do!" I replied.

"But if God wants everyone healed, how in the world is anyone ever supposed to die?" he asked. You see, someone had planted wrong thinking in his head.

But now hath he obtained a more excellent ministry, by how much also he is the mediator of a better covenant, which was established upon better promises.

—Hebrews 8:6

That just hurt my heart. I thought, *Here's a man who has given his life to serve God on the mission field. Now that he's come back home, he's waiting to get sick so he can go home to be with the Lord!*

So I told the man, "Sir, I don't mean to be disrespectful, but I believe we ought to have it at least as good under the new covenant as God's people did under the old covenant. Back then, men of faith who served God lived long, healthy lives. They'd come to the end of their lives, lay hands on their families to bless them, drew up their feet in the bed, said goodbye, and took off for heaven." (Gen. 49:33.)

We need the same revelation if we want a long, satisfied life: We don't have to be sick to die. We can go to our heavenly home in perfect health.

Confession

I'll live a healthy and useful life for God and go home when I'm satisfied.

How Does God Perfect the Saints?

And he gave some, apostles; and some, prophets; and some, evangelists; and some, pastors and teachers; for the perfecting of the saints, for the work of the ministry, for the edifying of the body of Christ.

—Ephesians 4:11,12

Some people say, "I believe God wants to use sickness to perfect us." Well, if that's been God's method of perfecting the Church, He's failed miserably. If sickness were supposed to be the perfecter and the teacher of the Church, then every Christian ought to be thoroughly furnished unto all good works. If that were God's plan, then He missed it big time.

Some might say, "Yeah, but sickness ought to make you more pious." No, sickness doesn't bring out piety in people; it brings out their worst. If you've ever been sick, you know that. Sickness makes you mean, ornery, and cantankerous.

The idea of God using sickness for our benefit is simply wrong thinking. God doesn't want us sick. It's not part of His plan for us. He never planned for sickness to perfect us, correct us, or make us more pious.

God gave us the Word of God to correct and instruct us. He sent the Spirit of God to live inside us to teach, lead, and guide us. And if we go a step further, Ephesians 4:11 says God gave ministry gifts to perfect the saints.

So the maturing of the saints doesn't come through sickness. God designed it to come through the Word, the Holy Ghost, and the ministry gifts.

Confession

My God wants me well! He sent the Holy Ghost, the Word, and the ministry gifts to instruct me in His ways. I receive those gifts and become a mature saint, walking in God's best.

Sickness Is Not Your Teacher

How do we learn about the things of God? By spending time in prayer and fellowship with the Holy Ghost and in study of God's Word.

I hear people say all the time, "I learned so much from being sick." I admit people have learned things while they were sick, but they didn't learn *because* they were sick. They learned because they fed on the Word of God and prayed. It may have been the first time they took time to do that in a long time. That's why a lot of folks mistakenly relate sickness to learning—they never took the time to study and pray *until* they got sick.

Take my yoke upon you, and learn of me; for I am meek and lowly in heart: and ye shall find rest unto your souls.

—Matthew 11:29

We'd be a lot better off if we learned to feed on the Word and pray when we're well. We'd learn just as much, and it would be a lot less painful.

Someone once said to me, "Yeah, but God made me sick and wanted me in the hospital because I witnessed to someone while I was there."

But God is intelligent, and so are we. I believe as we wait before God in prayer, He can drop in our hearts to witness to someone in the hospital while we're well. Too often we rationalize everything, trying to figure it out in our heads. Let's just stick with the truth found in the Bible and accept God's promise of health and healing every day.

Confession

The Holy Spirit, my teacher, shows me in the Word that Jesus took my sins and my sicknesses. I'm so glad for His help and to walk in the blessing of health.

Be Willing To Change

*For I am the Lord,
I change not.*

—Malachi 3:6

Lillian B. Yeomans was a medical doctor who lived many years ago. She was raised from her deathbed by the power of God and turned in her medical license and started practicing medicine with the Great Physician. She had amazing results.

Dr. Yeomans made a statement that stood out to me: *If you're praying or believing God for something that belongs to you in the Word, and you don't see something start to change in three days, then you start changing.*

If something belongs to us, God's already paid for it. He's redeemed us, delivered us, and healed us. So when we see the answer to our need in the Scriptures, we latch on to God's promise with the hand of faith and say, "Father, You said it, I believe it, and I receive it!"

But if time passes and our answer hasn't manifested, something may have to change. Perhaps sin or disobedience is keeping us from receiving from God.

Some people say, "I'll keep standing. I'll keep doing what I'm doing until God changes." Then they sit and do nothing, waiting for God to change.

That won't work. You have to accept that God can't change, Jesus can't change, the Holy Ghost can't change, and the Word can't change. So if something has to change—that something has to be you.

Ask the Lord if you need to change in some area. That will put you in motion. And as the Lord reveals the changes you need to make and you make them, you'll receive the results you desire.

Confession

Jesus bought and paid for my healing with His own precious blood.
I'll change when I need to, and I'll receive the results I desire.

Jesus Was Bruised for Us

How could it please the Father to bruise Jesus? I'll tell you how. It pleased the Father for Jesus to be bruised because it provided healing and health for all His people. Jesus would die, descend into hell, and be resurrected in three days with a new, glorified body, free of all sickness and pain. From that day forward, God's people wouldn't have to suffer sickness, pain, or disease.

Jesus was made sick so we might be made well. He went down to hell so you and I could live eternally with Him. He left heaven so you and I could be welcome there. He left the throne room of God so we could go there in His name any time we wanted.

And I tell you what, Jesus is alive and well and doing fine today! He's not hurting anymore. He took all the benefits of redemption, wrapped them up, put a bow and ribbon on the package, wrote our names on it, and said, "Here—pick these up any time you need them."

Jesus was bruised so you and I wouldn't have to be. The price has been paid. Healing and health belong to us!

Yet it pleased the Lord to bruise him; he hath put him to grief: when thou shalt make his soul an offering for sin, he shall see his seed, he shall prolong his days, and the pleasure of the Lord shall prosper in his hand.

—Isaiah 53:10

Confession

Healing belongs to me! Jesus' body was broken so I could walk in divine health. God was pleased to accomplish His redemption plan, and He's pleased when I walk in that plan by faith.

Jesus Paid the Price

Yet it pleased the Lord to bruise him; he hath put him to grief: when thou shalt make his soul an offering for sin....

—Isaiah 53:10

Several years ago, I heard that one of my relatives was very sick. Her husband said the doctors couldn't figure out what was wrong. She'd been in for surgery two or three times, and there was nothing more they could do. Sickness had spread throughout her entire body, but they didn't know exactly what it was and couldn't get rid of it. Doctors weren't even sure she would live.

After prayer, she went in for surgery one more time. But when they opened her up, they couldn't find a trace of any sickness except in her appendix, which they removed. She's been healthy ever since.

As I pondered her situation, I thought, *That's a good picture of what God did for us! Just as it pleased God to get that diseased appendix out of my relative's body, it pleased Him to send Jesus to pay the price for our sicknesses.*

You see, sickness was destined to destroy the entire body of Christ. But God took all sickness and condensed it into Jesus' body.

That's why it pleased God to bruise Jesus. Thank God for His love. In a moment of time, all the disease of mankind was centered in one Man. Jesus willingly paid the price for our sins and sicknesses. He paid the price for you and me to walk in health today.

Confession

God so loved the world that He gave Jesus. Jesus so loved me that He willingly paid the price to set me free from sickness and disease. Praise God, I am free.

Be Careful How You Hear

And it came to pass on a certain day, as he was teaching, that there were Pharisees and doctors of the law sitting by, which were come out of every town of Galilee, and Judaea, and Jerusalem: and the power of the Lord was present to heal them.

—Luke 5:17

God's power was present, but none of the Pharisees and doctors of the law were healed. They weren't there to receive; they were just looking for a reason to accuse Jesus.

But what about the woman with the issue of blood? She heard of Jesus, pressed through a crowd, touched His garment, and was healed. "Jesus, immediately knowing in himself that virtue had gone out of him..." (Mark 5:30). Yet that same virtue, or power, was available to everyone in the multitude, but only this woman was healed.

Now look at Luke 6:17-19. A great multitude "came to hear him, and to be healed of all their diseases.... And the whole multitude sought to touch him: for there went virtue out of him, and healed them all" (vv. 17,19). This time the entire multitude was healed.

All three of these accounts talk about the power Jesus was anointed with, but these three stories each had a different result. *Hearing* was the difference. In Luke 5, the religious leaders refused to hear, so no one was healed. In Mark 5, the woman heard, believed, and received. And the multitude in Luke 6 all "came to hear him, and to be healed," and they were.

It's a pattern in Jesus' ministry: Those who heard and acted in faith *always* received.

Confession

What I hear and how I act determine what I have in my life. My faith increases daily to receive all God says is mine—including healing.

When God's Compassion Flows

As [Jesus] went out of Jericho with his disciples and a great number of people, blind Bartimaeus, the son of Timaeus, sat by the highway side begging. And when he heard that it was Jesus of Nazareth, he began to cry out, and say, Jesus, thou son of David, have mercy on me. And many charged him that he should hold his peace: but he cried the more a great deal, Thou son of David, have mercy on me.

And Jesus answered and said unto him, What wilt thou that I should do unto thee?

The blind man said unto him, Lord, that I might receive my sight.

And Jesus said unto him, Go thy way; thy faith hath made thee whole. And immediately he received his sight, and followed Jesus in the way.

—Mark 10:46-48,51,52

Blind Bartimaeus wouldn't stop; he just kept crying out: "Have mercy on me! Have compassion on me!" And that divine compassion started to flow.

Jesus turned and asked, "What do you want?"

Bartimaeus replied, "That I might receive my sight." And he did!

When God's compassion flows, miracles happen. Jesus had compassion on the multitudes, and He healed them all. (Matt. 14:14.)

Sympathy feels sorry for people, but God's compassion causes His love to flow to meet needs or produce miracles in people's lives.

We have that same divine love shed abroad in our hearts. It's time we let that sweet love of Jesus flow forth to a sick and dying world. People are looking for love and compassion. When compassion begins to flow through us, God's power flows. And when God's power flows, miracles happen.

Confession

God's love and compassion haven't changed; they flow *to* me and *through* me to heal and deliver.

Call on God's Mercy

When Bartimaeus called on the mercy of God in Mark 10:46-52, Jesus said, "What do you want Me to do for you?" (v. 51).

Bartimaeus touched the heart of God when he called on His mercy. During Jesus' ministry, many people called on God's mercy. When they did, blind eyes were opened, deaf ears could hear, the oppressed were set free from evil spirits, and the sick were healed of sicknesses and diseases.

For thou, Lord, art good, and ready to forgive; and plenteous in mercy unto all them that call upon thee.

—Psalm 86:5

What good does it do us to know that fact? Well, Psalm 86:5 says that God is plenteous in mercy unto all those who call upon Him. His mercy endures forever, and He doesn't turn away anyone who calls upon Him. So just as people called on His mercy 2000 years ago, we can call on His mercy today and have the same results.

There's a time to rise up and operate in our own faith for our healing and other needs. But there are also times when we just need to get down to business and say, "Lord, have mercy on me. Because Your mercy endures forever and You give to all who ask, have mercy on me."

God's mercy is ready to manifest in your life as health, freedom, strength, liberty, wisdom, and everything else you need. When you touch God's heart by calling on His mercy, He will manifest His mercy to you—spirit, soul, and body.

Confession

My God is the Father of mercies and the God of all comfort.
My God is plenteous in mercy to me because I call
upon Him. His mercies are new to me every morning.

Following the Holy Ghost

How God anointed Jesus of Nazareth with the Holy Ghost and with power: who went about doing good, and healing all that were oppressed of the devil; for God was with him.

—Acts 10:38

God anointed Jesus with the gifts of the Holy Ghost. The gifts were working through Jesus when He walked through the crowd at the pool of Bethesda and asked a man, "Is it your will to be healed?" The man said, "I have no man...." But Jesus said, "Get up and walk anyway," and the man was instantly healed. (John 5:1-15.)

Many times Jesus just walked into a situation and delivered a miracle. In Mark 7:32-35, a deaf man with a speech impediment was healed. In Mark 8:22-26, a blind man at Bethsaida was healed. God sent Jesus to those individuals with the gifts of the Spirit in operation. But Jesus couldn't turn those gifts on and off at will. If He could have, He would have healed everyone in the place every time.

You see, God may not want to manifest Himself through the gifts in each case. If He did, people might begin leaning on the manifestations more than God's Word.

So Jesus must have had His "spiritual antenna" up all the time, checking to see how the Holy Ghost wanted Him to minister healing. We should do the same.

"But that was Jesus," you may say. Yes, but Jesus laid aside His mighty power and glory to minister as a man anointed by God. So if that worked for Jesus, it will work for us! He's the same Holy Ghost who leads and heals today, and He dwells in us

Confession

The Holy Spirit guides me to receive my own
healing and to minister healing to others.

Don't Consider the Circumstances

How could Abraham "stagger not" at the promise of God? A 90-year-old woman and a 100-year-old man having a child? That was a big promise! So how was he able to not stagger? I mean, today many stagger at "by Jesus' stripes, you were healed."

"Being not weak in faith, he *considered not* his own body." The word *considered* in the original Greek means "to observe" or "to perceive."[1] So you could say it this way: "And being not weak in faith, he *observed not* his own body now dead, when he was about 100 years old."

Abraham didn't sit there and think about how his body felt. He didn't dwell on how old his body was. He didn't say, "Oh, Lord, I'm 100 years old, and Sarah is 90. It's just not going to work."

Now, Abraham didn't deny the problem; he simply ignored it. Abraham didn't observe his own body or the deadness of Sarah's womb. *He was dwelling on the answer instead of the problem.* That's why he could "stagger not" at the promise of God. And as Abraham filled his heart with the goodness and faithfulness of Almighty God, he became fully persuaded that what God had promised, He was also able to perform.

And being not weak in faith, he considered not his own body now dead, when he was about an hundred years old, neither yet the deadness of Sarah's womb: He staggered not at the promise of God through unbelief; but was strong in faith, giving glory to God.

—Romans 4:19,20

Confession

Being not weak in faith, I consider not my own circumstances.
I consider not my own body or any symptoms. I'm strong in faith,
knowing what God has promised, He's also able to perform in my life.

Keep Your Eyes on the Answer

...Abraham lifted up his eyes, and saw the place afar off. And Abraham said unto his young men, Abide ye here with the ass; and I and the lad will go yonder and worship, and come again to you.

—*Genesis 22:4,5*

If you always have your eyes on the answer and consider only what God said, you'll overcome in the end, regardless of your situation. A good example of this principle is the story of Abraham.

Abraham's miracle child, Isaac, was born to him and Sarah because they "staggered not" at God's promise. But Isaac wasn't the fulfillment of the promise; he was just the means to the fulfillment. God didn't say, "I'll give you a son." He said, "I have made you the father of many nations." (Gen. 17:4; 22:17.)

But in Genesis 22, God told Abraham to offer Isaac as a burnt offering to Him. Abraham would've been in trouble if he'd been walking around saying, "I know I'm the father of many nations because I have a son." If he thought that way, he would've responded, "Lord, I can't do that. Isaac has to live, or I can't be the father of many nations."

But Abraham was absolutely convinced if he sacrificed his son, God would have to raise him from the dead to fulfill that promise. (Heb. 11:17-19.) So Abraham told the servants, "Both of us will go up, and both of us will come back." And both of them did!

Don't take your eyes off the answer—off Jesus and the Word—for anything—whether good or bad. Even when your body feels better, don't dwell on that. Instead, be fully persuaded that what God says is exactly what will come to pass.

Confession

Whether my body feels good or bad, I keep my attention
focused on God's healing promises at work in me.

Finishing What Jesus Began

Jesus says we're to do even greater works than the works He did while He walked on the earth. But how can we? Jesus explained how: "The Father that dwelleth in me, he doeth the works" (v. 10).

The greater One living in Jesus did the works. Jesus always made that clear, saying, "Everything I do is My Father's will. My meat is to do My Father's will. I do what I see My Father doing."

Then Jesus said, "I'm going to leave, but I'm going to send the Holy Spirit, the Comforter, and He'll live within you. Then it won't just be Me doing the works of the Father all alone. Thousands of believers will preach the Gospel and lay hands on the sick all over the world. My people will do even greater works because I'm going to be with My Father."

Verily, verily, I say unto you, He that believeth on me, the works that I do shall he do also; and greater works than these shall he do; because I go unto my Father.

—John 14:12

In Acts 1:1, Luke talks about "all that Jesus began both to do and teach." Jesus began to love and forgive people, to teach people, and to lay hands on the sick and see them recover. But He couldn't do the job all alone, so He sent His Spirit to empower you and me to carry on His work. He has never stopped the ministry He began; He's continuing through His Church today. It's up to us to get the job done!

Confession

I help continue the work Jesus began: teaching and loving people, and laying hands on the sick so they'll recover. But it's my Father dwelling in me by the Holy Ghost who does the work.

Get in the Life Raft of Deliverance

[The Father] has delivered and drawn us to Himself out of the control and the dominion of darkness and has transferred us into the kingdom of the Son of His love.

—Colossians 1:13 AMP

When we were delivered from the kingdom of darkness, we were delivered from Satan's rule and authority and everything that's a part of his evil kingdom.

That means we've been delivered from spiritual death, disease, bad habits, oppression, and poverty. We don't have to wait for God to do it; it's already been done. We just need to receive and walk in our deliverance.

If I were out in the middle of a lake drowning and my father threw me a big inner tube to hang on to, I'd grab hold of it! I wouldn't say, "Well, I just don't know if I can take that. You know, I'm the one who fell in the lake, and I probably deserve to be out here. I'd better just see if I can make it through." If I said that, my father would probably get a little perturbed at me.

I can't imagine what God must think when we do the same thing spiritually. He's delivered us from the power of darkness and translated us into the kingdom of His Son. Yet some sit around nursing their symptoms, saying, "Well, I don't know if God wants me healed. He may want me to learn something from this sickness."

No, He's thrown us a life raft! He wants us to climb out of that sickness and disease and just float on in to safety and health.

Confession

I've been delivered from the dominion of darkness.
I don't have to be sick anymore. I walk in freedom,
safety, and health because I'm in God's kingdom.

He's Returning for a Healthy Bride

Jesus Christ, our soon-coming King, is coming back for a bride.

Well, how many grooms want to come back for a bride who is sick and emaciated? How many grooms say, "Well, Honey, I hope you're good and sick now so I can take you to the altar"?

No, Jesus wants a healthy bride. He's coming soon as the King of kings and Lord of lords, and He plans to return for a bride who is without spot or blemish. (Eph. 5:27.) That means in part that He wants to come back for a bride who's walking in health. That's His will!

So receive the healing Jesus purchased for you on the Cross. Walk in the divine health that belongs to you as part of the Church, the bride of Christ. Make sure you're preparing for the Bridegroom's return!

To the end he may stablish your hearts unblameable in holiness before God, even our Father, at the coming of our Lord Jesus Christ with all his saints.

—1 Thessalonians 3:13

Confession

I'm a part of the Church, the bride of Christ. The Bridegroom has clothed me with the garments of salvation, and I walk in all that salvation includes: health, wholeness, deliverance, and safety.

Sanctifying Your Food

For every creature of God is good, and nothing to be refused, if it be received with thanksgiving: for it is sanctified by the word of God and prayer.

—1 Timothy 4:4,5

When our food is sanctified by the Word and prayer, we can eat anything without harm if we partake of it with thanksgiving.

After eating some food back in the bush country, I can tell you from experience this verse is true. I didn't know what we ate and decided it was better not to ask. Janet and I just ate the food in faith and didn't suffer any kind of ill effects from it.

We haven't experienced any problems from eating unknown foods in other countries. We've always walked in divine health. Why? Because every time we sit down to a meal, we say, "Thank You, Father, that this food is sanctified by Your Word and prayer." The food can't harm us then. We also frequently travel on the road. When I think of some of the restaurants we've eaten at along the way, I'm sure glad that prayer works.

The only way you could experience a stomach problem after that kind of prayer is by opening the door to the enemy through fear or worry. And the solution to that is found in 2 Timothy 1:7: "For God hath not given us the spirit of fear; but of power, and of love, and of a sound mind."

Fear always opens the door to the enemy. And when it comes to food, we never have to fear because God has given us a way to eat safely in faith.

Confession

I sanctify my food with the Word and prayer.
I've been redeemed from the curse of the law,
which includes every disease known to man.

Light the Fuse of Faith

The power of God can be defined as the ability to act supernaturally and miraculously. According to this verse, our faith is to stand in the strength of God's divine power to remove every yoke of bondage from our lives.

But is there anything we can do to cause the power of God to manifest?

Power is released through faith. Faith is the fuse that releases the explosive force residing in God's power. Confession lights the fuse. You can put the fuse in, but it does no good unless you light it.

So confess the Word, and light the fuse of faith. Release God's power to perform miracles in your life!

My speech and my preaching was not with enticing words of man's wisdom, but in demonstration of the Spirit and of power: that your faith should not stand in the wisdom of men, but in the power of God.

—1 Corinthians 2:4,5

Confession

Speaking from a believing heart releases God's power on my behalf.
I say to my mountain of difficulty, pain, or sickness: "Be removed and cast into the sea!" I don't doubt in my heart, but believe what I say shall come to pass. And according to the Word, I have what I say.

Gain Possession of God's Word

My son, attend to my words; incline thine ear unto my sayings. Let them not depart from thine eyes; keep them in the midst of thine heart. For they are life unto those that find them, and health to all their flesh.

—Proverbs 4:20-22

God is telling us how to find health and abundant life. But these benefits don't work for everyone; God's promises are conditional. What's the condition? He said His words are life *to those who find them.*

I used to think when God said, "unto those that find them," He meant unto those who look up three or four Scriptures in a concordance and read them a few times and maybe even make some notes. But you won't qualify as one who has grasped the Word just by reading a few verses a few times and making lists of Scriptures.

To find doesn't mean just to locate. Actually, it means everything but locate. *To find* means "to attain or acquire, to get a hold upon, to have, to take hold on."[1]

God is telling you to do more than just locate Scriptures. He said His words are life to those who *attain or take hold of them.* In other words, *God wants you to stick with His Word until His Word sticks with you.*

Jesus desired the same thing for His disciples. In Luke 9:44, He instructed them, "Let these sayings sink down into your ears...."

God's Word begins to work for you when it becomes rooted and grounded in your heart. So gain possession of the Word and watch it come to pass.

Confession

As I take hold of and gain possession of God's Word, it becomes life to me. I believe God's promises, and they come to pass in my life.

Believe God With Your Heart

Let these sayings sink down into your ears.

—Luke 9:44

In today's civilized societies, we've spent a great deal of time educating our minds far beyond our spirits. So when we start reading the Bible, our minds often say, "I've got this already. I don't need to study anymore." Unfortunately, that usually means we've grabbed hold of the Word *with our minds and not with our hearts.*

The only way to believe God's Word with the heart is to spend time *feeding* on it. You have to get the Word rooted deep in your heart *so that its truth becomes more real than the doubts in your mind.*

A lot of people just mentally assent to the Word. In other words, they agree with Scripture in their heads. But you cannot have faith or believe God until the Word is planted in your heart.

You see, you cannot believe God with yout mind. And you certainly can't believe God with your body. God is a Spirit, and you must believe him with your spirit or with your heart.

When God's Word takes root in your heart, you can be strong and believe it even in the face of big obstacles. Some of the greatest faith victories come when you're believing God with your heart while doubts are firing at your mind and symptoms are firing at your body like machine-gun bullets. Plant God's Word in your heart, believe it, act upon it, and win your victory.

Confession

God's Word is life and medicine to my flesh.
I plant it in my heart. I act on it in faith and it works.

Follow God's Instructions

And be not conformed to this world: but be ye transformed by the renewing of your mind, that ye may prove what is that good, and acceptable, and perfect, will of God.

—Romans 12:2

In order for the Word to work successfully, we must be sure we're following God's instructions. Many are deceived because they *only attempt* to stand on the Word and believe God for their healing.

I remember some of my early experiences of endeavoring to stand on the Word. When I first believed God to heal me of the flu, the sickness didn't go away for about seven days.

All the while, I knew if I were to let the sickness run its own course, it would also take about seven days. This frustrated me, until one day I realized I'd been doing something wrong. I'd been standing on the right Scriptures. I had them all located and memorized, but the Scriptures weren't *planted on the inside of me.* I had some *head knowledge,* but my *heart hadn't grasped* the Word.

How do you plant God's Word in your heart? Read the Word over and over, study the Word, meditate on the Word, confess the Word—and keep on doing it.

It's so important for the Word to drop from your head to your spirit or heart because faith is of the heart. *As a matter of fact, the difference between victory and defeat in the Christian life is the eighteen inches between your head and your heart.* Is the Word planted in your heart? The answer to that question determines whether or not the Word will work for you.

Confession

I plant God's Word deep inside my heart. No matter what obstacle I face, I believe God's Word is true and gives me the victory.

Pain Doesn't Change God's Word

Sometimes people ask me, "I still have pain in my body. How can I believe I'm healed?" But it doesn't matter whether or not there's pain in your body. Pain doesn't change the promise of God.

This book of the law shall not depart out of thy mouth; but thou shalt meditate therein day and night, that thou mayest observe to do all that is written therein....

—Joshua 1:8

Let me ask you this: Does the pain in your body affect the fact that Jesus is coming again? No. Regardless of the symptoms or circumstances we deal with in life, we're always "waiting for the coming of our Lord Jesus Christ" (1 Cor. 1:7).

Well, if your pain doesn't affect one of God's promises, then it doesn't affect another of His promises. If it doesn't affect God's promise of Jesus' soon return, it doesn't affect the fact that by His stripes you were healed. (1 Peter 2:24.)

You see, as we start believing God's Word, it will begin working the change we desire in our symptoms, our circumstances, and our problems.

How do we develop our faith in the Word? We feed on it. That means we read it, study it, think about it, meditate on it, and mutter it to ourselves. Soon our hearts will be so full of the Word that our faith in God's promises will drive every remnant of pain and sickness away.

Confession

Even when my body is in pain, the Word of God is still true.
I walk by faith and believe I'm healed from head to toe.

God Isn't Our "Heavenly Butler"

For therein is the righteousness of God revealed from faith to faith: as it is written, The just shall live by faith.

—Romans 1:17

Someone once said to me, "You faith people make God sound like a heavenly butler."

I replied, "Let me ask you something. Suppose you meet someone on this earth who has unlimited means. As he gets to know you, this wealthy person decides he likes you and buys twenty years' worth of everything money can buy—cars, homes, everything.

"Then the rich man says to you, 'Now, I've bought everything you could ever want for the next twenty years. If you need it, want it, or desire it, just come and knock on the door. I have it in a big warehouse, and it's for you.'

"Now, if you went to the door and said, 'I could sure use such-and-such,' would you be pushing that person around or treating him like a 'butler'? No, you'd be taking him at his word."

You might say, "Well, if God spoke to me like that, I'd believe Him." But He did! God gave you sixty-six books called the Bible and spoke to you in every one of those books! He said, "By Jesus' stripes, you were healed," so healing is yours. He said, "God supplies all your needs," so all your needs are met.

We're not pushing God around. Don't be concerned about that. He's big enough to handle Himself. No one pushes or controls God.

So just take God at His Word and choose to believe that what He has said, He will do.

Confession

I go to the Word, my spiritual "warehouse," and obtain
the benefits God has already provided for me.
I take God at His Word and believe healing is mine.

The Table Set Before You

Thou preparest a table before me in the presence of mine enemies: thou anointest my head with oil; my cup runneth over.

—Psalm 23:5

Some folks think the table in Psalm 23:5 refers to the marriage feast of the Lamb in heaven. But that can't be right. The marriage feast of the Lamb won't be in the presence of our enemies— there won't be any enemies in heaven.

No, God has prepared a table before you right in the presence of your enemies down here on earth. Sickness may come running up, ready to attach itself to your body. But you have a table set before you with a big plate of bread right in the middle. When sickness presents itself, you can say, "God prepares a table before me in the presence of my enemies. Healing is the children's bread. So, pass the bread, please!" (Mark 7:25-30.)

Everything you need is spread before you on that table. You have the fruit of the Spirit. You have the milk of the Word to help you grow in God. You have the meat of the Word to make your spirit strong.

So take advantage of the table set before you. No matter what enemy comes to harass you, just sit down at the table and feast on the Word and the children's bread. You'll be well taken care of, and there's not a thing in the world your enemies can do about it.

Confession

A table is spread for me in the midst of my enemies.
I feast on God's Word, and it's life to me and medicine
to all my flesh. So please pass the children's bread.

Watch Your Attitude Before God

And [Jesus] spake this parable unto certain which trusted in themselves that they were righteous, and despised others: Two men went up into the temple to pray; the one a Pharisee, and the other a publican. The Pharisee stood and prayed thus with himself, God, I thank thee, that I am not as other men are, extortioners, unjust, adulterers, or even as this publican. I fast twice in the week, I give tithes of all that I possess.

And the publican, standing afar off, would not lift up so much as his eyes unto heaven, but smote upon his breast, saying, God be merciful to me a sinner.

—Luke 18:9-13

I believe Jesus is trying to show us the difference between the two men's attitudes here. The Pharisee arrogantly boasted, "I do this and that and everything else, God; Your blessings belong to me now." The other man just humbly prayed, "Lord, I don't deserve anything on my own. Please just be merciful to me."

It's true we need to stand up in our righteousness. We're to come boldly before the throne of grace, and believe and confess the Word in faith.

But we shouldn't come with an arrogant attitude like the Pharisee, saying, "You owe me!"

God's mercy, compassion, and grace provided everything we have in Jesus Christ, and His blessings are a gift. Because of God's grace poured out upon us, we can say, "If we believe and say what His Word says, it will come to pass."

So be bold when you go before God, but always keep a watch on your attitude. Remember, it's only by God's grace that you stand.

Confession

I'm grateful for all the redemptive blessings Jesus purchased for me.
I choose to walk in each one of them.

Blessed Are the Merciful

The best thing you can do if you need healing in your body is to start praying for other people to be healed.

Jesus said, "Blessed are the merciful." What are you doing when you're praying for the sick?

Blessed are the merciful: for they shall obtain mercy.

—Matthew 5:7

You're showing God's mercy. "Blessed are the merciful." How are the merciful blessed? "For they shall obtain mercy" (Matt. 5:7).

People all through the Gospels cried out for mercy, and the blessing they received was healing. You will receive God's healing mercies as well, as you minister God's healing mercies to others. This is confirmed in Ephesians 6:8, where it says, "Knowing that whatsoever good thing any man doeth, the same shall he receive of the Lord, whether he be bond or free."

Paul states a spiritual principle here: If you're doing good things, the same good things will be given back to you. Therefore, the best thing you can do when you need healing is to thank God that healing belongs to you and then start finding people to minister to. Go pray for the sick.

Be out doing the work of the ministry, fulfilling the Great Commission, whether your body hurts or not. As you get busy seeking first the kingdom of God and His righteousness and ministering God's mercy to others, the healing mercies of God will be added to you. (Matt. 6:33.)

Confession

Jesus is my healer. I show His mercy to people and help them receive, and I obtain the healing mercy I need.

A Treasure Hidden for Us

And he taught them many things by parables, and said unto them in his doctrine, Hearken; Behold, there went out a sower to sow.

—Mark 4:2,3

Jesus began teaching a crowd of people in parables. Later when alone, His disciples asked Him the meaning of the parable of the sower. In essence they said, "We don't understand what You're talking about."

Jesus said to them, "Unto you it is given to know the mystery of the kingdom of God: but unto them that are without, all these things are done in parables" (v. 11). Then He continued, "Know ye not this parable? and how then will ye know all parables?" (v. 13).

Jesus was saying, "If you gain understanding of this parable, everything else will open up to you."

Some people read the Bible and say, "I don't understand the Bible. It's Greek to me."

Well, that's why God gave us the Holy Ghost—to translate, interpret, and teach the Word to us. The reason many people have trouble understanding the Word is that they've never let the Holy Ghost be the teacher. They try to read the Bible with their own understanding.

But the Word is revelation truth. Verse 22 AMP says, "[Things are hidden temporarily only as a means to revelation.] For there is nothing hidden except to be revealed, nor is anything [temporarily] kept secret except in order that it may be made known." God's revelation truth was hidden not to keep it from us, but to keep it for us.

Every time you open your Bible, ask the Holy Ghost to teach and reveal it to you.

Confession

The Holy Ghost teaches and enlightens the Word to me.
I've planted the Word in my heart, and it's bearing rich fruit.

Don't Be a "Have-Hearder"

Jesus is teaching the foundation on which the entire kingdom of God operates: sowing and reaping.

In these verses, Jesus begins to explain, "These are they by the way side, where the word is sown; but when they have heard, Satan cometh immediately, and taketh away the word that was sown in their hearts."

How was Satan able to do that? Look at the phrasing: "...but when they *have heard*...." Jesus says they are *"have-hearders."* He doesn't say, "They're hearing it"; He says, "They *have heard* it." Satan stole away the Word so easily because the person quit hearing God's Word and started hearing something else.

I remember when I thought I knew everything there was to know about Mark 11:24. I'd heard hundreds of different messages about that one verse. Then at one meeting, the minister said, "Open to Mark 11:24," and I just shut off my mind. About six weeks later, I couldn't figure out why that verse wasn't working for me. Then I realized I had turned into a "have-hearder."

People often say, "I don't need to *hear that again.*" But we must hear every part of God's Word *continually.* What we hear today will bear fruit tomorrow.

Behold, there went out a sower to sow.

And it came to pass, as he sowed, some fell by the way side, and the fowls of the air came and devoured it up.

And these are they by the way side, where the word is sown; but when they have heard, Satan cometh immediately, and taketh away the word that was sown in their hearts.

—Mark 4:3,4,15

Confession

I'm a hearer, not a "have-hearder." I continually hear the Word.
And as I act on God's Word in faith, it bears much rich fruit in my life.

"Stony Ground" Hearers

And some [seed] fell on stony ground, where it had not much earth; and immediately it sprang up, because it had no depth of earth: but when the sun was up, it was scorched; and because it had no root, it withered away.

And these are they likewise which are sown on stony ground; who, when they have heard the word, immediately receive it with gladness; and have no root in themselves, and so endure but for a time: afterward, when affliction or persecution ariseth for the word's sake, immediately they are offended.

—Mark 4:5,6,16,17

We've all seen these "stony ground" people. They hear God's Word and then get really excited. They say, "Oh, man, this is so good! I've been looking for this for years!"

But these people are also "have-hearders." They don't settle down and *continue* to hear the Word so the Word they've heard never really takes root in them.

The minute persecution and affliction come along for the Word's sake (and they will), these people stop hearing the Word and start hearing the persecution and affliction. In six months, we wonder where they are. They've just blown away with the wind.

As soon as you get a revelation in the Word, the thief will try to steal it away through persecution and affliction. If you're not careful, you'll end up saying, "Well, I tried that, and it didn't work."

Jesus said these people endure only for a short time because they have no root in themselves. (v. 17.) God's Word takes root in us by hearing and hearing. What we hear regularly is what bears fruit in our lives.

Confession

I attend to God's Word, so it's rooted and grounded in my heart. When symptoms attack my body, His Word rises up to heal me.

Watch Out for Thorns

How could anything gain enough strength or power to choke the Word and cause it to become unfruitful? The cares of this world, the deceitfulness of riches, and the lusts of other things don't have enough strength in themselves to do it. It's what we do with those "thorns" that causes them to choke the Word in our lives.

This person starts out right. He's hearing and feeding on the Word of God, and the Word is starting to grow and bear fruit.

Then suddenly the cares of this world show up, and he starts listening to them. The deceitfulness of riches and lusts of other things follow right along, and soon he's feeding on them instead of God's Word. The "thorns" enter in and choke out the Word, making it unfruitful in his life.

Several years ago, I was trying to share the Word and pray for a man in a hospital. The man finally said, "I guess I was just *born* bad ground."

No, there's no such thing as being born bad ground! *You decide* what kind of ground you'll be. Will you be the kind of land that never bears fruit, or good ground that bears a return?

And some [seed] fell among thorns, and the thorns grew up, and choked it, and it yielded no fruit.

And these are they which are sown among thorns; such as hear the word, and the cares of this world, and the deceitfulness of riches, and the lusts of other things entering in, choke the word, and it becometh unfruitful.

—*Mark 4:7,18,19*

Confession

I'm good ground. I seek the riches of my inheritance in Christ.
The Word is planted in my heart and is bearing good fruit.

How To Be "Good Ground"

And other [seed] fell on good ground, and did yield fruit that sprang up and increased; and brought forth, some thirty, and some sixty, and some an hundred.

—Mark 4:8

How do you make sure you're good ground? Start out hearing God's Word. When the thief comes to steal it away, keep on hearing the Word of God. When persecutions and afflictions come because of the Word, (and they will come), keep hearing what God says.

First Peter 4:12 says, "Beloved, think it not strange concerning the fiery trial which is to try you, as though some strange thing happened unto you." What do you do when the fiery trials come? You keep on hearing the Word.

The cares of the world will try to distract you, but keep on hearing the Word. The deceitfulness of riches and the lusts of other things will try to get in your way, but just keep hearing the Word and plowing through. One day the fruit of that Word will start popping up on the other side of all the trials and distractions of life. You'll reap a harvest that's thirty-, sixty-, or even a hundredfold.

The Bible says, "My son, attend to my words; incline thine ear unto my sayings" (Prov. 4:20). If we want healing in our bodies, we must incline our ears unto His sayings. We must hear God's Word coming from the pulpit, from teaching tapes, CDs, TV, radio, and most importantly, from our own mouths.

Someone may ask, "How long do we hear the Word?" All through eternity; it's that good. It's not a chore—it's a pleasure.

Confession

What I hear controls the fruit in my life. I desire the fruit of divine healing, so I won't be distracted from hearing God's Word.

Shine Forth the Light of God

The margin in my Bible more accurately translates the word *candle* as lamp or light. Psalm 119:105 says, "Thy word is a lamp unto my feet, and a light unto my path." So this passage in Mark is talking about God's Word. Is the Word to be put under a bushel or a bed instead of set on a candlestick?

Jesus is saying it's not meant to be hidden or stuck on a shelf. It's meant to be on a stand, where it can shine forth and give life to everyone. In other words, God wants His Word to get on the inside of us so it can start producing life on the outside.

How do we get God's Word off the pages of the Bible and operating in our lives? How do we become living epistles, known and read by all men? (2 Cor. 3:2.)

The Word shines forth when we take time to hear and feed on it. The more we hear the Word, the more the Word gives us light, truth, and understanding. Then we're able to pass its truth on to others.

And he said unto them, Is a candle brought to be put under a bushel, or under a bed? and not to be set on a candlestick? For there is nothing hid, which shall not be manifested; neither was any thing kept secret, but that it should come abroad. If any man have ears to hear, let him hear.

—Mark 4:21-23

You see, we're God's billboards on this earth. As the Word produces life in us, we shine forth to those around us.

Confession

As I hear God's Word, the Holy Ghost reveals Scriptures to me.
God's light and life are in me, shining forth so others can see.

Live on the "More Besides" Side of Life

*...Take heed what
ye hear: with what
measure ye mete, it
shall be measured
to you: and unto
you that hear shall
more be given. For
he that hath, to
him shall be given:
and he that hath
not, from him
shall be taken even
that which he
hath.*

—Mark 4:24,25

Jesus explains in this passage that what we hear determines the kind of fruit we bear in our lives. Too often people listen to the wrong things, meditate on the wrong things, and feed on the wrong things.

Jesus said, "Take heed what you hear." *The Amplified Bible* makes verse 24 even clearer:

> And He said to them, Be careful what you are hearing. The measure [of thought and study] you give [to the truth you hear] will be the measure [of virtue and knowledge] that comes back to you—and *more* [*besides*] will be given to you who hear.

I don't know about you, but I want to live on the "more besides" side of life. We decide whether we live on the "barely-getting-along" side or on the "more besides" side.

But notice this: Jesus says, "More [besides] will be given to you who hear." Will more be given to those who beg and plead or to those who pray all the time? No. Although it's important to pray, prayer will do no good unless we're doing what Jesus tells us to do. "More besides" will be given to us only when we set ourselves to hear the truth of God's Word.

Confession

I continually hear God's Word, and "more besides" is
given to me in every area of my life as I hear and obey God's Word.

God Has Said

Jesus said, "All things are possible to him that believeth" (Mark 9:23). The only qualification He gave us is that we must *believe.*

Many would say, "Dear Lord, why did You make it so hard to believe?"

And yet, believing is the product, or the offspring, of God's Word planted in the human heart. Our problem hasn't been our lack of ability to believe; it has been not knowing *what* to believe. Believing has always seemed like an abstract, intangible mystery.

Who hath believed our report? and to whom is the arm of the Lord revealed?

—Isaiah 53:1

Someone says, "Man, I'm trying to believe God."

"What are you trying to believe?"

"I'm trying to believe God!"

But God gets more specific, and asks, "Who hath believed *our report?*" In any given situation, we need to find out what God is saying and believe His report.

In the Garden of Eden, God told Adam, "But of the tree of the knowledge of good and evil, thou shalt not eat of it: for in the day that thou eatest thereof thou shalt surely die" (Gen. 2:17). Later the serpent beguiled Eve, saying, "Ye shall not surely die" (Gen. 3:4). Now Eve had two reports. Unfortunately, she chose to believe the serpent's report.

Whose report do you believe ?

We can either believe what the problem says or what God says. The serpent asked Eve, "Yea, hath God said?" (Gen. 3:1). Yes, He has. God has said something about every situation we'll ever run into. So if we want God's power revealed in our lives, let's believe His report.

Confession

God said that by Jesus' stripes I was healed. I choose to believe God's report. I fully expect His healing power to be revealed in my life.

Endnotes

MARCH 22
[1] Leeser, p. 256.

MARCH 26
[1] Leeser, p. 274.

APRIL 6
[1] Merriam-Webster's Collegiate Dictionary, 10th Ed., s.v. "redeem."

MAY 3
[1] Vine, s.v. "life," Vol. 2, pp. 336-338.

JULY 6
[1] Strong, "Hebrew," entry #3068, p. 47; entry #7495, p. 110.

JULY 8
[1] Strong, "Hebrew," entry #5375, p. 80.
[2] Strong, "Hebrew," entry #5445, p. 81.

JULY 9
[1] Leeser, p. 724.

JULY 17
[1] Rotherham, p. 224.

JULY 22
[1] Rotherham, p. 176.

SEPTEMBER 3
[1] Vine, s.v. "messenger," Vol. 3, p. 64.

SEPTEMBER 27
[1] Strong, "Hebrew," entry #1897, p. 32.

OCTOBER 16
[1] Vine, s.v. "profession," Vol. 3, p. 217.

OCTOBER 22
[1] Vine, s.v. "confess," Vol. 1, p. 224.

OCTOBER 30
[1] Strong, "Greek," entry #2476, p. 38.

NOVEMBER 22
[1] The Companion Bible, Appendix 101, part II, 14, pp. 146-147.

DECEMBER 9
[1] Strong, "Greek," entry #2657, p. 40.

DECEMBER 16
[1] Strong, "Hebrew," entry #4672, p. 70.

References

Bosworth, F.F. *Christ the Healer.* New York: Fleming H. Revell Company, 1877.

Leeser, Isaac. *Twenty-Four Books of the Holy Scriptures.* New York: Hebrew Publishing Company, 1998.

Merriam-Webster's Collegiate Dictionary, 10th Ed., Springfield: Merriam-Webster, Inc., 1995.

Rotherham, Joseph Bryant. *The Emphasized Bible.* Grand Rapids: Kregel Publications, 1959.

Strong, James. *Strong's Exhaustive Concordance of the Bible.* "Hebrew and Chaldee Dictionary," "Greek Dictionary of the New Testament." Nashville: Abingdon, 1890.

The Companion Bible. Grand Rapids: Zondervan Bible Publishers, 1964, 1970, 1974.

Vine, W.E. *Vine's Expository Dictionary of Old and New Testament Words.* Old Tappan: Fleming H. Revell Company, 1981.

Prayer of Salvation

God loves you—no matter who you are, no matter what your past. God loves you so much He gave His one and only begotten Son for you. The Bible tells us "...whoever believes in him shall not perish but have eternal life" (John 3:16 NIV). Jesus laid down His life and rose again so we could spend eternity with Him in heaven and experience His absolute best on earth. If you would like to receive Jesus into your life, say the following prayer out loud and mean it from your heart.

Heavenly Father, I come to You admitting that I am a sinner. Right now, I choose to turn away from sin, and I ask You to cleanse me of all unrighteousness. I believe that Your Son, Jesus, died on the cross to take away my sins. I also believe that He rose again from the dead so I might be forgiven of my sins and made righteous through faith in Him. I call upon the name of Jesus Christ to be the Savior and Lord of my life. Jesus, I choose to follow You and ask that You fill me with the power of the Holy Spirit. I declare right now I am a child of God. I am free from sin and full of the righteousness of God. I am saved in Jesus' name. Amen.

If you prayed this prayer to receive Jesus Christ as your Savior for the first time, please contact us on the Web at **www.harrisonhouse.com** to receive a free book.

Or you may write to us at
Harrison House
P.O. Box 35035
Tulsa, Oklahoma 74153

About the Author

Mark Brazee has taught the Word of God with unction and precision around the world for more than 25 years, sharing the message of Jesus Christ and the good news of faith and healing. Together, Mark and his wife, Janet, have traveled to more than 40 nations with these truths.

Today, the outreaches of Mark Brazee Ministries span a worldwide network of DOMATA Bible Schools as well as the U.S.-based DOMATA Tulsa.

Mark and Janet also pastor World Outreach Church in Tulsa, Oklahoma, where they base their ongoing outreach to the world.

Other teaching materials available include an extensive line of CDs and cassettes; books by Mark; music by Janet; and the ministry's quarterly *Vision Magazine.* For more information, or to request our catalogue or magazine, please visit **www.brazee.org**.

To contact Mark Brazee,
please write to:

Mark Brazee Ministries
P.O. Box 470308
Tulsa, Oklahoma 74147-0308

Or visit him on the web at:
www.brazee.org

*Please include your prayer requests
and comments when you write.*

Other Books by Mark Brazee

31 Days of Healing Devotional

Fear-Free Living in Dangerous Times

Does the Problem Look Bigger Than Your Faith?

Healing: Choice or Chance

Locking Arms for the Harvest—The Power of Partnership

Blood, Fire and Vapor of Smoke

Prayer, Power, and Prosperity

Preparing for His Glory

Processing the Plan of God Through Prayer

Fast. Easy.
Convenient.

For the latest Harrison House product information and author news, look no further than your computer. All the details on our powerful, life-changing products are just a click away. New releases, E-mail subscriptions, Podcasts, testimonies, monthly specials—find it all in one place. Visit harrisonhouse.com today!

harrisonhouse

The Harrison House Vision

Proclaiming the truth and the power
Of the Gospel of Jesus Christ
With excellence;

Challenging Christians to
Live victoriously,
Grow spiritually,
Know God intimately.